FIFTH EDITION

■Political Thinking

THE PERENNIAL QUESTIONS

Glenn Tinder

UNIVERSITY OF MASSACHUSETTS, BOSTON

HarperCollins*Publishers*

To Galen,
son and independent thinker

Sponsoring Editor: Lauren Silverman
Project Coordination, Text and Cover Design: R. David Newcomer Associates
Production: Michael Weinstein
Compositor: CFW Graphics
Printer and Binder: Courier Book Companies/Murray
Cover Printer: The Lehigh Press, Inc.

Political Thinking: The Perennial Questions, Fifth Edition

Library of Congress Cataloging-in-Publication Data

Tinder, Glenn E.
    Political thinking : the perennial questions / Glenn Tinder. —
5th ed.
        p.   cm.
    Includes bibliographical references and index.
    ISBN 0-673-52026-9
    1. Political science—History. I. Title.
JA81.T56   1991
320′.09—dc20   90-5179
                                                   CIP

91 92 93   9 8 7 6 5 4 3

The paradox is the source of the thinker's passion and the thinker without a paradox is like a lover without feeling: a paltry mediocrity.... The supreme paradox of all thought is the attempt to discover something that thought cannot think.

Søren Kierkegaard

Contents

Preface

There is one major difference between this and earlier editions of *Political Thinking*. I have tried to open up the discussion to issues posed by contemporary feminism. To this end, I have added a new question at the conclusion of Chapter 3. "Inequality and Equality": Should men and women always and in all ways be treated equally? Further, I have tried to make the text throughout sensitive to the concerns of feminists and of women generally. I have mentioned, and in some cases briefly discussed, these concerns at numerous points. And I have worked assiduously to update my use of language, eliminating masculine pronouns (except in reference to males), and doing away with such terms as *mankind*.

Needless to say, I do not take sides. My major assumption has not been that feminists are necessarily right, but that they deserve attention. Political thinking today cannot leave out the questions feminists pose, for they are fundamental. If I have succeeded, the present edition will be readily usable by feminists without being feminist in character; it will therefore be usable also by those opposed to feminism or not concerned primarily with feminist issues.

As a male, I felt a definite lack of confidence in my ability adequately to address feminist concerns. I told my editor that I needed a feminist consultant. He and the publisher responded generously, and Ruby Riemer, of New Jersey, a feminist writer and teacher, and a good friend, was engaged. She has accompanied me at every step, from recommending reading at the outset to checking the final draft. I have of course done my own writing, and have written only what I could understand and sincerely say. Hence, despite everything, I may here and there tread on feminist toes. If I do, however, it is not Ruby's fault; I would have done it far more often without her help. She has played an invaluable part, and what I have written would have been different, and worse, had it not been for her criticism and advice.

Apart from the introduction of feminist issues, the present edition is basically the same as the earlier editions. I have done a great deal of polishing; I have rewritten some passages; and I have tried to freshen the suggested readings at the end of each chapter. I think I have made some significant improvements. But the guiding idea of the first four editions—that political philosophy can advantageously be studied by paying more attention than is customary to the great questions underlying political thought and action—is unchanged in the present edition. And the writing style of earlier editions remains much as it was. And here it should be said that much credit for that style, so far as it was good, is due to Jack Beatty, an old friend, now a senior editor at *The Atlantic,* who not only provided valuable suggestions concerning the content of earlier editions but also helped me to remove many infelicities of style.

Glenn Tinder

■Introduction

This book may prove difficult and trying for some readers, perhaps especially for careful and probing readers. It is made up wholly of questions. Not only do I give no indication of the answers I accept, I am often as unsure of them as the reader is likely to be. As a result, *Political Thinking* has none of the satisfying finality characteristic of most books on political theory.

This is a warning, not an apology. The lack of finality is connected with the primary intent of the book. My purpose is to provide an introduction to political thinking, and I have tried to do this not by describing the great political philosophies of the past, but rather by helping each reader to engage in the activity of political thinking. This has necessitated asking questions but refraining from any effort to provide answers. Even when I could have—and this was not often—I have not offered any positions of repose.

It has been said that anyone who gives people the illusion that they are thinking will be loved by them, whereas anyone who actually prompts them to think will be hated. If so, some exasperation on the part of the reader (although I have tried not to cause more exasperation than is intellectually fruitful) will be a sign of this book's success.

Perhaps too much is said in universities about how exciting it is to think. Thinking undoubtedly has its excitements and satisfactions, but these feelings do not disclose its general char-

1

acter, and there is something very much wrong with the idea that they should. We do not think in order to enjoy ourselves but in order to understand life, which is troubling and problematic. We think because we are compelled to. And while thinking occasionally brings exciting discoveries, the periods in between these discoveries are likely to place heavy demands on the thinker's energy and patience. When thinking, we should not need to tell ourselves we are having an exhilirating experience; it should be enough to realize that we are behaving with the seriousness, rationality, and self-discipline that the human situation requires of us.

Such gravity is particularly applicable to *political* thinking in so tragic a time as the twentieth century. Should we find it enjoyable to ponder dilemmas that have cost uncounted millions of lives? The following pages are not supposed to be easy or uplifting. They are intended, rather, to introduce the reader to the trials of political thinking in an age of turmoil and doubt.

Once on the high seas of thought, however, a reader may feel that this book does not give enough instruction on how to navigate and remain afloat. How does a person go about thinking? I shall offer a few suggestions in this introduction. Help of this kind, however, is necessarily of limited value. Much of the trying nature of thought results from the impossibility of thinking according to teachable techniques. Although much is said about "teaching students to think," a teacher can do little more than offer encouragement and criticism. The appearance of an idea is a mysterious occurrence, and it is doubtful that anyone does, or ever will, understand just how it happens.

But a student can *learn* to think. My reason for saying that no one can be *taught* to think is to focus at the onset on the dependence of the entire process on the student's own solitary efforts. It is both the glory and the burden of thought that it is an exceedingly personal undertaking. The solitude of the mature thinker must be entered into immediately by the beginner. As the mature thinker thinks all alone, the beginner must *learn* to think all alone. Occasionally one may receive a gift of encouragement or useful criticism, but nothing is decided by these gifts. Everything depends on the capacity for solitary effort.

It follows that little instruction in the art of thinking can be offered beyond suggestions such as the following.

1. Do not try to arrive at ideas no one has ever thought of before. Even the greatest thinkers have rarely done that. The aim of thinking is to discover ideas that pull together one's world, and thus one's being, not to give birth to unprecedented conceptions. An idea is your own if it has grown by your own efforts and is rooted in your own emotions and experience, even though you may have received the seeds from someone else and even though the idea may be very much like ideas held by many others.

2. Be open. Ideas cannot be deliberately produced, like industrial products. They appear uncommanded; they occur, as we recognize when we say, "It occurred to me that..." You place yourself in a fundamentally wrong relationship with ideas if you assume you can control their appearance. You can only be open to them.

3. Do not hurry. Initial efforts to think about a problem are often completely frustrating. They may best be regarded as a tilling of the ground; time is required before anything can be expected to grow.

4. Make plenty of notes. It is easier to work with your mind if you are doing some corresponding work with your hands. It is often helpful to make notes on large pads where there is room for sketching out patterns of ideas. It can also be helpful to make notes on cards and then to cut up the cards so that each idea is on a small piece of card. These can then be laid out on a desk and rearranged. Often this process suggests new connections among your thoughts.

5. Beware of substituting reading for thinking. Reading about the thoughts of others is not the same as having thoughts of your own. To be sure, to engage in thinking you need some acquaintance with the thoughts of others. The great thinkers inspire, provoke, confirm, and in other ways help you do your own thinking. But to think you must at some point lay down the book and strike out on your own.

I have a final suggestion that I do not number with the five above because it must take the form, not of a briefly stated tip, but of a somewhat extended comment on the structure of political thought.

Most political ideas, perhaps all of them, are based on some particular conception of human nature. The conservative idea

that political authority should be strong and highly centralized, for example, is apt to be based on a conception of human beings as selfish and competitive; the liberal notion that
extensive social changes can ordinarily be brought about peacefully may arise from the premise that human beings are for the
most part reasonable. These examples are very simple, and in
an actual political philosophy the relations between the underlying conception of human nature and the superstructure of
political ideas may be far more complex; they do, however, illustrate the general structure that is implicitly or explicitly
present in almost every political theory.

What is the bearing of this observation on the question of
how you should go about thinking? Simply this: you will probably find that your mind is clarified and stimulated through ar-
ticulating this structure in your own thought. In the course of
political thinking you should occasionally pause to ask yourself how you view human nature and what implications this view
has for your political ideas.

You may feel that to ask in this way about human nature is to
face a mystery even darker than those encountered on the level
of political reflection. There are, however, two overriding issues
in this area, despite the infinite complexities of human nature;
you may initiate the process of thought by trying to respond to
these issues. One issue concerns the extent and origins of evil
in human beings: are we deeply and incurably evil, or is evil a
superficial and removable aspect of our character? The second
issue—less universally recognized nowadays than the first—
concerns the import of death: is an individual totally extinguished by death? Does the term *eternal life* correspond to
anything that we may actually experience?

Your response to the first issue will very largely determine
your ideas on such matters as how much freedom people
should have, to what extent historical progress is possible, and
the degree of violence necessary to bring about change. Your
response to the second issue decides in a general way your
whole conception of the purpose of life. If you believe that
death is complete extinction, you must somehow call on people
(using Nietzsche's words) to "be true to the earth"; if you do not
believe that death is extinction, you must see earthly politics as
significant only insofar as it helps or hinders people in working
out their relations with eternity.

Perhaps it is in order to say here that these ethical and metaphysical areas contain many pitfalls and surprises, and that we should be wary both of offhand answers and of facile inferences. For example, it is often assumed today that affirming the goodness of humankind, if an error, is a generous and harmless error. Hence political discussions are often punctuated with complacent expressions of trust in human nature. But this trust can have some paradoxical results. If people are fundamentally good, then how does there happen to be so much evil in human affairs? It is hard to avoid concluding that is must be because some people are exceptions to the general human norm. Thus Communists have tended to blame all the evil in the world on capitalists, and vice versa. It is apparent how sinister a line of thought this is, for the next step is deciding that to free the world of evil it is necessary only to eradicate the few who are the sources of evil. Through so natural a logic as this, a benign and generous judgment becomes murderous.

On the other hand, we should not lightly judge people to be evil, for if we believe that people are evil, how can we avoid being dominated by hatred and by hopelessness?

The issue of death also has its pitfalls. It has often been noted that to deny the finality of death can imperil freedom. This is simply because such a denial can only be based on religious faith, and religious faith readily takes the form of a dogma forcibly imposed on everyone.

It does not follow, however, that accepting the finality of death is safe and sets up no dangerous reverberations in the area of political thought. For example, it is doubtful that the idea that every individual is a repository of unique and measureless dignity would ever have arisen apart from the idea that every individual is immortal. The idea of personal immortality disentangled the human being from natural realities and set each of us above the whole natural world. That is why a person could not be regarded as a mere means, but had to be regarded as an end. A being that is not immortal, however, tends to sink back into nature and in some circumstances may be regarded, like any other natural reality, as a means rather than an end.

You may feel that you cannot possibly decide issues so vast. And of course you cannot, if deciding them means finding answers that are exact and sure, answers that are never altered and never doubted. But these vast issues do not concern something far away but rather the most immediate and intimate of realities—one's own self. Are we not in a position at least to hazard some guesses concerning the nature and destiny of persons, when we ourselves are persons? Can we live without making some assumptions concerning these matters? And if we are to make some assumptions, is it not best to bring them into the open and use reason to examine them?

But how are we to judge the truth of our ideas? This question can be asked not only about ideas concerning human nature but about political ideas in general. How can we test the validity of an idea that strongly appeals to us?

There are some standard and well-known tests: the idea must be consistent with other ideas we hold at the same time, and it should explain, or at the least be compatible with, all established, relevant facts. But even the most conscientious and dispassionate application of these criteria does not carry us very far. It can never, in the field of political theory, lead to proof; it probably will not lead to life and meaning. A set of ideas may be internally consistent and compatible with all known facts and still be dead and useless. In learning to identify the truth one needs to look beyond these standard criteria—but not toward another criterion so much as toward the idea of wholeness and integration that is implicit in the standard criteria.

An idea is living and important only so far as it brings us into relationship with ourselves and with reality, so far as it pulls things together. What is implied by the standards of logical consistency and factual accuracy is that nothing be suppressed and nothing ignored. An idea has the function of extending and integrating relationships. Hence, an idea that calls on us to ignore things we know or deeply believe to be true must be judged false or at least inadequate—it has a disintegrating effect on experience and being. A true idea is one that makes for inclusiveness and unity.

Feeling necessarily plays a great part in searching for the truth. Much that must be pulled together does not have the definite and conscious form of a fact or a belief. A great idea is one that symbolizes and unifies not only facts and beliefs that are clearly present to consciousness but also intuitions and impulses that have not been focused on and given form. The idea that does this is exciting. This may seem an invitation to be-

lieve whatever is pleasant or interesting. It must therefore be
added that thinking tries one's depth and honesty. We are
thinking deeply and well when we acknowledge and draw together into a single pattern all that emerges from our experience and emotions. Our search must be without sentimentality
or carelessness or fear.

As for the best way of using the present volume, the kind of
reading appropriate for most other books—that is, without long
pauses for reflection, discussion, and writing—should prove of
some value. Although the questions are posed without being resolved, they are linked together in a way that makes them a wan-
dering pathway over the terrain of political thought. Through
an ordinary reading you should gain some sense of the intellectual state in which political thinking originates.

This book is designed, however, not just to be read but to be
used—through discussion, writing, and prolonged reflection.
The questions are set forth not simply to inform you of the dilemmas of others but to draw you into dilemmas of your own.
This will happen only if, in addition to reading the book as a
whole, you dwell on at least a few of the questions and try to answer them. The questions are stated and arranged to facilitate
being used in these ways.

While I believe that reflection on politics is an end in itself,
this book may also provide help in studying the history of political theory. To understand the great thinkers requires getting
some sense of the interior of their minds, and doing this depends on feeling on your own the doubts and anxieties that
provoked them to thought. Only a rare and profound intellectual sympathy—or empathy—brought to the analysis of a particular thinker can make this possible. What *Political Thinking*
can do, I believe, is help readers gain a vantage point from
which such sympathy, gained from their own insight, or from a
teacher or a biographer, will become possible.

But are the questions we reflect on in the twentieth century
really the same as those that people reflected on in past ages?
Are there, in fact, any "perennial questions"? To ask this is to
raise the most serious doubt that political theorists are apt to
feel about the way ideas are dealt with in the following pages.
Most intellectuals today are deeply imbued with a sense of history. This means that they see ways of life and thought as continually changing and as differing from one historical period to

the next. They are keenly sensitive to the uniqueness of generations and centuries. Hence, in studying ideas they are inclined to say not merely that every era formulates its own particular answers, but also that every era asks its own particular questions. If that is so, it is an illusion to think that our questions are the same as Plato's or even as Locke's, and *Political Thinking* rests on a mistaken premise.

No one, of course, would deny that questions as well as answers do change with time. Every generation has certain unique concerns and perspectives and also certain unique ways of speaking and thinking; every generation asks some questions that were not asked by the preceding generation, and it asks old questions in new ways. This is very far from saying, however, that there are no enduring or recurrent questions. The complete denial of perennial questions is not at all implied by the mere fact of intellectual change and is, for several reasons, highly dubious.

If it were true, the ideas of the past would have no deep and compelling interest for us. They would not answer any of the questions we are asking. They would be mere relics, like the tools or weapons of a former age that we glance at with idle curiosity in museums. They would be unusable. But the truth is that civilized people do not contemplate political ideas of the past in a mood of detachment. The rediscovery of Aristotle, for example, was one of the great events of the Middle Ages; and Plato's presence in Victorian England may have been as consequential as his presence in post-Periclean Athens—his own historical period. The idea that there are perennial questions— questions grappled with in former ages that engage us vitally today—is not a mere assumption; it is a vivid experience.

One may go further and ask: if there were no perennial questions, would the ideas of the past even be comprehensible to us? In some formal sense, of course they would be; we could repeat the words in which they were cast. To comprehend an idea, however, it is not enough simply to think it; one must be moved by it, for ideas have emotional power and this power is part of their essence. This is why they are important in history. But can we be moved by an idea that answers a question we have not asked and feel no inclination to ask? If there are no perennial questions, then past ideas are not merely like ancient tools that we have improved upon; they are like tools designed to do something we no longer care to do.

Perhaps the greatest weakness of the idea that there are no enduring or recurrent questions, however, is that it ignores our common humanity and thereby flies in the face of common sense. Were not those who lived in ancient Greece finite, as we are, and subject to emotion and equipped with reason? Were not the inhabitants of the Middle Ages, like us, often in error intellectually and at fault morally? Did not human beings of the Renaissance and the Enlightenment encounter threats of disorder and the necessity of organizing a governing power? And do we not share with every age one profound similarity, bursting with implications concerning our common humanity: that we live in history? But conditions such as finitude, fallibility, and temporality occasion some of the most pressing questions that we ask. If those conditions are enduring, it is hard to avoid the inference that there are enduring questions.

While I believe that there are perennial questions, however, I certainly do not believe that I have perfectly identified and formulated them. The most that I would like to claim for *Political Thinking* is that it provides an impulse and sense of direction that will help a reader think about the political dilemmas of human existence and hence of all times rather than of our time alone. This caveat has a practical implication: the reader should feel free to ask new questions. Since the following set of questions does not purport to be definitive, one may appropriately respond to them not only by trying to answer them but by pursuing further any line of questions they suggest. The aim of this book is to engage the reader in intellectual movement, and asking questions is at the origin of all such movement.

CHAPTER 1

■ Why Engage in Political Thinking?

One reason for asking this question is that thinking is a peculiarly arduous and discouraging undertaking. Of course, it is often remarked that thinking is hard work. However, one who enters fully into the process of questioning set forth in the following chapters will discover that the difficulties of thinking are far more subtle and exasperating than those of mere hard work. You will probably find, for example, that the effort of thought at first is completely fruitless; to admit uncertainty, as you must do in order to think, may seem to leave you in a kind of void with no horizons in the distance and no solid ground underneath. Further, you will find yourself annoyingly liable to daydream and persistently inclined to think about other things than the question at hand. Finally, you will discover that the products of thought are intangible and often fragile. Ideas that have taken hours to develop may evaporate owing to a few remarks by a friend.

A thinking person is exceedingly vulnerable. Such a person must appear before others, not behind the armor and shield of books read and of ideas formulated by others, but in the nakedness of purely personal thoughts and doubts.

Nor are the long-range results of this nerve-racking effort likely to be unarguably good. It is not obvious that thinking is the way to moral elevation, or happiness, or even wisdom. More than two thousand years of philosophical doubt and disagreement have proved that thinking is not the way to unshakable and enduring knowledge. Undoubtedly, something tells many of us that it would be ignoble to refrain deliberately from thinking. But not everyone feels this qualm; as great a writer as Rousseau believed that through thinking we alienate ourselves from reality and from our own being.

Contemporary American culture reinforces our natural reluctance to think. Granted, verbal tributes are frequently paid to articles or speeches that supposedly "provide food for thought" or that "make people stop and think." But Americans today do not seem to assign much importance to thought that is of philosophical breadth and seriousness. This is indicated by how rarely a philosophical work is found on the best-seller lists. The political books that become widely known are mostly factual works, often written by journalists and concerned with immediate issues in domestic and foreign policy. Books addressing personal concerns are ordinarily designed to provide encouragement and guidance rather than understanding of the universal realities of personal existence. Signs of a society biased against serious thinking are found even in universities, where one might expect philosophy to flourish; here there are diverse intellectual currents, such as behaviorism and deconstructionism, which are subtly if not overtly antiphilosophical. But perhaps the most conclusive evidence of a prevailing disinclination to think is simply the devotion among Americans of hours of daily time to television entertainment.

Any society probably has an inherent bias against original thought. Social order depends heavily on tradition and habit, and these are apt to be weakened by genuine thinking. The execution of Socrates in Athens exemplifies this antagonism. Nevertheless, today in America two forces, both stronger than they have been in many times and places, intensify the normal antiphilosophical cast of society and deepen the reluctance of individuals to subject themselves to the uneasiness and labor of thought.

One of these forces is a strong propensity toward action. Americans have probably always had this propensity, which our environment necessitated and rewarded. Today this traditional American inclination has been reinforced by the multitude and gravity of the problems confronting us—problems such as urban disintegration and persisting racial injustice. Politically conscious Americans are intensely preoccupied with all the things that demand doing and are confident of our power to do these things successfully. This dynamic spirit is in many ways advantageous; despondency is avoided and great tasks are often accomplished. But it makes people impatient with reflection and disinclined to entertain questions that do not have immediate practical urgency. They seek programs of action.

The other antiphilosophical force particularly strong in present-day America is a thirst for facts, which, at least partially, is a result of the bias toward action. Most Americans want to know what is actually going on—in the schools, in the ghettos, in the nonindustrial countries. If asked, for example, whether human beings are essentially estranged (the first question considered in the following pages), they may wonder what that has to do with the deterioration of the inner city or the poverty of Africa and Asia and dismiss the question as irrelevant. This thirst for facts is no more inherently reprehensible than is the bias toward action. Facts can be verified and often put to practical use, which is more than can be said for most philosophical theories. But perhaps philosophical theories are important in other ways, a possibility not likely to be of much interest to those who are avid for information.

In sum, the paths of thought are not altogether inviting. Following them leads inevitably to toil and insecurity but not necessarily to solid answers or inner rest. Also, thinking goes against the grain of our culture, which continually presses on us the urgency of action and the need for reliable information.

Then why—to recur to the title of this chapter—engage in political thinking?

For one thing, some questions cannot be answered by any other means. For example, when does a person have the right to disobey the government? Can a government legitimately break moral laws if the welfare of the nation seems to require it? Should all social and economic inequalities be abolished? Questions of this kind cannot be answered without thought. Information bearing on them may come from social sciences, personal experience, history, or other sources. But only thought can determine what information is relevant and then use it in answering the questions.

But, many Americans might ask, must such questions be answered? Would we not be better off concentrating on the concrete problems at hand? The answer to both question is that to adopt any attitude at all toward reality, even one of concentrating on practical matters and spurning philosophical reflection, is implicitly to adopt a philosophical position. The very idea that practical problems should have priority over philosophical problems is philosophical—it can be formulated and defended only through philosophical reflection. Questions of the kind Americans are inclined to dismiss impatiently are imposed on us by our life. We have no choice but to answer them. Our only alternative is how we answer them: either reflectively and carefully or thoughtlessly and irresponsibly.

To put the matter in another way, only through ideas can we discern reality and enter fully into relations with it. An idea is a kind of light. If it were not for the great political ideas, our collective life would be immersed in darkness.

For example, it is apparent to most of us that Nazism was fundamentally wrong. This would not be apparent, however, were it not for ideas like the dignity of law and the evil of tyranny; and these are not innate ideas of the human mind but were formed by philosophers such as Aristotle, Cicero, and Locke. As another example, it is plain to nearly everyone today that the discrimination suffered by blacks in America is unjust. But why is this so plain? Comparable arrangements have prevailed in many societies for thousands of years and have been taken for granted by most of the members of those societies; one can cite, as an example, Aristotle's casual acceptance of slavery. The light in which we view America's racial situation comes from the idea of equality—an idea we probably would not possess had it not been for thinkers such as Locke, Rousseau, and Marx. Perhaps eight or ten ideas—these not innate in the human mind, but rather products of reflection—are the lanterns of political civilization; they enable us to discern the realities of collective life.

Both the action and the facts prized today by American culture presuppose ideas and the thinking that forms them. In order to act intelligently, we must have ends we are seeking to effect. What are ends, however, but ideas of a certain kind—conceptions of a desirable state of affairs? For example, during the last two centuries people have often protested and rebelled

in order to gain self-government. But for several millennia most people acquiesced in the rule of highly exclusive elites. The demand for self-government does not arise from human nature, but from an idea. Activist Americans, impatient of thought, stand on a groundwork of ideas that has been built by reflection. If that groundwork were removed, they and all their plans would fall into a void in which intelligent action would be impossible.

Something similar can be said of the thirst for facts. This thirst is not satisfied by indiscriminately gathering in every fact that happens to be noticed. Such research would only create a chaos of insignificant and unrelated atoms of information. Indeed, without ideas that tell us what is real and what is significant, it is doubtful that any such thing as a fact could be discovered, for facts do not just lie about like pebbles; their very existence depends on the power of mind to distinguish and relate. An interest in facts that deserves any respect at all is an interest in organized and significant knowledge, which cannot be available without ideas. Consider, for example, the amount of knowledge we possess about poverty. Would we possess this knowledge if the ideas of Marx and other socialists and social reformers had not inspired and directed its accumulation?

Of course, only a few great thinkers create the ideas that illuminate reality and thus guide action and research. But the fact that the most influential thinking is done by only a few does not mean that the rest of us need not think at all. For one thing, the great thinkers do not agree. They offer different and often mutually contradictory ideas. How can we decide which ideas to accept without doing some thinking of our own?

Further, even if we were willing to commit ourselves to certain ideas instinctively and uncritically, we probably could not understand them without having experienced some of the labor and doubt that have gone into creating them. What is meant, for instance, by the idea that human beings are equal? Clearly they are not equal in any measurable quality, such as intelligence or health or emotional balance. One may say that they are equal only in their rights before the law. But why should they be accorded equal rights before the law if they are in no respect equal in fact? The question need not be pursued. It is plain that for someone who has never reflected on the matter, the concept of equality can hardly have any intelligible content.

Thus, despite the emphasis in this book on questions rather than answers, my first response to the query, "Why engage in political thinking?" is that we do so to reach answers that cannot be reached in any other way.

This response, however, ignores one of the weightiest and oldest objections to philosophical thought—that the ideas it reaches must always be undemonstrable and uncertain. It follows that to engage in thinking is to entertain doubts that can never, through thought, be wholly overcome.

This objection seems sound. Few, if any, of the main political ideas held by a typical American or European at the present time can be proved; most of them can be severely shaken. Substantial arguments, for example, can be brought against even so seemingly unassailable an idea as the rule of law. As Plato argued, the rule of law inhibits the full application of intelligence to social problems; further, it may restrict the initiative and energy of the police and thus may enhance the difficulty of protecting property and persons. The reader will perhaps think of answers to these arguments but none that conclusively refutes them. Every important idea is attended by some inseparable counter-ideas; the idea of freedom, for example, calls to mind and can never altogether destroy or subordinate to itself the idea of authority. In reaching the "answers" referred to above, a number of counter-ideas must be more or less subdued; but they will prove recurrently troublesome and refractory to those who refuse to turn their "answers" into ironclad dogmas.

The history of political thought shows how doubt continually pursues thought and frequently overtakes it. There is no more agreement concerning political truth now than there was twenty-five hundred years ago, when political thinking began. There may indeed be less. This divergence of opinion sharpens our original question. Why engage in inquiry of a kind that can only lead to uncertain and disputable conclusions?

This is an exceedingly important question, for it asks whether it is worthwhile to try to reason about the ultimate ends and fundamental assumptions governing our lives in common. This, after all, is the business of political thinking. Clearly, your position on this issue will have a great deal to do with your whole conception of how society should be organized. At the same time, the question is very difficult. Like the other ques-

tions with which political thinking deals, this one, having to do with the value of political thinking itself, has no incontrovertible answer. I shall suggest three provisional answers that may enable us to ponder the perennial questions with some confidence that we are not wasting our time.

First, while political ideas and political philosophies contain subjective elements (like a work of art, a political philosophy is emphatically and thoroughly the creation of a particular person, lacking the impersonal authority of a body of scientific laws), they are not wholly subjective. Very simply, we cannot believe whatever we choose. We must take into account evidence and observe the rules of logical consistency. Granted, no great idea or philosophy is demonstrably true. But it would be easy to formulate an idea or a philosophy that is demonstrably false, either because it is contrary to unquestionable facts or because it is self-contradictory. The uncertainty of political ideas should not be exaggerated.

Further, however disputable the conclusions of thought may be, we cannot live as human beings without them. Ideas enable us to live by understanding rather than by instinct. Of course they also can cause us to live by illusions, but they do not compel us to; and even a false idea can be a step in the direction of truth. While it may seem unsatisfactory that our ideas are so vulnerable to doubt, it is far better to have doubtful ideas than to have none at all. The former state is uncomfortable but civilized, the latter barbarous.

The final reason why it is worth thinking politically is the most important but the most puzzling; hence it requires more discussion than the two reasons already cited. Regardless of any conclusions that are reached, thinking in itself helps us gain a humanity not available in any other way. We are thinking beings, and even through inconclusive thinking, we can gain access to our humanity. Our yearning for action and facts, although often expressing a strong civic conscience, threatens us with the brutalization that is inherent in thoughtlessness.

How is humanity gained through thought?

First of all, questioning and reflecting enable one to realize one's own being in its freedom and distinctness. "All deep, earnest thinking," Herman Melville wrote, "is but the intrepid effort of the soul to keep the open independence of her sea." Speaking again of the soul, or self, he added that "the wildest winds of heaven and earth conspire to cast her on the treacherous, slavish shore."[1] Today, we may think "the wildest winds of heaven and earth" to be fear, bigotry, and fanaticism, and we may see the "treacherous, slavish shore" as the ideologies, bureaucracies, and totalitarian states that abound in the twentieth century. To think is to stand apart and affirm one's own irreducible reality. Those who regard political thinking as futile should remember that the totalitarian regimes of our time have done everything possible to stifle such thinking. This is partly because they have wished to stifle individuality.

Thinking is not only the realization of the self through denial and doubt, but also a way of gathering together and tentatively defining the self. To reflect on a problem of philosophical scope is to call your strongest impressions and convictions into consciousness, to relate them to one another, and to test them. It is to think back on all you have read and experienced, trying to fathom its significance. Thinking is a summoning of the self. Hence the subjective character of philosophical thought, which makes it unverifiable, is not altogether a drawback. It may deprive philosophy of the universally compelling force of scientific law, but it reflects its personal nature. Struggling with and living with doubt has a role in the achievement of individual identity.

Moreover, thinking not only summons the self, it puts us in touch with others. If all serious and candid reflection is an admission that I may be mistaken, it is by the same token an admission that others may be right. In this sense, thinking is a communal state. It means breaking down the walls of dogmatic self-assurance and trying to enter into the minds of others. Strong convictions have undoubtedly had a part in the development of political philosophies, and convictions of some kind may be necessary for personal stability. Convictions that go unquestioned, however, divide human beings from one another. Those holding them become hard and self-enclosed— distorted embodiments of the quality we call "humanity." To think, we must question our convictions and overcome the contempt we often feel for those whose convictions differ from our own. In sum, if thinking sets the individual apart from others

---

[1]Herman Melville, *Moby Dick, or The Whale* (New York: Modern Library, 1930), p. 153.

in their conformity and slavishness, it also places the individual in the company of others in the incertitude and mystery of their existence.

Finally, some philosophers have held that thinking is a pathway to the consciousness of transcendence or of God. For atheists and agnostics, of course, this would make thinking a pathway to illusions, not humanity. Even those who believe in God may be surprised and perhaps offended by the idea that an activity destructive of certainty and leading to no definite conclusions can bring us into contact with God. Is not religious faith a state of absolute certainty, in which all doubts and questions are definitely set aside? Thinkers of great stature have held that it is not.[2] According to these thinkers, the things we are certain of are idols: God cannot be contained in a doctrine.

It can be argued that encouraging religious openness and awareness is one of the main ways in which thinking contributes to our humanity. There is no tension between God and the kind of independent personal being cultivated by thinking; rather there is a mysterious unity. The great German philosopher Karl Jaspers (1883–1969), one of the founders of modern existentialism, asserted flatly that "freedom and God are inseparable." And he added, in one of his typically difficult but provocative utterances, that "where I am authentically myself, I am certain that I am not through myself. The highest freedom is experienced in freedom from the world, and this freedom is a profound bond with transcendence.[3]

Through thinking, then, a person may enter into the mystery of being—the being of the self, of others, perhaps of transcendence. If this is so, fixed and definite conclusions are not only unnecessary, they are undesirable. One is nearer the truth when thinking—keeping the open independence of one's sea—than when securely housed in conclusions built on "the treacherous, slavish shore."

It is because a thinker is searching for truths of a kind that cannot be put into words that, as stated in the epigraph chosen for this volume, "the paradox is the source of the thinker's passion." A paradox is a statement that appears to be, whether or

---

[2] Among the major thinkers who have taken this position are Martin Buber, Gabriel Marcel, and Karl Jaspers, all of whom lived and wrote in the twentieth century.

[3] Karl Jaspers, *Way to Wisdom: An Introduction to Philosophy,* trans. Ralph Manheim (New Haven: Yale University Press, 1951), p. 45.

not it actually is, self-contradictory. For example, Rousseau's assertion that a human being can be forced to be free is a paradox, since we usually assume that being forced and being free are opposite states.

Not every paradox, of course, has value. The assertion that Julius Caesar was assassinated in 44 B.C. and in A.D. 1865 is formally a paradox. It is valueless, however, because it cannot in any way be true. It is simply senseless. A paradox worthy of a thinker's passion must contain a possible truth, as does the idea of being forced to be free. The nature of force and freedom, and the relationships between them, are highly uncertain. Hence the idea of being forced to be free, as startling as it is on a first encounter, is not a palpable absurdity.

Aside from containing a possible truth, however, the value of a paradox lies in the very fact that it is unacceptable. It compels us to keep thinking, to remain open to the mystery of being. A person cannot settle down and live comfortably with it. While Rousseau's statement makes us aware that force and freedom may not be as contradictory as they at first appear, it is not something we can accept, file away in memory, and never question. Again and again it forces us to think.

Handling paradoxes properly is a difficult and puzzling task. It is also a somewhat perilous task, for paradoxes can be used irresponsibly. They can be used as rhetorical devices, lacking serious meaning, intended only to impress listeners and to avoid significant communication. But this simply says that understanding reality—the self, others, and encompassing being—is a difficult and puzzling as well as a perilous task. And there is no need for being relentless and extreme in seeking paradoxical formulations; there is no need, for example, to go as far as a recent French thinker, Simone Weil, has urged. When thinking of something, she asserted, we should as a regular method of investigation immediately try to see in what way the contrary is true. Such a method might be effectively used by a person of genius—like Simone Weil herself—for most of us it would be hopelessly confusing. What is called for is only a kind of tenderness toward reality—a willingness to apply ideas gently, an openness to those who take issue with our ideas, and a resolve to keep thinking.

Readers of this book must be ready to suffer the yeses and the nos that will crowd about as soon as they read a question, that will solicit support from one side or the other, and that will not quickly disperse and leave them in peace. The great questions of political theory are perennial precisely because intelligent people through the ages have not found it possible all to side with the yeses or with the nos. To approach the ultimate realities to which these questions point, one must be prepared to put up with mixed feelings and a divided mind—to struggle against contradictions but to remember, as the epigraph states, that "all thought is the attempt to discover something that thought cannot think," and to keep in mind that understanding will not come in the form of an unequivocal answer. One must realize that the most important questions we can ask cannot be settled once and for all. One must be willing to entertain paradoxes, and that means being willing to put up with uncertainty. In this state of mind it may be found, unexpectedly, that uncertainty is illuminating.

In other words, a reader should not be discouraged by finding it impossible, in struggling with any of the questions that follow, to settle on a single answer. If two mutually exclusive answers appear in some sense both to be true, then thought has achieved a kind of success. It has found a paradox. Rather than being discouraged, one should look about and see whether the truth is not near at hand.

Today we possess awesome powers of action, as manifest in our command of nuclear energy, our exploration of space, and our industrial productivity. We also possess highly developed skills in accumulating and interpreting facts, as is dramatically evident in the scope and refinement of the physical sciences and in the vast quantities of data accumulated by the social sciences. But it is doubtful that we possess wisdom. Our lives are therefore carried on under an ineffaceable question: can we make our powers of action and our skills in research serve any valid ultimate purpose? The fear that pervades our time—fear of war, of poverty, of despotism, and of numberless other evils—shows how far we are from being able confidently to respond to this simple question in the affirmative.

I suggest that the wisdom demanded by our powers of action and research does not lie in knowing something beyond all doubt, as we feel we do when we adhere unwaveringly to a set of clear-cut and perfectly consistent principles, but in a certain kind of not-knowing—in an uncertainty that expresses both independent selfhood and openness to others. We all long for absolute assurance concerning what is true and right; we feel that our selfhood and our relationships are imperilled when that assurance is lacking. But the selfhood and relationships thus imperilled are false. They depend on an illusory certitude rather than on thought. This book is based on the premise that we humans are thinking beings. Only through thought do we affirm our rationality, our freedom, and our loyalty to being. Hence, if we learn to consider questions with clarity and determination and an open mind, we learn something that is irreducible to objective answers—the wisdom and poise of humane uncertainty.

CHAPTER 2

Estrangement and Unity

The word *estrangement* is used here to signify every kind of disunity among human beings. War among nations, conflict among classes, and personal alienation are manifestations of estrangement; hatred, indifference, and loneliness are emotions of estrangement.

Without estrangement, there would be no politics. The antonym of *estrange,* according to *Webster's Dictionary,* is *reconcile.* Following this lead, it may be said that politics is the art of reconciliation and that the need for this art always arises from some kind of estrangement. When the leaders of one nation covet territory held by another nation or when one class resents the easier life of other classes, demands are placed on political leadership. Of course, not every kind of estrangement necessarily gives rise to political demands; it is not clear, for example, whether the personal alienation so acutely felt in advanced industrial societies at the present time constitutes a political problem. The point, however, is that while not every situation of estrangement produces political problems, all political problems are rooted in situations of estrangement.

If estrangement is the fundamental condition for politics, it is also the fundamental condition for political thinking. If human beings were not estranged, whether in quiet loneliness or in active conflict, political thinking would not occur. We are impelled to ask about the ultimate forces and standards governing human relations only when those relations are strained or destroyed. The greatest achievements of political thought have for the most part been responses to social disintegration. Plato's *Republic* can be read as a meditation on the Peloponnesian War, in which the Greek cities not only fought one another for several decades but were also torn within by ferocious factional conflicts; Saint Augustine's *City of God* is an explicit commentary on the fall of the Roman Empire; Thomas Hobbes's *Leviathan* was called forth by the civil wars of seventeenth-century England, and Rousseau's essays were inspired by the degeneration of *l'ancien régime*, as manifest in the artificiality and loneliness of Parisian intellectual life and in the autocracy of royal officials.

Hence, we must begin our questioning by probing the nature of estrangement—by inquiring, for example, whether it is inherent in human nature and whether it can be counteracted or overcome.

The cardinal question about estrangement concerns its origin. Do such conditions as loneliness and conflict derive from the very nature of human beings, so that as long as the human species endures people will be estranged from one another? Or is estrangement caused by circumstances that can be altered or by human characteristics that can be eliminated without destroying anything essentially human?

1   Are human beings estranged in essence?

Today this question presses on us from various sides, although we do not often recognize it. For example, can we hope ever to achieve harmony and understanding among all the nations of the world? If human beings are not estranged in essence, perhaps we can. However, if we are thus estranged—if, for example, we have ineradicable aggressive impulses—a wise leader will not aim at anything so far-reaching as global understanding and unity. If human nature is such that our deepest satisfactions are experienced in war and conflict, then there is little use in dreaming of universal concord; we will accomplish enough if we can moderate hatreds and confine wars to limited areas and to the less destructive weapons.

The importance of this question is exemplified also in the conflict of races. Can we sometime achieve full integration? We can if racial hostility is not an expression of the human essence. But perhaps a human being is essentially an uneasy and suspicious creature who is put off even by superficial differences in others. If so, though we may be deeply convinced that racial differences are insignificant, we probably should not strive for integration; in these circumstances, absence of conflict, uniform justice, and decent conditions of life for everyone would be sufficiently elevated aims.

As fascism shows, it is possible to envision human nature in a way that invalidates even the goal of reducing conflict. War and racial domination, given a certain conception of human nature, may be the highest ideals.

The question of whether human beings are essentially estranged also presses on us through the alienation pervading contemporary middle-class life. Many people today feel that although their lives are superficially harmonious, they lack relationships that are substantial and significant. Such conditions as the disintegration of families and the mobility entailed by many jobs tend to make all personal links tenuous and impermanent. But would those who bewail the lack of community find, once they entered a community, that it is actually of little value or is even undesirable? Is defiant individuality perhaps of greater value, and should we cherish our solitude rather than merely endure it? Community is everywhere extolled. But is privacy perhaps a greater good? Such questions can be answered only by determining whether human beings are estranged in essence.

There are always more than two opposite answers to fundamental questions like this. However, in order to delineate sharply and concisely the issues involved in these questions, it will sometimes be convenient to discuss only the polar positions. This procedure will be followed here.

No one has so masterfully argued that people are essentially estranged as Thomas Hobbes (1588–1679), the mordant and witty English philosopher. The natural condition of our lives, Hobbes maintained, is one of war "of every man, against every man." Where there is no strong central government "to overawe them all," then "men have no pleasure, but on the contrary a great deal of grief, in keeping company." Life in such a state, Hobbes asserted in one of the most famous phrases in political theory, is "solitary, poor, nasty, brutish, and short."[1]

There are, so to speak, two levels of estrangement in Hobbes's philosophy. One level is psychological. People are estranged because they are essentially egotistical. One is concerned above all with the preservation of one's own life; a person also seeks such things as wealth and prestige. None of these benefits can be gained without power. Thus Hobbes attributed to human beings "a perpetual and restless desire of power after power, that ceaseth only in death."[2] We care nothing about others except as they can help or hinder us in reaching our private goals. Such self-centeredness is not perverse, nor is it avoidable: it is our true nature. To be human is to be concerned exclusively with personal interests and personal power.

Beneath the psychological level of estrangement is what can be called the ontological level. Ontology is the study of being; *ontological* refers to Hobbes's conception of the nature of being. Hobbes was a materialist, meaning that he saw every reality as wholly definable in terms of space, time, and the laws of causation. The universe is composed of objects in motion. A human being is simply one of the objects making up the universe, more complex than such things as rocks and trees, but not essentially different. What concerns us now is only one consequence of this view: unity among human beings, as we usually understand it, is impossible. Material objects are essentially external to one another; they cannot be united by bonds such as compassion, empathy, or common purpose. They can be united only in the sense of being put in the same place or forcibly joined together, as stones are in building a wall. Because Hobbes saw human beings as material objects, he concluded that they could be united only by the power of an absolute government.

Many thinkers have argued the opposing view: that human beings are essentially united. Probably the most influential of these was Aristotle (384–322 B.C.), the founder of political science. Aristotle came from outside the world of the Greek city-states (he was from Macedonia) and witnessed the fall of that

---

[1]Thomas Hobbes, *Leviathan, or the Matter, Forme and Power of a Commonwealth Ecclesiastical and Civil,* ed. with an introduction by Michael Oakeshott (Oxford: Basil Blackwell, n.d.), pp. 81–82.

[2]*Leviathan,* p. 64.

world. But from his vantage point he saw deeply into the prevailing political ethos and gave powerful expression to the ancient Greek feeling for the primary and pervasive significance of the city-state. For Aristotle, just as a leaf in its innermost nature is part of a tree, so a person by virtue of the human essence is a member of a city. "The man who is isolated—who is unable to share in the benefits of political association, or has no need to share because he is self-sufficient—is no part of the *polis* [the city-state], and must therefore be either a beast or a god."[3]

Aristotle did not carry the concept of unity to its logical extreme, the ideal of a global and completely egalitarian polity. People could not unite on any larger scale, Aristotle believed, than that of the city-state; moreover, even within the city-state only a few could attain the full unity of common citizenship, most people being fitted only to be artisans, laborers, or even slaves. Despite these qualifications, however, Aristotle's political thought is a sober and powerful denial that human beings are essentially estranged. Perhaps his most famous utterance is that "man is a political being," meaning that we cannot realize our essence in solitude and privacy but only in the company of fellow citizens.

But if, as Aristotle argued, human beings are not estranged by their very nature, why have peace and harmony always been so impermanent and elusive?

2 If human beings are not estranged in essence, why are there so many divisions and conflicts among them?

This question presents a simple (although not easily resolved) issue: if human beings are not estranged in essence, the divisions and conflicts among them must proceed either from human beings themselves or from circumstances external to them. Let us consider first the former alternative—that human beings cause estrangement even though they are not in essence estranged.

What could this mean? The answer is delineated as sharply as anywhere in the writings of Saint Augustine (354–430) a brilliant churchman and thinker, and author of one of the classics

---

[3] Aristotle, *Politics,* trans. Ernest Barker (Oxford: Clarendon Press, 1946), p. 6.

of Christian thought, *The City of God*. Augustine held that God did not intend us to live in a state of division and conflict, hence these conditions were not attributable to the human essence, which was created by God. There is estrangement because we have betrayed the human essence. This betrayal was what Augustine and many other Christians meant by "sin." We have carried out a tragic rebellion against the order of God's creation. In doing this we have rejected our nature as received from God and have become different in actuality than we are in essence. The unity of divine creation has been lost. Neither God nor the human essence created by God can be blamed for this dreadful derangement, but only human beings in their universal perversity.

As Augustine envisioned it, sin is not merely a *tendency* of the will; it is a settled and—humanly—unchangeable configuration of the will. We not only commit particular wrongs; we do so out of a confirmed disorientation of soul. But we are still responsible not only for the particular wrongs we commit but also for the state of will from which they arise. This primal responsibility is symbolized by the concept of original sin. Each of us is an alien within creation, divided from both Creator and fellow creatures. So far as human powers go, this condition is irreparable; at the same time it is our own fault. There is hope only in the grace of God.

Dark and censorious theology of this sort repels many people today. But Augustine's view is not just dogma; it conforms with a strange but common experience. We sometimes feel unable to resist doing things for which we nevertheless blame ourselves; we feel helplessly estranged (assuming that the acts for which we blame ourselves are in some way harmful to others), and at the same time we feel guilty of producing our estrangement.

Augustine's is a fearful and impressive philosophy, with its picture of humanity as a ruined race toiling in a world with no light aside from the gleams of God's mercy. Equally powerful philosophies, however, have been founded on the idea of human innocence. This idea is old because it is not only possibly true, it is pleasant. Augustine devoted much time and effort to attacking Pelagius, a monk who argued that we have it within our power to turn away from sin. But perhaps the most eloquent claims for human innocence are found in the writings of Jean Jacques Rousseau (1712–1778), a tormented genius who suffered unbearably from loneliness and was acutely conscious of the disorders of modern society.

Let us, then, ask Rousseau: if human beings are essentially united and have never betrayed their essence, how has history come to be filled with so much hatred and turmoil? The only possible answer is that they have in some way accidentally (and not from grave, inherent defects) become entangled in circumstances that have estranged them from one another. It was Rousseau's conviction that such a misfortue had occurred in the distant past. Early in the human career on earth, property and power came to be concentrated in the hands of a few. This did not happen because people were extremely evil, but it did subvert the natural decency of human beings and the natural harmony of human relations. Rousseau's confidence in humankind did not lead him to palliate the evils of society; on the contrary, he was one of the most bitter social critics of modern times. But he did not blame the dislocations of society on human beings—at least, not on the human essence or on an irreversible repudiation of that essence.

Augustinian and Rousseauean views of estrangement have had powerful reverberations in other spheres of political thought. For example, conceptions of the value of established institutions are determined largely by the alternative chosen. According to the Augustinian philosophy, a human being is a dangerous creature; existing social and political institutions may be imperfect, but insofar as they assure some kind of order, even if only through the pressures of habit and fear, they have some value. From a Rousseauean point of view, however, order alone is worth very little, for people are capable of far greater things; they can attain justice and happiness.

This is not to say that Augustine always and Rousseau never approved of established institutions. For Augustine, institutions are made by sinful humanity and are bound to have much evil in them; Rousseau thought that the original virtue in the human will had occasionally, as in the ancient Roman republic, escaped corruption and gained sovereign power. But for Augustine, heaven on earth is impossible and any order of life precluding the chaos implicit in human nature deserves appreciation. For Rousseau, on the other hand, because human innocence is not irretrievably lost, there is hope of earthly paradise or at least of earthly justice; but by this standard few actual societies can be seen as anything but mean and degraded.

Another way of stating the issue between Augustine and Rousseau is by asking whether the primary source of evil is human nature or human institutions. For Augustine, the evil in institutions is a result of the evil in human nature; Rousseau maintains the opposite, that the evil in human nature is a consequence of the evil in institutions. Thus for an Augustinian, the idea of humankind escaping the influence of institutions and recreating civilization is unthinkable, whereas for a follower of Rousseau, such a possibility is real.

This polarity suggests another. An Augustinian is apt to be conservative—not in the sense of revering the prevailing order but in the sense of fearing any effort to change it. To tamper with restraints grounded in personal habits and long-standing customs might unleash the disorder inherent in sinful human nature. A follower of Rousseau, on the other hand, can readily take revolutionary pathways. Our original innocence provides possibilities of historical reconstruction. For such reconstruction to occur, of course, humankind in its primal decency must somehow throw off the influence of the oppressive and corrupting institutions in which it is encased. But nothing in Rousseau's thought forbids the hypothesis that this liberation is possible through an act of revolutionary destruction. As it happens, Rousseau himself was not so carefree about revolution, and he did not in fact assume that any act of institutional destruction was an act of liberation. The explosive effect of his thought in history, however, derived primarily from the revolutionary implications of his psychology—implications Rousseau drew out cautiously, but his posterity exuberantly.

In America, students have sometimes adopted a revolutionary attitude or at least employed a revolutionary rhetoric. The established order contains enough evil, such as poverty and racial injustice, to warrant such an attitude. But is there enough goodness in human nature to warrant it? If Augustine is nearer the truth than Rousseau, then this radicalism, often infused with intolerance and self-righteousness, might lead to evils greater than those it attacks.

We have now considered the origin of estrangement—whether it lies in our essence, in a tragic rejection of our essence, or merely in accidental historical circumstances. This discussion puts us in a position to ask how estrangement can be overcome, or, if human beings are estranged in essence, how the conflicts among them can be moderated. In considering this question it may help to focus on a human faculty that political philosophers throughout history have seen as the primary source of unity and order, that is, reason.

3 ___ Can estrangement be overcome through reason?

There is no doubt concerning the consensus of the West on this question: it is strongly affirmative. Granted, in ancient Israel, one of the two major roots of Western culture, there was relatively little respect for reason, our overriding duty being to obey the commands of God. But God and human beings sometimes engaged in reasonable discourse; the Hebraic God was a God who listened and spoke. And in ancient Greece, the other source of our culture, the most powerful and prevalent theme of political thought was probably the idea that people can overcome conflict through reason. The Greek view won the day, and even Christianity became markedly rationalistic in the Middle Ages. The modern world thus inherited a strongly rationalistic tradition, which has been carried on most spectacularly in science and technology. While there have been some powerful revolts against the reigning rationalism, they have not come near to succeeding. Western society might still take as its motto the biblical injunction "Come, let us reason together."

This consensus rests, however, on the assumption that human beings in essence are united or at least that their interests at some point coincide. If they were essentially estranged and their interests altogether in conflict, then, of course, there would be little that reason could do. Far from drawing human beings together, reason would enable the most cunning and ruthless to gain advantage over others. No great political thinker (not even Machiavelli) has argued in favor of using reason in this fashion. But according to Plato, at least two intellectual figures well known in his own time, Thrasymachus and Callicles, did so. For these two men, as Plato depicts them, reason was a solvent of the irrational customs and baseless scruples that sometimes lured superior people into subordinating their own interests to the interests of others.

If at some point individual interests do coincide, however, then even if human beings are essentially estranged and care nothing about one another except as means to individual satisfaction, reason might draw them together by disclosing the underlying unity of their interests. Such an idea enters into one of the most enduring concepts in Western political thought, the idea that government is based on a "social contract." This concept is illustrated by the views of Hobbes. As we have seen, Hobbes regarded human beings as estranged in essence. Yet he did believe that everyone has an interest in peace and thus in effective government. Reason, he thought, could make this congruence of individual interests indisputably clear, thus saving people from the "war of all against all" into which they otherwise would plunge owing to their essential estrangement. For Hobbes, each person is concerned only with personal safety; but reason shows that the safety of each one necessitates obeying a goverment that secures the safety of all.

The Western faith in reason reaches its height with the denial of essential estrangement. The idea that through reason we can discern our common essence and from this source derive the laws that unite us is among the oldest and most durable principles of our heritage. In Plato it was the first principle of an elitist political philosophy built around the city-state; in Stoicism it became the basis of an egalitarian and universalist outlook; in the Middle Ages it retained its authority, although combined with the princples of orthodox Christianity; and in modern times it has been the theoretical foundation both of international law (limiting state power in its external application) and of constitutional government (limiting state power in its internal application). By using our reason, according to this view, we become members of a community that is not destroyed by the conflicts among nations and among classes. Our common membership in this universal society of reason enables us to subject power, with its ceaseless tendency to become brutal and limitless, to rationally certain and morally unchallengeable standards. If there is a single indispensable idea in our past, it is this one.

Nevertheless, several thinkers have viewed this idea either with reservations or with hostility. An indication of the power of the rationalist idea is that probably no great thinker has repudiated it altogether. But one who came near to doing so, and thus serves as a convenient example of the antirationalist position, is Edmund Burke (1729–1797), an Irish-born philosopher

winds of heaven and earth conspire to cast her on the treacherous, slavish shore."[1] Today, we may think "the wildest winds of
heaven and earth" to be fear, bigotry, and fanaticism, and we
may see the "treacherous, slavish shore" as the ideologies, bureaucracies, and totalitarian states that abound in the twentieth century. To think is to stand apart and affirm one's own
irreducible reality. Those who regard political thinking as futile should remember that the totalitarian regimes of our time
have done everything possible to stifle such thinking. This is
partly because they have wished to stifle individuality.

Thinking is not only the realization of the self through denial and doubt, but also a way of gathering together and tentatively defining the self. To reflect on a problem of philosophical
scope is to call your strongest impressions and convictions into consciousness, to relate them to one another, and to test
them. It is to think back on all you have read and experienced,
trying to fathom its significance. Thinking is a summoning of
the self. Hence the subjective character of philosophical thought,
which makes it unverifiable, is not altogether a drawback. It
may deprive philosophy of the universally compelling force of
scientific law, but it reflects its personal nature. Struggling with
and living with doubt has a role in the achievement of individual identity.

Moreover, thinking not only summons the self, it puts us in
touch with others. If all serious and candid reflection is an admission that I may be mistaken, it is by the same token an admission that others may be right. In this sense, thinking is a
communal state. It means breaking down the walls of dogmatic
self-assurance and trying to enter into the minds of others.
Strong convictions have undoubtedly had a part in the development of political philosophies, and convictions of some kind
may be necessary for personal stability. Convictions that go
unquestioned, however, divide human beings from one another. Those holding them become hard and self-enclosed—
distorted embodiments of the quality we call "humanity." To
think, we must question our convictions and overcome the
contempt we often feel for those whose convictions differ from
our own. In sum, if thinking sets the individual apart from others

[1]Herman Melville, *Moby Dick, or The Whale* (New York: Modern Library, 1930),
p. 153.

tions with which political thinking deals, this one, having to do with the value of political thinking itself, has no incontrovertible answer. I shall suggest three provisional answers that may enable us to ponder the perennial questions with some confidence that we are not wasting our time.

First, while political ideas and political philosophies contain subjective elements (like a work of art, a political philosophy is emphatically and thoroughly the creation of a particular person, lacking the impersonal authority of a body of scientific laws), they are not wholly subjective. Very simply, we cannot believe whatever we choose. We must take into account evidence and observe the rules of logical consistency. Granted, no great idea or philosophy is demonstrably true. But it would be easy to formulate an idea or a philosophy that is demonstrably false, either because it is contrary to unquestionable facts or because it is self-contradictory. The uncertainty of political ideas should not be exaggerated.

Further, however disputable the conclusions of thought may be, we cannot live as human beings without them. Ideas enable us to live by understanding rather than by instinct. Of course they also can cause us to live by illusions, but they do not compel us to; and even a false idea can be a step in the direction of truth. While it may seem unsatisfactory that our ideas are so vulnerable to doubt, it is far better to have doubtful ideas than to have none at all. The former state is uncomfortable but civilized, the latter barbarous.

The final reason why it is worth thinking politically is the most important but the most puzzling; hence it requires more discussion than the two reasons already cited. Regardless of any conclusions that are reached, thinking in itself helps us gain a humanity not available in any other way. We are thinking beings, and even through inconclusive thinking, we can gain access to our humanity. Our yearning for action and facts, although often expressing a strong civic conscience, threatens us with the brutalization that is inherent in thoughtlessness.

How is humanity gained through thought?

First of all, questioning and reflecting enable one to realize one's own being in its freedom and distinctness. "All deep, earnest thinking," Herman Melville wrote, "is but the intrepid effort of the soul to keep the open independence of her sea." Speaking again of the soul, or self, he added that "the wildest in order to gain self-government. But for several millennia most people acquiesced in the rule of highly exclusive elites. The demand for self-government does not arise from human nature, but from an idea. Activist Americans, impatient of thought, stand on a groundwork of ideas that has been built by reflection. If that groundwork were removed, they and all their plans would fall into a void in which intelligent action would be impossible.

Something similar can be said of the thirst for facts. This thirst is not satisfied by indiscriminately gathering in every fact that happens to be noticed. Such research would only create a chaos of insignificant and unrelated atoms of information. Indeed, without ideas that tell us what is real and what is significant, it is doubtful that any such thing as a fact could be discovered, for facts do not just lie about like pebbles; their very existence depends on the power of mind to distinguish and relate. An interest in facts that deserves any respect at all is an interest in organized and significant knowledge, which cannot be available without ideas. Consider, for example, the amount of knowledge we possess about poverty. Would we possess this knowledge if the ideas of Marx and other socialists and social reformers had not inspired and directed its accumulation?

Of course, only a few great thinkers create the ideas that illuminate reality and thus guide action and research. But the fact that the most influential thinking is done by only a few does not mean that the rest of us need not think at all. For one thing, the great thinkers do not agree. They offer different and often mutually contradictory ideas. How can we decide which ideas to accept without doing some thinking of our own?

Further, even if we were willing to commit ourselves to certain ideas instinctively and uncritically, we probably could not understand them without having experienced some of the labor and doubt that have gone into creating them. What is meant, for instance, by the idea that human beings are equal? Clearly they are not equal in any measurable quality, such as intelligence or health or emotional balance. One may say that they are equal only in their rights before the law. But why should they be accorded equal rights before the law if they are in no respect equal in fact? The question need not be pursued. It is plain that for someone who has never reflected on the matter, the concept of equality can hardly have any intelligible content.

Thus, despite the emphasis in this book on questions rather than answers, my first response to the query, "Why engage in political thinking?" is that we do so to reach answers that cannot be reached in any other way.

This response, however, ignores one of the weightiest and oldest objections to philosophical thought—that the ideas it reaches must always be undemonstrable and uncertain. It follows that to engage in thinking is to entertain doubts that can never, through thought, be wholly overcome.

This objection seems sound. Few, if any, of the main political ideas held by a typical American or European at the present time can be proved; most of them can be severely shaken. Substantial arguments, for example, can be brought against even so seemingly unassailable an idea as the rule of law. As Plato argued, the rule of law inhibits the full application of intelligence to social problems; further, it may restrict the initiative and energy of the police and thus may enhance the difficulty of protecting property and persons. The reader will perhaps think of answers to these arguments but none that conclusively refutes them. Every important idea is attended by some inseparable counter-ideas; the idea of freedom, for example, calls to mind and can never altogether destroy or subordinate to itself the idea of authority. In reaching the "answers" referred to above, a number of counter-ideas must be more or less subdued; but they will prove recurrently troublesome and refractory to those who refuse to turn their "answers" into ironclad dogmas.

The history of political thought shows how doubt continually pursues thought and frequently overtakes it. There is no more agreement concerning political truth now than there was twenty-five hundred years ago, when political thinking began. There may indeed be less. This divergence of opinion sharpens our original question. Why engage in inquiry of a kind that can only lead to uncertain and disputable conclusions?

This is an exceedingly important question, for it asks whether it is worthwhile to try to reason about the ultimate ends and fundamental assumptions governing our lives in common. This, after all, is the business of political thinking. Clearly, your position on this issue will have a great deal to do with your whole conception of how society should be organized. At the same time, the question is very difficult. Like the other ques-

and statesman whose *Reflections on the French Revolution* is a manifesto of modern conservatism. Burke candidly defended prejudice in place of reason. His writings show a belief in the essential unity of human beings that is as emphatic and unqualified as Aristotle's. But Burke did not trust reason to disclose the human essence. He thought that established customs and traditions reflected human nature far more accurately than did the abstract conclusions of reason; these customs and traditions, enthroned in the human mind, he called "prejudice."

We are not only too deep and complex to be adequately guided by reason, according to Burke; we are too dangerous as well. Burke had an Augustinian view of human nature. Order needs the support of habit and emotion, and thus it depends on institutions and traditions that are old, hallowed, and unquestioned. Prejudice is not only wiser than reason, it is also more powerful. For Burke, then, estrangement is overcome only through allegiance to venerable and awesome institutions. The claim to understand human nature imperils the mutual understanding and respect found only in humble submission to the traditions, customs, and institutions inherited from the past.

The aim of this book is to mark out the main pathways of political thought, not every possible pathway. I do not mean to suggest that there are only a few alternative routes that a reflective person logically can follow. Thought is (and should be) ingenious in finding untraveled ways. Nevertheless, the terrain of thought does impose certain common tendencies on all who start from the same basic principles. Accordingly, the rationalist and the Burkean positions divide philosophers into two broad groups that, despite differences within them, reflect two different ways of looking at the social and political world. The following polarities, in their typical forms, derive from this distinction.

1. *Moral absolutism* versus *moral relativism*. Moral absolutism is the theory that there are moral standards independent of the interests of individuals and societies and also of the standards that happen to prevail in any particular time and place. The main form of moral absolutism in Western history is the idea of natural law, according to which there is a universal and eternal law based on the human essence and discernible by reason. Plainly this idea expresses the conviction that reason does draw people together. Relativism has various forms, which vary according to what is held to determine morality,

and thus what morality is held to be relative to. One of its main forms is the principle that good and evil are defined by each society. Burke was not an extreme relativist, for he believed that certain standards are incumbent on human beings regardless of the rules prevailing in their societies. But his regard for custom and tradition led him naturally to accept moral variations among times and places that a rationalist might condemn.

2. *Uniformity* versus *organic unity.* Reason can discover only the general—that which is common to many particulars; consequently, rationalism readily gives rise to a conception of unity hard to distinguish from uniformity. In contrast, thinkers like Burke are likely to be particularly open not only to the societal differences that are sanctioned by moral relativism but also to those individual differences—for example, in character, talent, and vocation—that are coordinated in the organic unity of the group. A clear expression of this polarity can be seen in Aristotle's protest that Plato erased essential differences among persons in order to unite them. "It is," Aristotle complains, "as if you were to turn harmony into mere unison, or to reduce a theme to a single beat."[4]

3. *Radicalism* versus *conservatism.* To believe that we can comprehend human nature rationally may lead to the notion that we can and should destroy all those ancient institutions that rest on mere prejudice and rebuild them in accordance with rational designs. Rationalism in this way gives rise to radicalism. Such pride before the majestic, enigmatic past infuriated Burke. He set against it the conservatism that necessarily follows from the principle that the human essence is disclosed only through custom and tradition. The kind of order built through generations of prudent statecraft and spontaneous life cannot be deliberately and swiftly constructed according to the counsels of reason, as Burke saw it. If you are fortunate enough to live within such an order, all you can do—and this is your overriding duty—is to respect and guard it.

To guard against oversimplification, however, it seems appropriate to take note of one of the "untraveled ways" that, as I remarked earlier, human thought is ingenious in finding. Contemporary feminists are apt to shy away from both the rationalism running through the Western political tradition and the

---

[4] *Politics,* p. 51.

kind of irrationalism inherent in subordinating critical judgment to established customs and ancient traditions. It is easy to
see why feminists are not inclined toward the latter, toward reverence for old customs and traditions; these have practically always sanctioned the subordination, if not the outright oppression, of women. The use of critical judgment in relation to the
past and present order of society is vital to the social changes
that feminists seek. Still, critical judgment is based on reason.
Why, then, it may be asked, should feminists shy away from rationalism, which means simply emphasis on reason?

The answer seems apparent. A faculty—reason—that from
the time of Aristotle to the present seems to have lent itself
readily to defining and justifying what feminists see as rank injustice is almost bound to be questioned. The purported universality of male generalizations and rules strikes feminists as
dubious. Traditional rationalism appears one-sided and in its
one-sidedness inhuman and unjust.

But what would feminists put in place of rationalism? Not irrationalism, ordinarily. It is not reason itself that is apt to be rejected by feminist writers but what they believe is an undue reliance on reason. They see this imbalance as characteristic of
male-dominated culture and envision a broader form of discernment, sensitive not only to the features common to many
situations—features it is the function of reason to grasp—but
also to features that are unique and thus beyond the scope
of reason.

The feminist critique of rationalism has been reinforced by
psychological studies indicating that female perceptions of reality differ significantly from male perceptions. Females of all
ages are apt to be attuned to the possibilities inherent in particular situations, regardless of what those situations have in
common with other situations, whereas males are inclined to
appeal to general rules. Faced with a moral problem, females
typically are responsive to the unique and concrete character of
the problem, while males search for a universal standard in accordance with which the problem can be resolved. Females display empathy, males logic; females try to elicit harmony, males
to do justice.

Perhaps no single word is adequate to designate the quality
that feminists would add to reason, but words like "intuition"
and "sensitivity" suggest what they seemingly have in mind.

The point, at any rate, is that feminists often attribute to women an insight into the particularities of time and place and personality, an ability to enter imaginitively into situations and sympathetically into the lives of individual persons, that men either do not possess or have allowed to atrophy. They believe that such insight, brought fully into the public realm, might enable us to right the imbalances seen in traditional rationalism. In answer to the queston before us, then—can reason overcome estrangement?—feminists answer that alone it cannot; it needs to be fused with, or in some other way supplemented by, another kind of discernment, a kind more fully developed—in present-day societies at least—among women than among men.

To reflect on the power of reason in relation to estrangement may lead one to an even broader question. Can human powers of any kind overcome estrangement, or are we dependent on something beyond humanity? Asking this brings us to an issue that people today generally ignore. The spiritual atmosphere of our time seems to be one of religious doubt along with human self-confidence. It is widely assumed that we neither need to, nor can, call on anything beyond our own faculties for resolving our tensions and discords. But is this assumption so plainly true that it cannot be questioned? In the past, one of the most persistent and widespread convictions has been that a stable and decent society must be built on some kind of religious foundation. Numberless generations in all parts of the globe have assumed that people can be properly related to one another only if they are properly related to the divine.

We must ask whether this is so.

4   Do we need religious faith to overcome estrangement?

Three general positions in relation to this question can be conveniently distinguished. The first is the self-confident humanism of modern times, often accompanied by atheism or agnosticism and by suspicion of organized religion. No historical lesson has sunk more deeply into the American mind, it seems, than that drawn from the religious wars of Europe and the Puritan theocracy in Massachusetts: religious faith can be divisive and despotic. This conviction has been reinforced for many by the secularism of Marx and other radicals. For Marx, religion was "the opium of the people," and socialists have traditionally dismissed it as "pie in the sky." The serious allegation behind such rhetoric is that religion makes people indifferent to the worldly suffering of others and in this way is an enemy of community.

This humanism is ascendant today. Almost all responsible people nowadays assume that the time has finally come, after long ages during which the majority of human beings lived in squalor and ignorance, to meet the pressing needs of everyone. Our powers of organization and production make poverty intolerable; we must now care for one another in a measure that corresponds with our powers. Most of those sharing this ideal, however, make the crucial assumption that its realization need not be hindered and may even be helped by the weakening of religious faith during the past few centuries. After all, when people felt closely united with the divine, they were usually very imperfectly united with one another; often they were horrifyingly cruel to one another. Now perhaps the love and devotion we once bestowed on God can be bestowed on each other.

The humanist vision of unity can be a moving one. In its light we see ourselves as inhabiting a vast, indifferent universe, clinging together in our cosmic loneliness and interdependence. Even most of those who still believe in God seem to feel that such a vision will suffice, as religious faith declines, to undergird our common life.

In view of this humanist consensus, it is striking that the political thinkers of antiquity and the Middle Ages for the most part believed that unity among human beings depends on unity with God. The first great political philosophy set forth in the West, that of Plato (427?–347 B.C.), exemplifies this viewpoint. Plato is among the greatest figures in the world's spiritual history, standing with such teachers as Confucius and Buddha, and his philosophy is marked by a dramatic consciousness of our separation from, and dependence on, transcendent realities. If the injunction implicit in most twentieth-century social commentary is "Forget the transcendent and concentrate on one another," the injunction implicit in Plato's major work in political theory, *The Republic,* is "Know first the transcendent, then consider one another."

Beyond all we can see, hear, and touch, Plato believed, there is a source from which these things draw their reality and value. He called this simply "the Good." He likened the Good to the sun, which makes it possible for all living things to grow and be seen, suggesting that the Good makes it possible for all things to exist and be known. Like all the rest of reality, humanity is looked upon from this point of view. The being and worth of humankind are reflections of the Good, and human beings and their needs can be understood only in the light shed by the Good. Accordingly, a major theme of *The Republic* is that organizing the best human life is possible only through supreme knowledge, under the sun of all being. Thus human affairs are centered on the transcendent. Those who are separated from this ultimate principle of life, value, and truth cannot possibly attain authentic unity. Plato would find the twentieth-century notion that we should ignore ultimate realities and concentrate on building a good society as absurd as we would find the suggestion that we disregard the laws of physics in order to expedite the exploration of space.

Not long after the time of Plato, Stoic philosophers began to develop a far more ecumenical and egalitarian concept of unity than Plato's. More will be said about this concept further along. The point to be made here is that this new concept of unity still rested on religious foundations. For the Stoics, the entire universe was divine. The duties that bind human beings to one another are imposed by the divine order they inhabit. In this sense there is unity among human beings only through the omnipresence of the divine.

The Platonic-Stoic conception of the dependence of society on religion is the second general position relating to the question we are discussing (the first was the humanistic outlook). What distinguishes it from the third position is its reliance on human initiative. The divine is considered to be inert and merely available; it is humans who act. For adherents of the third position, that of orthodox Christianity, it is God who acts.

Before exploring this difference, it should be noted that the two positions agree in making unity among human beings dependent on unity with the divine. In the Christian view a person is a worthy object of love owing to a sanctity that comes from God. For Paul, the first Christian theologian, we (or at least all Christians) are "members of one another"; but this is only because we have been created and redeemed by God. It would have been as unthinkable to Paul as to Plato that human beings should love one another, or even respect one another, simply for what they are in themselves rather than for the divine splendor they reflect. The only authentic unity, borrowing Augustine's phrase, is that of "the City of God."

Nevertheless, the orthodox Christian idea of the relation of the divine and the human differs greatly from that held by Plato and the Stoics. For the Greek thinkers a human being can ascend to God; this is a power inherent in reason. For Christians, however, the idea of a human ascent to God was an expression of pride. It was foolishly and sinfully unrealistic. The distance between humankind and God is far too vast for us to be able to cross it. Through sin we have removed ourselves from God's presence and crippled ourselves as spiritual beings; thus unity with the divine is dependent on divine initiative. For Christians this initiative was taken in the life, death, and resurrection of Jesus.

In sum, the idea of the ascent of humanity has been replaced by the idea of the descent of God. As a result, the conquest of human discord came to be viewed very differently from the way it was represented in the philosophy of the Greeks. For Plato and the Stoics it was sufficient that the divine was real; human beings could find their way to the high plateaus of divine reality and build their cities there. Even for those Greeks who emphasized the dependence of human harmony on the divine, all cities were in their origins thoroughly human. Christians necessarily disagreed. No real community could be founded by human beings. Only God could break the chains cast by original sin and enable human beings to unite. The unity of one human being with another, no less than that of a human being with God, was dependent on God's merciful descent into the morass of disorder and alienation that human beings have created. Community originates in the action, not merely the availability, of the divine. This is why any true city is a "City of God."

Today many people find it hard to take ideas of this kind seriously. But for many centuries they were taken very seriously indeed, and we would have to be quite complacent to assume that it is the advanced state of the modern mind that makes the profoundest concerns of earlier ages so incomprehensible to us.

Are we more dependent on religious faith than we realize? What do we mean, for example, when we speak of the dignity of the individual? This is perhaps the key phrase for expressing the modern ideal of community; each human being, according to this ideal, deserves respect and hence fair treatment, regardless of race, faith, or class. Few people would attack this standard. Perhaps because it calls forth a sense of the ultimate or perhaps because of cultural conditioning, it has immense authority. On the basis of a humanistic outlook, however, does it make any sense? Jews and Christians believe that "God created man in his own image."[5] According to the Christian faith, God is concerned with the eternal destiny of each individual. One may find such patterns of belief incomprehensible or implausible, but they did provide a context in which it makes sense to speak of the dignity of the individual.

If the divine is nowhere in the picture, however, what qualities entitle every individual to the deep respect that is called for when we speak of dignity? If there is no Platonic sun of being, no God, can there still be glory in every human being? People today readily say that there can be. Is it apparent, though, to the dispassionate eye of observation and reason? This is doubtful. Dignity is not a plain empirical fact that we can perceive in human beings as we can perceive the color of their hair and the shapes of their noses. But if the dignity of every individual is not a plain empirical fact and cannot be derived from any principle concerning the transcendent, then is it anything at all? Is it real?

It would be well for us in the twentieth century, if we could answer this question, for the individual seems to be threatened from all sides. "The organization man," "the lonely crowd," "the revolt of the masses," and like phrases are well-known signals of alarm in which writers have expressed the pervasive sense that the individual is being engulfed and lost. But how can we save the individual if we really do not know what we mean by "the dignity of the individual"?

Nowhere is this question posed more dramatically than in the writings of Fyodor Dostoevsky (1821–1881), the great nineteenth-century novelist, and one of the prophets of our troubled times. For Dostoevsky the issue lay between two radically antagonistic ideals, that of the "man-god" and that of the "God-man." The former is the ideal of a person who has repu-

---

[5]Genesis 1:27. Except where noted otherwise, biblical quotations are from the Authorized (King James) Version.

diated God and embarked on the enterprise of elevating human beings to the status of God. Dostoevsky held this to be a logical and inevitable outgrowth of atheism. Its results, however, were far from the global compassion invoked by humanitarian atheists and agnostics in the twentieth century. He thought that the denial of God was in effect also a denial of the dignity of individuals and of the authority of all moral laws. Thus the man-god would become a criminal, a nihilistic revolutionary, or a tyrant.

Not only did Dostoevsky reject the atheism and agnosticism so common at present; he also rejected the widespread sentiment—shared even by believers—that whether a person is an atheist or an agnostic is purely a private matter. On the contrary, he maintained that these attitudes imperil even the minimal decencies. Dostoevsky would say that the God-denying humanitarians so numerous today simply have not yet realized the real meaning of their loss of religious faith.

The God-man, in Dostoevsky's mind, was an entirely different matter. Christ is the original God-man. The ideal of the God-man is that of human beings exalted to divine status through the mercy of God rather than through their own assertiveness. The ideal can be realized only through Christianity. Hence the decline of Christianity, more pronounced in the twentieth century than it was in Dostoevsky's time, as Dostoevsky prophetically foresaw, was in his eyes an all-engulfing catastrophe.

The four questions so far discussed have enabled us to consider human relations in their most general character. We have asked about both the source and the healing of estrangement. We have asked whether human beings are estranged in essence, and if not, how the human essence has been lost and can be restored.

To reflect on such questions it is necessary to ask what the human essence is—to ask about our nature and destiny. Hence we should recall the idea suggested in Chapter 1 that the self, others, and transcendence are fundamentally mysterious. Accordingly, human nature cannot be objectively and finally understood. "Man," as Karl Jaspers has written, "is always more than he knows about himself."[6]

[6]Karl Jaspers, *The Perennial Scope of Philosophy,* trans. Ralph Manheim (New York: Philosophical Library, 1949), p. 60.

Jaspers's statement reminds us of something else discussed in Chapter 1—the role of paradoxes in our thinking. If a human being "is always more than he knows about himself," any statement concerning human nature can be added to or contradicted. In speaking of the individual and society, therefore, you must always be tentative, inviting further inquiry and avoiding claims that the whole truth is already known. Even though your own self seems the most intimately known of all realities, in theorizing about it you must be wary of the conclusive yes and the conclusive no. In asking about the ultimate nature of a human being, you are striving, as the epigraph states, "to discover something that thought cannot think."

In reflecting on these questions, therefore, you must be open to some puzzling possibilities. For example, perhaps human beings are neither estranged nor united in essence; or perhaps they are both. The words we use for discussing and thinking about such matters seem better suited for dealing with things like stones and bricks than with human beings, and it may be that they do not allow us to express the truth unambiguously. This may be true also of the relationship of human beings with the divine. And in trying to understand why there is social conflict and how far reason can help to overcome it, we may in like fashion be dealing with realities that we cannot finally and unequivocally state in words.

This should not make you feel that thinking is hopeless, however. Rather, it should encourage you with the thought that when the question you are struggling with begins to seem insoluble, you may be getting close to the truth. Nor should you feel that it would be useless to try to choose one side or the other (although, of course, there may be several sides to choose among). You cannot think without doing that, and most of the great philosophers do choose a side. But deciding on an answer should never mean closing your mind to the other side. It was to avoid this that Plato put his "answers" in the form of dialogues, conversations, and that he often did not permit these to reach any definite conclusions. There was always room for further thought and discussion.

I could end the chapter here and move on to other areas of thought. Some of the ideas discussed may become more alive, however, if we see how they apply to the most serious divisions among humans. Over the centuries, the two most profound and unbridgeable divisions have been those among peoples (city-states, empires, and nations) and those among classes. These will be the subjects of the final two questions of this chapter.

5___Should all peoples be united in a single global society?

The history of thought discloses two extreme and opposed responses to this question. Both are old and enduring; both appear in ancient as well as in modern times.

Greeks in the age of Socrates and Plato believed that a political order as large as the modern nation-state was incompatible with a fully human life. Aristotle's assertion that "man is a political being" expressed a widely shared conviction; it was commonly assumed, however, that people can live according to their political nature only in states that are small. To live in a large state or in an empire is to be governed from a distant center and thus to be a subject rather than a citizen. In Aristotle's vision, people are united by a universal essence, yet only a parochial state, the *polis,* enables them to realize that essence and the unity it implies.

This is plainly a vision in which the idea of a global society is threatening and antihuman. It is a vision that has recurred with increasing frequency in modern times, as people have sought ways of escaping the impersonality and inhuman scale of industrial civilization. Rousseau reaffirmed the basic standard of ancient democracy—that a state should be small enough for the citizens to meet regularly in a single assembly. Since his time, some of the most idealistic thinkers have felt that only through breaking up the vast states and organizations of the modern world could community be saved. And in contemporary America most radicals seem to believe that the only way to a new humanity is through drastic decentralization. Indeed, the ideas of community and face-to-face association have become virtually equivalent in many minds. From this point of view, for all humankind to constitute a single society and live under a single government would be catastrophic.

Another kind of idealism, however, is inspired by a very different vision: one of all human beings, with no peoples or races excluded, living in common humanity in a global polity. This conception, like its opposite, that of face-to-face democracy, arose in ancient times. It was developed by the Stoics after the city-states had been incorporated in empires. The *polis* is replaced in the thought of the Stoics by the *cosmopolis*—the cosmic *polis*. As we know, Stoics saw the universe as a divine order; this order is present in laws that can be apprehended by reason; we are all therefore citizens of a universal city. Here the principle that there is a universal human essence takes a very logical political form, the ideal of a universal human community. Not surprisingly, Stoicism was the principal philosophy embraced by the most effective strategists of universal order that the world has known—those who administered the Roman Empire and shaped the Roman law.

Christian thinkers during antiquity and the Middle Ages were even more universalist than the Stoics; typically they envisioned humankind as united not only by natural law but also by a divine plan of redemption. These two forms of unity, they thought, should be recognized and acted upon both through some kind of universal political order and through the Catholic (that is, world-embracing) Church.

The Roman ideal of universal and eternal peace and the Christian ideal of one global faith linger as a bitter longing in the twentieth century. These ideals glimmer faintly in international law and in the United Nations. They deepen the horror that we feel before the maelstrom of nationalism, fanaticism, and war that has filled the history of our times.

One of the most powerful restatements of the universalist outlook is found in the philosophy of Marx. Nations are held by Marxists to be organizations of a doomed class; the workers will establish the lasting and all-encompassing unity that eluded both the Roman Empire and the Roman Church. But how far we are from realizing this ancient dream is indicated by the contributions of Marxism itself to the passions pitting us against one another.

Which do we really want, associations so small and personal that they might, as Aristotle believed, be bound together by friendship, or a peace so inclusive and just that in its compass all humankind is one community? Is our ideal Athens or Rome? These two visions have been invested with such splendor by their idealistic defenders that we may feel let down when reminded that many prefer what we now have, the nation-state system that crystallized about five hundred years ago. This is another alternative to a global society.

Is the nation-state just the wrong size—too large for personal relations and too small for global concord? Most people prior to the Reformation would have said that it is, and many today would agree. The nation-state is vast and impersonal; individuals and their intimate, spontaneous relations seem to be nothing in the face of the nation and its demands for money, soldiers, technicians, and submissive workers. The hatred that some students have felt for "the Establishment," the draft, the Pentagon, and so forth, probably arises in part from their sense of the vulnerability of personal relations before the overwhelming and omnipresent power of the nation. At the same time, however, no single nation can guarantee global peace, and thus national might is dedicated above all to war; nations bring the impersonality of the global state, but not its security and peace. Professors and students seem to have felt these defects keenly; in universities today the nation-state has few warm friends.

During the past two centuries, however, it has been one of the chief objects of human devotion, and not only on the part of the worst human beings. People of intelligence and high ideals have been nationalists, among them the great German philosopher Georg W. F. Hegel (1770–1831), whose ideas had an impact on Marxism, liberalism, and practically every other major strain of modern political thought.

Hegel believed that for a community to have any real life it must have some significance in history, it must play a part in the affairs of the human race. In the past, it is true, small associations had been able to do this; Athens is the outstanding example. Hegel believed, however, that life now had to be conducted on a larger scale. The nation-state could attain a degree of power and of inner diversification beyond the reach of smaller associations. At the same time, however, a community should not be coextensive with that vast and miscellaneous collection of people we call "humankind." It would then have no identity as a particular community. To have this identity, it must be distinct from other communities—in a position to define itself through its differences from them and to test itself against them in war. On these grounds, Hegel looked on Athens and Rome—the small and the universal—as stages that have been left behind in the progressive development of humanity. The climax of history, he thought, would occur in the era of nation-states.

These political bodies took on a religious grandeur in Hegel's thought. A nation is of greater reality and value, he held, than any individual human being. And in one of the most notorious propositions in the literature of political thought he referred to the nation-state as "the Divine Idea as it exists on earth."[7] Hegel has been condemned and derided for such statements, but he was only saying explicitly and philosophically what many modern nationalists have felt.

Hegel was more extreme, however, than it is necessary to be in order to defend the nation-state. It is possible to feel that polities no larger than the ancient city-state are in most circumstances too small to be economically viable, militarily defensible, or culturally profound and diversified, and yet also to feel that it would be presumptuous and oppressive to place the entire globe under one set of institutions. These polar attitudes might lead one to favor something on the order of the present nation-state—a polity that is large but less than global.

From this point of view, the nation, with all its flaws, may seem an indispensible medium for uniting the individual with others. Only as a member of a nation can a person enter into the full range of human relationships—those involved in family, vocation, military responsibilities, and so forth. You can hold this view while admitting that your nation is very imperfect and that your fellow citizens (and presumably you yourself with them) have much to be forgiven. There is, in short, a sober and repentant nationalism that rejects not only the ideal of a single, global society but also the national self-glorification expressed by Hegel.

Who is more nearly right—the Athenian citizen, the Roman-Christian universalist, or the modern nationalist? Each one speaks for an indispensable condition of unity and life. Each makes a reasonable argument.

Let us now, by means of a final question, reflect on unity among classes.

---

[7]Georg Wilhelm Friedrich Hegel, *The Philosophy of History,* rev. ed., trans. J. Sibree (New York: Wiley, 1900), p. 39.

6   Should all class distinctions be abolished?

If we assume that unity is good and our end is to overcome estrangement, this question presents us with two subordinate questions. The first is whether class distinctions necessarily stand in the way of unity. It is possible to argue, after all, that unity depends on the coordination of differences; if that is so, a properly arranged set of class distinctions might be a prerequisite rather than an obstacle to unity.

The second subordinate question we confront is whether it is possible to abolish all class distinctions. There is a dilemma here. If no unity can be achieved without abolishing classes, and if unity is good, it follows not only that classes should be abolished, but also that this has to be done through violence, for classes that are in no way united would be unable to agree peacefully to their own abolition. But the use of violence itself promotes class distinctions by advancing those who command the violence into a separate and dominant class. This dilemma, perhaps, is the contradiction—as fatal as any that Marx saw in capitalism—that has wrecked the promise of the Russian Revolution.

As we consider the question of abolishing classes, then, keep in mind both the relationship that class distinctions bear to unity and the possibility that the very project of abolishing classes is self-defeating.

The call for the abolition of classes contained in the research and thought of Karl Marx (1818–1883), the major intellectual source of socialism and communism, has shaken Western institutions more profoundly than any utterance since the Reformation. The key to Marx's attitude lay in the importance he attributed to economic conditions. Marx held that our ideas and feelings—in truth our whole nature—are shaped by our economic situation. What people think and feel is decisively influenced by what they do for a living. A person must work in order to live, but in order to work must accept a place in the economic system. That place will determine a person's entire situation in life. It is manifest from history and from anthropological and sociological studies that human nature is not fixed but is malleable. We may infer that the character of human beings will be shaped by circumstances inherent in their work.

This view may at first glance seem innocuous and sensible. It implies, however, that classes must be composed of completely different kinds of people and that they cannot possibly be united in a single community. Marx identified classes in economic terms because his emphasis on the formative power of economic circumstances allowed no other differentia to be of primary significance. The main class division is between people who own nothing and thus have to work and people who own property and thus command the resources on which the lives of all others depend. Between these two groups there is not simply a divergence of interests or ways of life. One is tempted to say there is a divergence of species, for their different economic situations make them entirely dissimilar in character.

Reverting to the concepts we have been discussing in this chapter, this differentiation amounts to a denial (1) that there is a common human essence uniting people and (2) that there are common faculties, such as reason, by which this essence can be discerned.

As for the first point, according to Marx a human being cannot be identified with any abstract, changeless idea of human nature. Rather, we *are* what we *do;* hence our nature is defined by our work. Those who do different kinds of work, therefore, such as wage laborers and capitalists, must be fundamentally different in nature and have little or nothing in common. As for the second point, even if there is some very general human essence by virtue of which both laborers and capitalists are human, there are no common, impartial faculties powerful enough to define this essence accurately and to bring everyone to respect it. Our ideas and feelings about life as a whole are products of our economic situation; this must also be true of our ideas and feelings about our own essence. Thus not only are owners and workers basically different in nature, they have different conceptions of themselves.

It is apparent that for Marx there could be no unity among the classes even if there were no serious conflict of interest dividing them. As a matter of fact, however, Marx believed that there was such a conflict. Owners of the means of production (primarily factories in the era of industrialism) are compelled by the system of production to oppress the workers. In other words, all systems of production, aside from communism, are essentially exploitative. It follows that the exploited cannot remain satisfied with moderate reforms but are driven to attack the entire economic order within which they live and work. The owners are, of course, the custodians and beneficiaries of the established order. Thus the two classes are not only different; they are antagonists in a deadly war.

Any social order claiming to unite all classes is, therefore, basically fraudulent. Ruling classes always claim that the populace accepts their governance and the ideology behind it; but this is no better than an effort to disguise the despotism they impose. The liberal democracies, in Marx's eyes, were covert dictatorships run by capitalists. They cannot, as they pretend to, establish the rule of the people, inasmuch as the interests of those being ruled are in fundamental and ineradicable opposition to the interests of their rulers.

Thus Marx provided one answer to the question of whether class divisions are an obstacle to unity. What about the question of abolishing these distinctions? How can this be done without using violence in such a way that new distinctions arise while the old are being suppressed?

Here Marx appealed to what he saw as the natural course of events. History was moving irresistibly, he believed, toward the abolition of private ownership and toward a society without classes. This movement does not depend primarily on deliberate human planning, but arises from tensions inherent in the capitalist system. Thus a group using force to abolish classes, when the time is ripe, would only serve as a midwife for history and would not need to embark on the kind of sustained and systematic violence that might create a new class. And since Marx thought that economic circumstances form human beings, common ownership of the means of production would give rise to a cooperative human type and bar the rise of a new governing class.

Among the philosophies opposed to Marxism in the matter of class relations, two principal kinds can be distinguished: the conservative and the liberal.

In the conservatism of Edmund Burke, class divisions are assumed to be just and necessary. Societies need ruling groups, and some people, because of innate ability, education, and other advantages that cannot in the nature of things be enjoyed by everyone, are particularly well fitted to be members of these ruling groups. Not only are class distinctions justified, but the lower classes can see that they are justified. Thus the conservative idea is that of unity *through* class distinctions, which is the possibility noted at the outset of this discussion: class distinctions are a prerequisite, rather than an obstacle, to unity. Class lines required by a sense of justice shared by all classes are not lines of estrangement but rather articulations of the structure giving unity to the whole.

To put this in terms of the central concepts of this chapter, through loyalty to common traditions and customs, all classes participate in the "prejudice" that unites them. This prejudice discloses the human essence, on which unity is based. Here the human essence is realized not through the absolute uniformity and equality envisioned by some radicals, but by the simultaneous diversity and unity of classes.

In this view, there is no point in asking how to abolish these classes, for they should not be abolished but preserved. Conservatives point to the apparent impossibility of abolishing one class system without creating a new one as evidence that class distinctions are natural and inevitable and that it is vain to oppose such necessities with will and violence.

The most effective opposition to Marxism has probably come from those who hold that while justice does not sanction the division of society into separate and unequal classes, all classes can perceive the requirements of justice and can be brought to cooperate in eradicating class distinctions. This is the central idea in liberalism like that of Franklin D. Roosevelt and John F. Kennedy. In answering the question of whether class distinctions necessarily stand in the way of unity, most liberals would agree more nearly with Marx than with Burke. Granted, many liberals would be satisfied with moderating class distinctions rather than totally doing away with them. Nevertheless, liberalism is generally on the side of equality and is not easily reconciled with the Burkean idea that class differences contribute to social unity.

As for the possibility of attaining this goal—the possibility of abolishing class distinctions—liberals generally differ from both Marx and Burke. They feel that class distinctions cannot be abolished (or moderated) by force, but that nevertheless they must be abolished (or greatly moderated). The means of doing this is the community of reason that transcends class divisions. The classes should unite not in accepting society but in reforming it. All classes should come together in a single community, as called for by conservatives, but not in one that remains what it has always been; they should come together rather in a reforming community, a community that is imperfect but gradually perfects itself.

Two ideas we have discussed are at the core of the liberal outlook: that people are essentially at one, and that reason enables them peacefully to realize their unity. A common essence and common rationality have greater force than the economic system. Owners may not gladly give up unfair privileges, but reason and legal pressure can bring them peacefully to do so. Marx's basic premises—that people are made by their economic situation and that the classes are in mortal conflict—rule out the possibility of any such understanding between owners and workers. This is why Marx was a revolutionary rather than a reformer; unity would normally have to be created through violent destruction of the owning class. Liberalism, in contrast, rests on the idea that economic estrangement is not total estrangement; a common human essence dictating harmony and common rational powers making this harmony accessible remain in spite of class divisions.

This faith has been of immense historical importance. It has been professed in one way or another by most of the governing parties in the Western democracies during the present century and it has provided the main ground on which the totalitarian extremes of fascism and communism have been opposed. But is it valid?

For most of us who are not hungry and cold, liberalism is a more *appealing* faith than Marxism. It does not tell us that we live in a doomed society or that we are obliged to take on the burdens and perils of revolutionary action. It regards all persons with affection and hope.

But is liberalism a *truer* faith than Marxism? It requires some complacency to say without hesitation that it is. We see more and more clearly how skillfully, through the several decades of social reform that began with the New Deal in 1933, the owning classes have preserved their wealth and privileges. Further, we see now that under the governance of these classes, our cities have decayed, nature has been debauched, and the wealth of the nation has been spent in a futile and barbarous war (Vietnam) and in deadly nuclear competition. It is no longer easy to count on peaceful reform or to regard all human beings with liberal affection and hope.

But most of us cannot stand on the Marxist side, either, without serious misgivings. These are occasioned above all, perhaps, by the implications of Marx's vision of the warfare of classes. If capitalists and workers are irreconcilable enemies, has humankind any prospect except despotism and terror? After all, Marx presented a somber picture of the human situation. He did not succumb to despair because he shared the typical nineteenth-century faith in the common people and in historical progress. But today our faith in the common people has been shaken by such phenomena as the vulgarity of popular culture; our faith in progress has been ravaged by the catastrophic events of our time. In these circumstances, Marx can prompt despair.

These changing circumstances have affected the assumptions and expectations of many twentieth-century Marxists. The workers no longer are relied upon to usher in a new society; historical progress is seen, not as assured by natural economic evolution, but as dependent on the revolutionary will of oppressed and alienated groups, such as Asian peasants; and popular culture, rather than being left to fade with economic changes, is subjected to a probing intellectual critique. Calling forth these revisions is the realization by contemporary Marxists that workers and capitalists are not as sharply differentiated or opposed as Marx had thought, and the recognition that capitalism and its way of life have been accepted by most workers about as emphatically as by the owners and managers of capitalist enterprises.

This realism and flexibility on the part of his followers has gained Marx an enduring vitality. He represents an alternative to liberalism, even in circumstances apparently in conflict with some of his original ideas. Is it really Marx, however, who lives in the thought of followers who have almost wholly lost his sense of the alienation and the mission of the working class? Has Marx inspired a view of things that, however worthy of consideration, he would neither recognize as his own nor view with sympathy?

In concluding this chapter, it should be pointed out that all the doubts arising from this question and the preceding one are expressions of the simple issues set forth in the first four questions. Let these be restated. Are the hatred and violence of the twentieth century mirrors in which we see ourselves as we basically and inescapably are? If not, how have such misfortunes come to pass, and how can we gain and enact a deeper vision?

Through what faculties? And through what powers—those of human beings alone?

■ Suggested Readings

(This list, like possible readings listed at the end of other chapters in this book, is intended merely to be suggestive—to help instructors think creatively about suitable reading. As the slightest perusal will show, it is far from comprehensive. Titles are listed chronologically, and most are available in paperback or other inexpensive editions.)

Plato. *The Symposium*
———. *The Republic,* Books I–IV
Aristotle, *Politics,* Books I–III, VII–VIII
Saint Augustine. *The City of God,* Chapters 11–14
Saint Thomas Aquinas on Politics and Ethics. Ed. and trans. Paul E. Sigmund
Dante Alighieri. *On World-Government (De Monarchia)*
Hobbes, Thomas. *Leviathan,* First Part
Rousseau, Jean Jacques. *The Social Contract*
Kant, Immanuel. *The Fundamental Principles of the Metaphysic of Ethics*
Burke, Edmund. *Reflections on the French Revolution*
Paine, Thomas. *The Rights of Man*
Marx, Karl. *Economic and Philosophical Manuscripts*
Dostoevsky, Fyodor. *The Brothers Karamazov*
Durkheim, Emile. *Suicide*
Buber, Martin. *I and Thou*
Freud, Sigmund. *Civilization and Its Discontents*
Bergson, Henri. *The Two Sources of Morality and Religion*
Silone, Ignazio. *Bread and Wine*
Berdyaev, Nicolas. *Slavery and Freedom*
Fromm, Erich. *Escape from Freedom*
Niebuhr, Reinhold. *The Nature and Destiny of Man,* Vol. I
Weil, Simone. *The Need for Roots*
Arendt, Hannah. *The Human Condition*
Marcuse, Herbert. *Eros and Civilization*

CHAPTER 3

▪ Inequality and Equality

The problem of inequality carries us into the center of modern political conflicts. The history of recent times could be told largely in terms of the rebellion against privilege and power that began with the French Revolution in 1789. Socialism and communism have both been deliberate, sustained assaults on inequality; twentieth-century upheavals in Asia and Africa have been inspired by a determination that wealth and power shall not be monopolized by white people. In America, the black rebellion against white supremacy has been perhaps the most significant event since World War II. And pervading the Western nations, the feminist movement has brought under attack not only institutions that for millenia have confined women to subordinate and restricted roles in society but also the philosophical principles buttressing those institutions.

Granted, changes have occurred in the last two centuries, inequality is a less flagrant fact of life than it has usually been in the past. Traditional aristocracies have largely disappeared; the physical lives of most people, in the industrial nations, have become considerably more comfortable and secure than in earlier ages; governments in most Western countries have come to depend for their power on the votes of the populace at large; and the predominant styles and values in many societies have become those of the common people. Even within recent decades, discrimination based on race and gender has been reduced in fact and rendered almost indefensible in theory.

Although we do not yet understand the full significance of these changes, it would be impossible to claim that they are meaningless; and they may be leading us into—or already have led us into—a new era of history. Nevertheless, marked inequalities of wealth, power, and status remain in every nation; the lives people lead are shaped throughout by where they stand within these economic, political, and social hierarchies; and where they stand, in turn, is heavily influenced, and often determined, by such accidents as whether they were born white or black, or male or female.

Thus, inequality and equality are not merely abstractions that can be safely and responsibly ignored, even if one prefers not to think about them. They have so much to do with the history of our times and with the circumstances in which each of us lives that we are compelled to think about them.

The logical starting point for this undertaking is a question that parallels Question 1, which asked whether it is in the fundamental nature of things or the result merely of historical circumstances that human beings are estranged. Here it must be asked whether, beneath all the inequalities incorporated in the social and political order, human beings are really—by nature and not just by convention—unequal.

7   Are human beings unequal in essence?

Certainly, human beings are unequal in most physical and psychological characteristics. They are unequal in health and intelligence and emotional balance and in so many other ways that it would be tedious to try to list them. It is easy to see, however, that these unassailable facts are far from deciding the issue.

To start with, we must ask whether such apparently *natural* inequalities are in reality merely the result of *social* inequalities. May not poor health, for example, derive from the inadequate nutrition that often accompanies poverty, and may not low intelligence merely reflect the illiteracy of an impoverished household? In some cases, yes. It does not seem, however, that all inequalities can be traced to social causes. After all, inequalities are manifest among people who have been shaped by the same conditions. Among those who have been raised in the most favorable physical circumstances, some are healthier than others, and among those who have had the greatest educational advantages, some manifest greater intelligence than others. There seems to be no escaping the fact of natural inequality.

Still, a shadow of doubt remains. No two people ever grow up within *exactly* the same circumstances, and differences that appear minor to an outside observer may be decisive for those molded by them.

Concerning another aspect of the matter, the doubt is greater. Do inequalities we can measure pertain to the essence of the human being measured? For example, in gauging intelligence are we gauging the entire capacity of consciousness or only the ability to carry on intellectual operations that happen to be emphasized in our culture? Our doubts about judgments of inequality may go deeper than this. Let us assume that an absolute standard of intelligence has been discovered, so that when we measure intelligence we are truly measuring the entire capacity of consciousness. Does even a measurment of this kind pertain to the essence of the human being measured? Is intelligence—or any other particular quality—part of the essence of a human being?

The question may be put in this way: is it possible that someone who is markedly and demonstrably inferior to most others in health, intelligence, emotional balance, and other qualities is yet *in essence* equal to everyone else? The idea sounds strange. But we seem to be saying something of this kind when we say that there is an inherent dignity in every individual or that each person should be treated as an end and not merely as a means.

In our age it may seem that idealism is on the side of equality and that there is something cynical in the idea that human beings are essentially unequal, for to say that they are essentially unequal is to say that they are unequally human. Nevertheless, some of the most exalted figures in Western intellectual history have been willing to say this. Aristotle is a good example. He envisioned humankind as a great natural hierarchy, with the main determinant of rank being the degree and kind of reason a person possesses. At the summit of this hierarchy are those preeminent in their powers of general understanding, such as scientists and philosophers. Beneath them are natural citizens, who are rational enough to manage political affairs in company with many others of their kind, and then natural artisans and workers, who should be excluded from political affairs. At the base of the hierarchy are people who have only enough reason to perform services for others; these are slaves by nature. Aristotle defined humanity in terms of reason; hence, to have only enough reason to be an artisan or worker is to be deficient in humanity, and to be a natural slave is to be hardly human at all. Aristotle would have regarded as a dangerous absurdity the Christian notion that a person unfit for science, philosophy, or political activity may nevertheless be equal in essential humanity to the greatest scientists, thinkers, and leaders.

Aristotle would also have regarded as a dangerous absurdity the modern suspicion that no such hierarchy of the kind he envisioned in fact exists, that being an able physicist, for example, is not inherently nobler than being an able carpenter, and that the life of a philosoher may embody disabilities, such as habituation to abstractions, that prevent it from being unambiguously superior to the life of a farmer or laborer. And he would most certainly have been disconcerted by the notion that many scientists might find equal fulfillment as artisans, that many artisans may possess scientific talents and proclivities, and that whether one is a scientist or an artisan, a philosopher or a farmer, may depend more on the chances of life (particularly by such chances as skin color and sex) than on one's natural level. Aristotle would have been particularly offended by the idea that women are not at all inferior to men in either their intellectual or their practical abilities. It was manifest to Aristotle that women were in the same general category as slaves and children.

But if Aristotle oversimplified, exaggerated, and in some cases grossly misunderstood the inequalities distinguishing human beings, it does not follow that he was in principle wrong. It does not follow that human beings are simply equal or that a society that treated them as equal would work. Hence the matter must be pursued. To do this, let us begin by noting that views affirming essential inequality usually assume one of two main forms. For some, the superiority of the few consists in their relationship with a sacred and transcendent reality—with the Good or with God. This relationship shapes their mind and character. It may be said, consequently, that the superior few are superior in sanctity. One of the greatest proponents of this outlook was Plato. In Plato's vision a few stood above all others in their capacity for philosophical understanding (it is noteworthy that these might be women as well as men; it was not from Plato that Aristotle, who learned much else from Plato, learned his disdain for women). What made philosophical understanding important, however, was that it consisted primarily in knowledge of the Good. The preeminence of philosophers lay not in philosophical ability in itself but in gaining that which philosophical ability made possible: entry into the divine essence of all things.

This view is more paradoxical and harder to understand than it may at first seem. The human essence, in terms of which superiority is defined, is not contained within the individual as a separate and self-enclosed entity; rather it lies within the relationship of the individual and the Good. Therefore, the philosopher's essential superiority to others does not consist in superior intelligence but in the transcendental relationship to which intelligence provides access.

For certan other thinkers the excellence of superior people is purely worldly. It consists in such qualities as political genius, artistic mastery, and athletic prowess. Excellence does not depend on any sort of transcendental relationship but is entirely within the person.It might be said to consist, at least for some thinkers, not in being *related* to the divine but in *being* divine.

The works of Friedrich Nietzsche (1844–1900), a writer of exceptional power, tormented by a prophetic vision to which hardly anyone in his time paid any attention, constitute an extreme and moving statement of this belief. Nietzsche was convinced that one condition determined the spiritual atmosphere of his time and the duty of serious people: an awakening to the unreality of God. His melodramatic proclamation of this condition—"God is dead"—is by now a familiar phrase. This condition compels us to cast off the self-destructive humility imposed on us by Christianity and to affirm our full worldly being. What does this mean? What is the nature of our worldly being? According to Nietzsche, it is "the will to power." Being is power, and it is our nature to transcend ourselves ceaselessly and to search for greater and greater power. Hence, if we are now to affirm ourselves, taking up the cosmic room, so to speak, that once was filled by God, we must unapologetically dedicate ourselves to the enhancement of our power. This did not necessarily mean political activity and war; a great artist, Nietzsche thought, might be more powerful—in better command of the materials being worked with—than a Roman emperor. But it did mean inequality.

Nietzsche repeatedly and with utmost bitterness attacked the idea of equality, which he saw as one of the devices by which the masses, in their pettiness and rancor, crush human greatness. The average person is weak, and the grandeur of humanity thus depends on those with the daring and strength to raise themselves far above the vast herds of common people. Now that God is dead, human existence depends for its splendor and significance on the few who, rather than worshipping transcendent gods, become gods themselves. These few would not necessarily be white or racially pure. Human superiority was a matter of culture and spirit, not race. It is worth noting, however, that the superior few would always be men; Nietzsche unapologetically, even stridently, called for male mastery and female subservience. In many ways, Nietzsche was exhilaratingly free of ancient prejudices; in his views of women, however, he clearly exposed himself to the charge that he failed in what he was above all trying to do, to think anew. At any rate, Nietzsche's philosophy as a whole amounts to a repudiation of the idea of equality. A concept that was for ages a basic—if largely unobserved—principle of Western thought is cast aside. Human relations must once more, as in ancient times, be shaped by domination and rank.

Plato and Nietzsche, both maintaining that human beings in essence are unequal, are among the greatest names in the history of the Western spirit. Despite their authority, however, one of the most irrepressible and potent ideas ever conceived is that all inequalities are insignificant; in essence, human beings are equal. Without this idea the modern attack on inequality would not have occurred. There probably would have been no French Revolution; socialism and communism would perhaps not have arisen, nor the revolutions in Russia and China have occurred; blacks in America and Africa, landless peasants in Asia and the Philippines and Latin America, might not have set out to transform their situations. Without the idea of equality, there perhaps would have been no feminist rebellion against the ways in which established institutions discriminate—much to the disadvantage of women, feminists believe—between the sexes. Of course, what might have happened in history, but did not, can never be surely known. It is quite certain, however, that if the idea that human beings, regardless of all external features, are equal had never entered anyone's mind, the face of the civilized earth would look very different than it does today. What is the basis of this idea?

Nietzsche was right in associating belief in equality with belief in God. The first philosophical defense of equality seems to have come from the later Stoics, with their religious reverence for cosmic order. Human beings were held to be equal in that every person could understand the demands of the moral law, demands implicit in the divine harmony of the cosmos. In this way, human beings were equal in their relationships with the divine. Moreover, if the idea of equality was planted in the Western mind by the Stoics, it deepened its roots and grew under the care of the Christians. Here, too, equality was grounded, not on the claim that human beings are similar in character or intelligence or some other worldly quality, but on their relationships with transcendence. For Christians, transcendence meant God, and God was merciful toward all persons, regardless of worldly excellences and distinctions. Every person was formed by God, and every person, having betrayed these divine origins, was offered redemption. In the face of the glory and hope surrounding God's descent into the world, all natural and social distinctions—health, intelligence, and beauty no less than rank, power, gender, and wealth—faded into irrelevance.

Transcendentalism remained in the concept of equality that helped to inspire the rise of modern liberalism and democracy. John Locke (1632–1704), for example, who defended the establishment of constitutional (that is, lawful or limited) government in England and who influenced the framers of the American Constitution, clearly did not believe people to be equal in their observable qualities. They were, for Locke, equal only in the rights received from God. In like fashion, Thomas Jefferson (1743–1826) asserted that human beings were *created* equal and that they were endowed *by their Creator* with inalienable rights. Thus the idea of a sanctity received through a relationship with the divine is the basis not only of a certain conception of essential rank and inequality, as in Plato, but also of the traditional idea of essential equality.

Among the great political thinkers only one, Thomas Hobbes, maintained that in their purely worldly qualities people are essentially equal. However, his argument is not likely to appeal to those who, without believing in God, believe in the dignity of the individual, for in Hobbes's view people are less deserving of equal respect than of equal disdain. Our equality lies in our common subjection to human limitations and desires and, above all, in our common subjection to death. Hobbes sardonically pointed to the equalizing power of death with the observation that anyone can kill anyone else (a point tragically illustrated in the assassination of President Kennedy, apparently the attempt of a profoundly alienated young man to rise forcibly above obscurity and insignificance). And not only are we all mortal; we all are governed by the egotistical desire to postpone death as long as we possibly can. This is where the interests of human beings coincide, despite their essential estrangement, making it possible to organize a society that is advantageous for everyone. Hobbes's egalitarian outlook did not rest wholly on death; he looked skeptically on all the supposed virtues and merits in which people take pride and he deftly punctured human pretensions. He conveyed the impression, however, that death was the sovereign equalizer. While in the eyes of Christians all worldly rank and excellence melted into insignificance before God, before the glory of divine mercy and omnipotence, in the eyes of Hobbes this happened before inescapable death.

Hobbes's unusual view aside, the foundation of traditional egalitarianism is religion. Where does this leave contemporary humanity, which doubts the existence of God and the soul but is convinced of the dignity of the individual? Many people today assent to Nietzsche's declaration that the time has come for us to rely on our own intelligence and courage and not on God. But most of those people refuse to take seriously Nietzsche's insistence that when it comes to intelligence, courage, and other qualities we presumably need in order to take the place of God, we are drastically unequal. Instead, they continue, with Christians, to exalt the common person.

Does this make sense? Can one make a case, on empirical grounds, and without any reliance whatever on religious presuppositions, that all human beings are equal? *All* necessarily includes criminals and alcoholics, the retarded and the insane, the diseased and the aged; it includes those who are filthy and personally repellent and those who are unable or unwilling to fulfill any useful function in society. Counting every one of such persons and looking unsentimentally and irreligiously at the simple facts, can it be argued that all human beings are equal? The question is important partly because today the ancient religious foundations beneath the idea of equality have been largely abandoned. Socialism and communism, for example, are typically more or less irreligious (liberation theology is an exception); peasant uprisings have commonly been led by Marxists, who, as such, are atheists; feminist writers do not, for the most part, appeal to religious principles. How thin is the ice on which this great multitude of rebels is skating?

Perhaps it is not fair, however, to suggest that we stand in an either-or situation—either equal before God or unequal in a godless universe. A powerful strain in Western thought holds that human beings are equal by virtue of the fact that they are all rational beings. Those holding this view typically see reason as a moral rather than a practical faculty; it enables us to formulate laws governing our behavior. It is reason, for example, that leads us to insist that all persons in like circumstances be treated alike. Thus, admitting that people are unequal in some of the uses of reason—for instance, in writing books or playing chess—it may be argued that they are equal in their capacity for judging whether they and others have been treated fairly. If this is true, it is not necessary to choose between religious egalitarianism and agnostic, or atheistic, elitism. Whether God exists or not, all persons could discern with equal force and depth the requirements of justice and thus make equal claims to take part in political affairs and share in the common life.

But again we face the recurrent question: is this true? Certainly it may be. It has been accepted by numerous distinguished philosophers, among them Immanuel Kant. Still, if reason were a moral faculty, one would expect all who are capable of reasoning to be moral. As we all know, however, they are not. And if moral inequalities occur among people able to reason (even though they should not, according to the original hypothesis), one would expect evil people to be deficient in reasoning ability and good people to be exceptionally rational. But again, we all know that some criminals are highly intelligent and that tyrants may be cunning and astute. On the other hand, we do not assume that saints will display intellectual brilliance or uncommon intelligence, although some of them have. It appears, then, that morality depends on something more, if not other, than reason—perhaps on certain emotional or character traits. But can that "more" be added without undermining the principle of equality?

The question, then, remains: does the idea of equality necessarily presuppose that of transcendence? Can we claim that all people are equal without appealing to something beyond the realities we can see and measure?

The issue is involved in some of the most pressing concerns of our time. Despite centuries of equalization, inequality remains a stubborn and shameful reality. It is manifest in the acute poverty that persists even in a country as wealthy as the United States, in vast concentrations of private wealth, in the immense hierarchical organizations that dominate economic life in the industrial nations, and in the overwhelming power that has accumulated in the hands of governmental executives, exemplified strikingly by the American presidency. It is manifest also in the economic and educational deprivations still, in spite of all recent progress, suffered by blacks and hispanics in America. Inequality is evident, finally, in a host of disabilities and inequities still suffered by women. The question is whether under these circumstances the cause of equality is doomed by the secularism of its defenders, that is, by their inability to appeal to any source of dignity beyond the plain empirical character of the average person, with all of its manifest limitations and faults.

However you respond to this issue, the position you take will shape your views of how society should be organized. Let us consider this aspect of the matter.

8   If some human beings are essentially superior to all others, how and by whom can they be identified?

First, it must be asked whether the best human beings, if such there be, can be identified at all. We are strongly tempted to assume without thought that they can, for it is humbling and exasperating to think that, grounded in the depths of human nature and destiny, there may be a hierarchy of excellence but that we cannot bring it to light. Those I esteem most highly may stand very low in this hierarchy and those whom I ignore or condemn may be, in a manner of speaking, ontological princes. I myself may be far more base and contemptible (or, of course, far more admirable) than I realize. Such a view of things may seem strange, but—assuming that excellence can consist in a transcendental relationship—it has been held by many people, most of them Christians who accepted the doctrine of predestination. Only God, they believed, could determine one's true worth, and God's judgment would be handed down only at the end of time. The difficulty of living in the face of so dismaying an uncertainty, however, is indicated by the anguish of devout people at the thought that, if not they themselves, some whom they love—husbands, wives, friends—might be eternally condemned and lost. And aside from the personal anguish likely to arise from the idea of an invisible hierarchy of excellence, there is the political consternation: how can we reasonably arrange for the distribution of power if we cannot distinguish between the better and the worse?

Plato, Aristotle, and Nietzsche all provide a measure of reassurance. Granted, our casual judgments may be in error, and serious mistakes may thus be made—especially in democracies, where reliance is placed in masses of ordinary people, who lack the time, training, information, and all else needed for making accurate judgments. Nonetheless, the true rank of human beings can be humanly known and the order of society can be regulated accordingly.

Still, one must wonder. Even if excellence is entirely worldly, consisting in visible qualities, such as political sagacity and artistic genius, it seems that human beings may often fail to see it. Abraham Lincoln, ranked by most present-day historians as the greatest American President, was regarded by many of the best-informed people of his time as an oaf and a buffoon. Impressionist painters whose works now seem enchanting to most viewers were occasionally, while at their easels in the streets of Paris, spat upon by passers-by.

If excellence consists not in visible, worldly qualities but in a relationship with transcendence, is not our fallibility magnified? How can we have reliable knowledge of any such relationship? Can one be sure even of one's own relationship with God or the Good? These questions are likely to be particularly persistent and sharp to those who believe, like orthodox Christians, that our relations with God depend not on our own intentions and powers, but on God's. Who among us can anticipate and announce the decisions of God? "Judge not, that ye be not judged."[1] The most dramatic symbol of God's nullification of human rank is the crucifixion of Jesus: one who died ignominiously with two thieves was, in the faith of Christians, the Lord of the human race.

In order to proceed with the discussion, however, let us set aside these doubts and assume that excellence can be recognized. By whom? There is much sense in the notion that if there are absolutely superior human beings, the only ones who can identify them are others of like superiority. To argue otherwise is to suggest an anomalous defect in the superior people—their lack of ability to recognize superiority—and an anomalous virtue in their inferiors—their possession of that ability. Thus, in Plato's plan for government by philosophers (those who have ascended to the Good), philospher-rulers—who might be women, in Plato's plan—would be chosen by philosopher-rulers. This is partly because Plato conceived of the philosopher as not merely superior but virtually perfect; hence no electorate composed of those inferior in philosophical excellence could possibly have grounds for challenging the philosopher's judgment. But a similar logic works, although not quite so irresistibly, in an aristocracy where the leading class is conceived to be merely superior to other classes without being perfect; the superiority of the aristocrats disqualifies every competing electorate. In short, the idea of a self-chosen elite, given elitist premises, is natural and logical.

The paradoxical idea is that of an elite chosen by their inferiors, and it is a surprising fact in the history of thought that this idea has been supported by a number of distinguished thinkers. The main form of the idea is the principle that government is legitimate only with the consent of the governed. This principle was common both in ancient times and in the Middle Ages, long before the rise of modern democracy. It is true that it grew less out of confidence in popular judgment than out of the moral conviction that people cannot be rightfully subjected to power without their consent. But this conviction could not

[1] Matthew 7:1.

have had any practical effect without some confidence in the good sense of the people. Thus a number of thinkers who believed in government by a superior few trusted sufficiently in the many to accord them the right of consent. The preeminent minority was to be identified, at least to the extent of being freely accepted, by the common majority.

The trouble with vesting electoral powers either in the few or the many is that neither is infallible or even nearly so. This fact makes it easy to understand the charm of an impersonal process. For example, one of the most alluring features of the doctrine of *laissez-faire,* or "free enterprise," is the idea (not insisted upon by sophisticated defenders of the doctrine, but arising spontaneously and inevitably) that those who succeed in a free market are those with personal qualities deserving of wealth, status, and power. Competition automatically sifts out the superior people. It can be objected, of course, that financial success is not a reliable indicator of general human excellence, and perhaps not even of economic acumen (since it can be caused by luck or trickery). It cannot be doubted, however, that the ideal of the free market has attracted support partly because it seems to some a reasonably accurate way—a way invulnerable to the hazards of human judgment—of singling out the best and most intelligent people.

It testifies to the charm of an impersonal process that opponents of market economics devised their own system for evading human fallibility. This is the so-called merit system for appointing and promoting civil servants. The principal alternative to the free market is govermental intervention, and opponents of laissez-faire generally favored larger and more efficient government. This could be achieved, it was thought, by appointing people to official positions solely on the basis of examinations open to all aspirants to governmental service and by advancing people to higher rank on the basis of performance in office and without regard to party affiliation. The main cause of an incompetent officialdom is party favor and bias, and those would be largely eliminated by a well-designed merit system.

Faith in impersonal ways of elevating elites has been severely shaken—by economic crises and by the absence of clear cultural or spiritual distinction, or even political sagacity, among business leaders (in the case of laissez-faire) and by the rise of large, inefficient, and unwieldy bureaucracies (in the case of the merit system). Where does this leave us? The reigning democratic ethos tells us to trust the judgment of the people. Yet hardly anyone does, as is evident in the widespread contempt for those raised up by popular judgment—the politicians. Thus, contemporary uncertainties compel us again to ask: if there are superior people, how can we find them?

In order to think fully about this question one must ask not only who—or what process—will decide, but also what standards will be used. What are the surest manifestations and most reliable signs of human superiority?

The most common answer given in the past is hard for most people now to take seriously: the best are to be found among the wellborn. This belief was widespread during antiquity and the Middle Ages. Even John Locke, the principal theorist of modern liberalism, apparently assumed that government would generally be carried on by a hereditary aristocracy. The major reason people were able to accept birth as a reliable indicator of virtue and governing capacity for so long probably lies in their belief in "breeding." The connotations of this concept are both biological and cultural. A person with breeding supposedly has inherited superior psychological and physical potentialities and presumably has been disciplined and educated in ways that bring those potentialities to their fullest realization. A titled member of a traditional aristocracy thus might be looked upon as an embodiment of centuries of biological selection and cultural development.

The aristocratic ideal is not absurd. This is shown by its workability during many generations and in many civilizations. It is shown also by its acceptance in our own time by so intelligent and skeptical a man as Nietzsche. Few of us today, nevertheless, would willingly embrace it. We are too sensitive to its overtones of race and privilege; we are democratically unsentimental about titles and skeptical of inherited wealth and power.

But what better signs of superiority are there than birth?

The modern world has one large answer to this question, an answer very widely accepted, although it means different things to different people. This is performance. Superiority, it may be said, is defined by *action* rather than *being;* it is what one has done that counts. There are many types of performance—political, military, and academic, for example. Most es-

teemed in recent centuries, perhaps, has been business performance; it was regarded by early Calvinists as a sign even of the
kind of excellence prized by God. The American people have
occasionally taken military success as a sign of excellence; this
is exemplified in General Eisenhower's two terms in the presidency. It must be said, however, that while virtually everyone
agrees that superiority must be determined by performance,
there is little agreement as to what kind of performance is decisive. It is a commentary on the fragmentation and uncertainty
of modern civilization that no human activity has preeminence. This fact lessens the practical and political force of our
esteem for performance.

Despite our uncertainties, however, there is a popular concept
that sharply focuses such beliefs as the superiority of a few and
the importance of empowering them. It is that of *meritocracy*.
Gradations of excellence are assumed to exist and to constitute the only reasonable basis for social organization. The concept of meritocracy includes no precise specifications concerning the kind of performance determining excellence or the way
it can best be judged. But meritocracy is commonly an ideal of
technological and administrative efficiency. Excellence is
thought of as scientific, industrial, and managerial rather than
artistic, religious, or heroic. Competence is more important than
inspiration. The concept tends toward ideological neutrality. A
conservative and a reformer both might believe in the hierarchy
of merit. But meritocracy is more apt to be favored by conservatives than by reformers for it is premised on a concept of justice
in which equality means little but equality of opportunity. Thus
the standards of meritocracy are often invoked against programs of racial justice that would compromise the apportionment of power and position strictly on the basis of competence.

The idea of meritocracy provides a timely focus for thought.
By reflecting on it one might come to grips with all of the main
issues touched on in the last few pages: Can superior people be
identified? If so, by whom? Through what processes? And by
what standards?

These are formidable questions, however, and the reader
may begin to despair of finding answers to them. Let us, therefore, go back to the beginning and try another path. This path
starts out with a rejection of the premise underlying this entire
discussion, that some human beings are essentially superior to

all others. On the contrary, human beings are essentially equal. This assumption requires us to consider an entirely different set of questions. To begin with, if human beings are essentially equal, must they be socially, economically, and politically equal?

9   If human beings are essentially equal, are all conventional inequalities wrong?

Conventional is used here as an antonym for *natural*. All the inequalities resulting from the laws and customs of the social order are conventional; such inequalities include those of social status, power, wealth, and honor. Of course, it is possible to argue that in a good society the conventional inequalities would be natural as well. But if human beings are essentially, or naturally, equal, then all inequalities are purely conventional.

The idea that human beings are essentially equal, strange to say, had been in the Western mind for over a thousand years before it motivated a serious attack on conventional inequalities. Neither Stoics nor Christians sought to abolish even slavery, let alone other established ranks. Their restraint came partly from their belief that nothing mattered except the state of a person's soul, which was not necessarily affected by rank in society. It stemmed also from their belief that the order of society was sanctioned by God and hence was not to be attacked by human beings. The resulting social attitude was disrespectful yet submissive. The inequalities inherent in the established order were at once condemned and tolerated—condemned because they clashed with the principle of equality and tolerated because of their ultimate insignificance and their dependence on divine permission.

However, once people thought that social conditions do affect the morals and the ultimate happiness of individuals, and that social conditions are not sanctified by God, the idea of equality began to shake the hierarchies of the established order. The idea was like a volcano that had lain dormant so long people had forgotten the fire and lava underneath and had built villages on its sides, but that suddenly began to erupt, pouring destruction on all the habitations around it.

Let me restate the logic of this upheaval. If human beings are essentially equal, if the denial of their essential equality will not be compensated on another plane of being but does grave and irreparable harm, and if the social order is a product of human will rather than divine will, then privileges and power that cannot be justified in terms of the public good are intolerable. About two hundred years ago, it began to seem that all of these conditions existed. The idea of equality was no longer dormant.

In the eruption that followed, the two principal thinkers—the volcanic figures of modern thought—were Rousseau and Marx. Both expressed a new sense that the individual's whole life and nature are shaped by society; for beings without transcendental soul or transcendental life the social order is an all-encompassing fate. Both thinkers, moreover, reflected the loss of faith that society is governed by God and the growing conviction that there is nothing to alleviate worldly injustice or to ease our responsibility for correcting it. These attitudes, combined with the idea of equality, moved both thinkers to challenge priests, aristocrats, kings, and (borrowing a phrase of Santayana's) all other "dominations and powers." We live today amid institutional ruins that Rousseau and Marx did much to produce, and we hear all around us the continuing reverberations of their assault on established institutions.

It is hard not to share their outrage. It is by no means clear that human beings are unequal in essence; at least it does not seem clear enought to justify the inequalities in wealth, power, and privilege that have prevailed in practically every society. Nor is it clear that religious faith obliges us to acquiese to injustice. From the standpoint of faith, the rectification of injustice is no doubt a matter of less desperate importance than it is from a purely worldly standpoint. Nevertheless, religion does not require—or, perhaps, even allow—writing off the world, and the idea that established injustice is always divinely sanctioned is the product of a particular religious culture, not a necessary inference from religion as such.

Thus, whether your basic stance is that of faith or worldliness, it is not farfetched to see the subjection and deprivation suffered by the masses throughout history as a continuing outrage perpetrated by the "respectable" elements heading society.

All the same, people do seem to be unequal in important characteristics, such as intelligence and emotional balance, whether as a result of inequalities of essence or inequalities of social condition. Furthermore, the working of society seems dependent on inequalities of power and rank; planning can be done and action initiated only by a few. For these reasons, even while feeling the anger Rousseau and Marx felt over the inequalities that have been relentlessly imposed on people throughout history, we may draw back from the project of establishing total equality.

Rousseau and major followers of Marx have manifested this ambivalence. Rousseau and Marx alike stood for the general principle of radical democracy, government carried on either directly by the people or by represenatives held closely to the immediate will of the people. In drawing up actual governmental plans, however, as he once did for the government of Poland, Rousseau was willing to sanction inequalities of wealth, rank, and power. Some of Marx's followers have felt compelled to make even more far-reaching concessions of this kind, including the establishment and justification of what may be a new kind of class dictatorship.

Hesitations about equalization are poignantly evident among women in our time. The experience of a great many women has revealed harsh discords between nature and convention. They have been conscious of potentialities stifled by the conventional specification that the home is the woman's sphere and raising children her proper vocation. Many have consequently been bitterly rebellious. Yet convention in this case has moorings of a sort that convention does not always have: distinctive biological capacities and social expediency. Many women have been strongly desirous of bearing children. But as most societies are presently organized, it is often difficult for mothers to arrange for the care, by anyone but themselves, of the children they have borne. In addition, some experts in child care have questioned whether it is possible for anyone but the mother to provide the kind of attention and love a young child needs. Hence, many women have felt compelled, either by existing social structures or by conscience, to conform in some measure with an order of things they find, if not flagrantly unjust, at least personally burdensome.

We shall return to this dilemma later in the present chapter; and in the following chapter we shall look again at the whole puzzle of equality from the vantage point of power. Meanwhile, we may reflect further on the ideal of equality by considering its relationship with two other ideals, those linked with it in the rallying cry of the French Revolution: "Liberty, Equality, Fraternity." Let us begin with liberty.

10   If all conventional inequalities were abolished, could liberty survive?

Most of us spontaneously answer that it could, for liberty and equality have together been among the chief political goals in modern times. The Minutemen of Lexington and Concord are heroic symbols of one of the first efforts to reach these goals. In 1789, only a few years after the end of the American Revolution, the French Revolution began. That revolution, in spite of the Reign of Terror and in spite of its denouement (the rule of Napoleon, followed by the restoration of the monarchy), has become a legend representing the human quest for both liberty and equality. A few have criticized this quest, to be sure, but they are a small minority, standing aside from—or occasionally in the path of—the major movement of modern thought and hope. Most of us, as part of this movement, assume that liberty and equality are fully harmonious.

Is it sensible, however, to assume that our political ideals in no way confict with one another? Few of us have personal goals that are completely harmonious. In our private lives we often have to give up one thing we desire in order to gain something else. Why should we think public life is any different? The very fact that we are finite beings suggests that we can not gain everything that we seek. We may, then, have to choose between liberty and equality; or if we choose both together, we may have to satisfy ourselves with a severely limited measure of each.

Such doubts do not arise merely from speculation, but are provoked by experience. The pursuit of equality seems to have been, in some ways at least, destructive of liberty. During the French Revolution, the attack on aristocratic privileges and powers led within a few years to the terrifying ascendancy of the Committee of Public Safety, under Robespierre, and, within a few years of the downfall of Robespierre, to other forms of authoritarianism. In the twentieth century we have seen the Communist drive toward equality eventuate, in the Soviet Union and elsewhere, in exceedingly cruel and repressive regimes.

Admittedly, the French and Soviet experiences do not conclusively demonstrate that liberty and equality are in conflict. While the quest for equality led in both cases to the suppression of liberty, the quest did not in either case succeed; equality was not achieved. To be sure, old inequalities were destroyed, but new ones were rapidly established. Thus it can be argued that liberty is lacking in the Soviet Union primarily because equality is also lacking.

But another kind of experience in modern history suggests the incompatibility of liberty and equality. This experience is found in societies that have come much nearer to equality than did those arising immediately from the French and Soviet revolutions. Some of the most careful and intelligent observers of society have been convinced that in places like America and Great Britain progress toward equality has seriously imperiled liberty. This has been seen as less a political than a social development. John Stuart Mill (1806–1873), a logician, economist, and political theorist, and one of the most highly respected minds of Victorian England, was alarmed by the way in which egalitarianism seemed to place an increasingly despotic power in the hands of the majority—a power exercised more often through public opinion than through government—and to draw ever narrower boundaries around individual liberty. Alexis de Tocqueville (1805–1859), the author of a great study of American democracy, developed views strikingly similar to Mill's from his observations of American society and politics. Tocqueville was on the whole sympathetic to the ideal of equality; moreover, he believed that the gradual advance of equality was historically inevitable. He studied America because he thought that America had come nearer to equality than had any other country and might therefore enable him to perceive the practical consequences of equality. One of the principal consequences, Tocqueville thought, was the weakening of liberty, owing not so much to governmental interference as to the censorious and ever-present eye of the populace. Tocqueville and Mill were among the first to note the appearance of a phenomenon many twentieth-century writers have seen as a dominant reality of our time, the despotism of the masses; here liberty is lost through social conformity.

While some have questioned whether liberty and equality go together, others have held that they cannot be separated. Wherever there is inequality, they maintain, it is at the expense of someone's liberty. Mill and Tocqueville were not the only ones in the nineteenth century to feel that in their time liberty was not as ample or secure as many assumed. Another was Karl

Marx. The personal liberty enjoyed in the industrialized countries was, for Marx, little better than a hoax. People were legally free to do such things as work for whom they pleased and live where they liked. But most were lucky if they could work at all, even for wages that barely kept them alive and in dirty and dangerous conditions. And their living quarters were almost always cramped and squalid. Legally free, they were actually enslaved. They were not enslaved, however, because equality had turned out to be unexpectedly antithetical to liberty, but, as Marx saw it, because there was no equality. The French Revolution had overthrown feudal rulers—kings, aristocrats, and bishops—but had replaced them with rulers whose despotism was colder and more relentless, although concealed behind governmental and legal forms ostensibly guaranteeing liberty. These new rulers were the industrial bourgeoisie. Only by overthrowing the new tyrants of manufacturing and finance could the promise of the French Revolution—liberty and equality together—be realized.

Marx thus assumed liberty and equality to be interdependent. Many of his most determined opponents deny that this is so. One of the chief points of contention in this controversy is capitalism. Marx believed that capitalism created the kind of highly developed industrial order that would render both liberty and equality accessible but that capitalism had to be replaced by socialism before humankind could lay hold of these benefits. Capitalism could lead us to the gates of a truly liberal and egalitarian order, but only socialism could enable us to enter. Marx's opponents, many of them, assert that liberty and equality are in conflict, but that capitalism provides as large a measure of each as is practically attainable.

The side you take—that of Marx or of capitalism—depends partly on how much you expect of the world. Can human potentialities be fully realized? Followers of Marx usually assume that with the abundance provided by advanced industrialism, they can. This will mean the enjoyment of both liberty and equality. Opponents of Marx often assume that even at best the world offers only limited chances for human fulfillment. We can gain liberty and equality only in part and only in an uneasy balance.

The overall question pertains not only to capitalism and the arguments of Marx, but also to the conformity feared by Tocqueville and Mill, and is not for sociologists and economists alone to answer. It is a question on which every individual can reflect. One can judge on the basis of daily personal experience whether the liberty one supposedly possesses is genuine and complete. One also can judge what threatens or infringes upon that liberty. One not only *can* but *must* do these things, for this is nothing less than trying to understand the quality of one's own life and the forces that shape it.

Some people say that liberty and equality have been reconciled in the United States in equality of opportunity. They acknowledge that many inequalities still exist—inequalities of wealth, power, and social standing—but claim that the way to the top is open to everyone. Without creating the injustice that would be inherent in giving equal rewards for unequal performances, and without establishing the despotic government that would be necessary to achieve "equality of result" (actual equality in wealth, power, and social standing), American society provides everyone with opportunities for the fullest realization of personal potential. This, they argue, is the only kind of liberty or equality that matters. But is such an achievement possible even in principle? Can liberty and equality be genuinely reconciled in equality of opportunity? It would be difficult to answer either question with a confident yes.

Equality of opportunity is an appealing goal. This is partly because it seems at first glance that anyone who fails to use opportunities equal to those of everyone else does not deserve any other kind of equality. Equality of opportunity is appealing also because it seems to remove the tensions inherent in balancing liberty and equality. This means each person will have an initial grant of liberty, but if that liberty is squandered it is not the business of government or of anyone else to set things right. The trouble is that inequalities of result necessarily produce inequalities of opportunity. For example, people in business who start with no advantage over others and accumulate a fortune not only bestow an immense advantage on their children but personally enjoy enhanced opportunities in increasing degree as their fortune grows. To assure complete equality of opportunity, it seems, it would be necessary to assure complete equality in every condition of life. Thus, equality of opportunity is an alluring phrase, but it does not solve any problems. The United States may have produced as acceptable a mix of liberty and equality as is humanly possible. It is doubtful, however, that it has produced a mix in which nothing of either component is lost.

The French Revolution celebrated not only liberty and equality but also "fraternity." Having considered the relations of equality and liberty, let us turn to those of equality and "fraternity." In doing this we shall reflect on the general place of equality in the context of modern ideals, and we shall also link the concerns of this chapter with those of the preceding one, for "fraternity" may conveniently be considered in terms of estrangement. "Fraternity" is community, the conquest of estrangement.

We shall not ask, as in the preceding question, whether equality and community are compatible. A better question is called forth by certain recent writings. Some thinkers say that inequality is the primary form of estrangement. According to them, the most drastic division among human beings is for some to have power over others, for some to be wealthy while others are poor, and for some to be continually honored and flattered while others live under an everlasting shadow of neglect and disdain. These views suggest that estrangement might be conquered by doing away with inequality. Is this possible?

11 If all conventional inequalities were abolished, would estrangement disappear?

This is one of the most important questions of the present time because it bears closely on the problem of humanizing industrial society—of making a mechanical civilization considerate of the fragile, nonmechanical being of persons.

Radicals and reformers, such as English socialists and American liberals, have traditionally seen the solution to the problem of industrial inhumanity in the idea of equality. The sharp lines between classes seemed the most inhuman aspect of industrialism. Class lines separated people even more drastically than they had been separated under feudal and monarchical regimes. Class lines also seemed to delineate the basic situation that permitted industrialists to impose on the workers such long hours and such low wages that their lives may have reached greater depths of misery than those experienced by the serfs and slaves of earlier ages. It was easy to conclude that the abolition of inequality would, in effect, be the conquest of estrangement.

The advance of industrialization, however, has cast doubt on this conclusion. One of the most bitter and persistent complaints in highly industrialized societies has been over, not class distinctions and inequities, but personal alienation. Both the rich and the poor, it is said, make up a lonely crowd, and the rich are about as lonely as the poor. It is tempting to respond, and it may be true, that loneliness is far more bearable for the rich than for the poor. The fact remains that a major grievance of industrial life does not, on the face of it, concern the inequality that radicals and reformers have always taken to be the primary derangement of unreformed societies. This grievance has been with an estrangement that seems to affect the relations even of those who, economically, socially, and politically, are equal. Thus, middle-class suburbanites in America apparently feel estranged not so much from the lower classes or the upper classes but from one another.

These conditions explain why we must ask whether the estrangement suffered today is traceable to the inequality traditionally attacked by radicalism. As the preceding remarks suggest, there are two quite different views on this matter. These call for thorough examination, for the future of industrial civilization depends on our capacity to decide correctly between them.

Rousseau and Marx represent the side of traditional radicalism. Both were acutely aware that something in modern life was weakening and severing the relationships of people to one another and to the physical world. Rousseau's *Confessions* is a poignant account of a lifetime of personal alienation; Marx's *Capital* could be described as a detailed analysis of the fragmentation of life wrought by capitalism. But the root of the matter, for both thinkers, was inequality—an inequality that was merely conventional, that was not in accordance with the human essence. Beneath the many estrangements human beings suffer is one great estrangement from which all the others grow—that between the few who own most of the property and control the government and the many who own little or nothing and are the helpless subjects of an alien political power. As a consequence of this split, a communal and creative life is practically impossible—not only for the miserable multitudes

but even for the rich and privileged, who are forced into a pampered and sterile defensiveness. The only way in which humankind can gain wholeness of life is by abolishing the distance between the few and the many.

In short, the conventional inequalities do not accord with the underlying human essence. They are in violation of the nature of humankind and disruptive of genuine relationships. Abolishing these inequalities, therefore, is the prerequisite for overcoming estrangement.

During the last century, however, some highly individual but profound and influential thinkers concluded the opposite: that by making people equal, we may deepen estrangement. One of the earliest and greatest of these thinkers was the Danish religious philosopher Søren Kierkegaard (1813–1855), who probably did more than anyone to implant in modern consciousness such concerns as commitment and "the leap of faith." The kind of estrangement that mattered most to Kierkegaard was estrangement from God. He thought this was likely to be reinforced by equality. His argument was directed against what is now called mass society, that is, society in which individuality is censured and suppressed not by government alone but by a bigoted and inquisitorial populace, by "the masses."

Kierkegaard was disturbed by what he saw as the disappearance of genuine individuals, persons capable of passion and decision. Only individuals can be Christians, for authentic Christianity depends on the decision, setting one apart from all others, to base one's whole life on the Christian hope of eternal happiness. To be a Christian merely because everyone else is a Christian is, in truth, not to be a Christian at all. For Kierkegaard the leveling that seemed to be occurring everywhere around him manifested the movement of humankind into a state in which everyone was merely a passive reflection of everyone else. This was necessarily a movement away from Christianity.

In this sense, equality meant estrangement from God. Does equality nevertheless unite human beings? Not for Kierkegaard and probably not for anyone adhering very seriously to a religious creed. A person's relationship with the transcendent must determine all other relationships. Its disruption propels a person into an isolation that is total, even though the resultant anguish may be partially relieved by behaving and thinking like everyone else. In Kierkegaard's case, authentic selfhood

depends on religious faith. If faith is lacking, selfhood is lacking too, and unity among selves is necessarily precluded. The uniformity Kierkegaard abhorred was a sign not of unity but of deep estrangement among human beings.

The fading of the conventional inequalities inspired doubt or fear, rather than expectations of reunion, in other thinkers as well—thinkers who were quite different from Kierkegaard and also different from one another. For example, Tocqueville, whose observations on America we have already discussed, was interested primarily in the social and political consequences of equality; his interests were more historical than religious; and his style, in contrast with Kierkegaard's ardor and irony, was one of cool penetration. But Tocqueville saw in America things Kierkegaard too would probably have seen had he visited America: a dearth of bold and distinctive individuals, and attenuated human relationships. Nietzsche, too, belongs in this company. He was, as already noted, an atheist, and in this way very unlike Kierkegaard and Tocqueville; yet he felt a horror much like theirs before the rising tide of equality. Finally, in the twentieth century, José Ortega y Gasset (1883–1955), a cultivated Spanish philosopher who shared little of Kierkegaard's single-minded faith, Tocqueville's fascination with social and political institutions, or Nietzsche's hatred of Christianity, expressed the spirit of all three when he denounced "the revolt of the masses." Equalization threatened our very humanity. These thinkers, with all of their idiosyncracies, agreed that equality presses the individual into conformity with the masses and thus creates alienation from one's own real nature. Someone alienated from the self cannot help but be alienated from others, even though such a one may appear to be exactly like them. Paradoxically, then, as equality is attained, unity is lost.

This view is not necessarily conservative. The critics of mass society have not ordinarily insisted on the preservation of traditional institutions or aristocratic rank. But all have refused to accept the common radical principle that doing away with conventional inequalities will end or even alleviate estrangement.

In what direction, then, should we move today? Radicals, although typically concentrating on class conflict, do not deny that estrangement has become more profound with the advance of industrialization. But they do deny, thereby separating themselves from the critics of mass society, that any real equal-

ization has come about in the process of this development. Under the egalitarian surface of things, they see the same class warfare that Marx wrathfully delineated a century ago. Contemporary radicals therefore hold, with Rousseau and Marx, that we should move toward true equality.

Those on the other side, to their own disadvantage in public debate, do not agree among themselves on any single response to estrangement, nor do the various responses they suggest have the simplicity and clarity of the radical response. Many recommend that we treat inherited traditions and institutions with great care and respect, although, as noted earlier, the critics of mass society are by no means uniformly conservative. Others hope for the rise of new authorities and leaders. In general, however, their mood is strongly marked by historical resignation. They see no completely reliable solution to the problem of estrangement and do not pretend to provide us with one. What they try to do, rather, is to illuminate our situation, thus preparing one to carry on a solitary life of resistance, in order both to salvage one's own humanity and to be open to a future that may be far better than the present, and could even be resplendent, although it is beyond our foresight or control and must be given us by destiny or God.

In concluding, let me suggest alternative lines of thought for those who would like to explore the possibilities without following the usual pathways either of radicalism or of conservatism. One will probably appeal primarily to those of radical temperament. It begins with the idea that what we need to overcome estrangement is not equality, pure and simple, but a particular kind of equality. What kind is the question. That there is such a question was indicated by no less an authority than Marx himself when he warned against a kind of communism in which "the role of *worker* is not abolished, but is extended to all men."[2] From this vantage point one can see the possibility of a more subtle radicalism than that of many self-styled radicals. Such a radicalism might free its followers from the tiresome compulsion to show that the reality behind every undesirable situation is the exploitation of one class by another. It also

---

[2]Karl Marx, *Economic and Philosophical Manuscripts,* trans. T. B. Bottomore, in Erich Fromm, *Marx's Concept of Man* (New York: Frederick Ungar, 1961), pp. 124–125. The italics are Marx's.

might induce radicals to be less ready than they usually are to assume that any measure of equalization is bound to make life better.

The other line of thought begins with the idea that it is a particular kind of *inequality* that is needed to overcome estrangement. Starting with this idea, you might hold a course clear of both conservatism and resignation, affirming the future as uncompromisingly as do radicals. You would reflect on the future, however, in terms of a new aristocracy. What kind of aristocracy? This, like the earlier question—what kind of equality?—is the question demanding reflection. Are scientists qualified to form a new aristocracy? Philosphers of some particular persuasion? Professors and students? Is the progress of technology perhaps creating an aristocracy of technicians? There are a number of possibilities, all implying that our task is not equalization but the establishment of new dominations and powers.

The mystery of our nature—that we are always, as Jaspers says, more than we know about ourselves—is never more evident than when we discuss the idea of equality. That idea itself may be considered a paradox. Few would assert that it is literally true; human beings are conspicuously unequal by almost every standard of comparison. The claim that they are equal is hardly possible without invoking something incomparable in every person. In other words, egalitarianism is likely to admit that in what we know about ourselves we are unequal but to assert, with Jaspers, that we are more than we can know about ourselves; in that "more" we are equal. This implies the paradox that though in every observable and measurable quality we are unequal, in our ultimate being we are nevertheless equal. By contrast, those who oppose equality are likely to be more "realistic," and to maintain that it is neither just nor practical to ignore the manifest inequalities among people.

These are only tendencies, to be sure. To make out that egalitarianism spurns objective reality altogether, or that inegalitarianism is oblivious of—or blind to—mystery, would be a great oversimplification. There are realistic arguments for equality, such as the waste a rigidly hierarchical society makes of the talents that turn up in the lower classes, or the arrogance and conformity that can destroy the spirit of a securely established aristocracy. On the other side, writers skeptical of equality sometimes see the mystery and grandeur of humankind as symbolized in an aristocracy of some sort. Nevertheless, the tendencies remain—egalitarianism often appealing to what we are beyond all we can observe and prove about ourselves, with the other side insisting that neither practicality nor justice allows us to ignore actual inequalities.

Today, we are forced by a variety of conditions to think about equality—by throngs of homeless people in every American city, for example, and by the persistence of racial prejudice and injustice. There is one condition, however, that forces us to think more deeply than we probably otherwise would, and that is the position of women. Clearly, it is not a position of perfect equality with men. Should it be? To ponder this particular issue seems a fitting way of concluding our consideration of the general issue of inequality and equality.

12   Should men and women always and in all ways be treated equally?

It may seem questionable to suggest that the position of women forces us to think more deeply than we otherwise would. How so? Should we not think deeply about the position of blacks, for example? In some ways, no doubt, we should. It is manifestly unjust and oppressive, yet it endures. Why is change so slow? What must be done? Here are serious subjects for thought. Still, it does not seem that the situation of blacks challenges political thinking quite so fundamentally as does the situation of women. There are no arguments worth considering in support of the situation of blacks. As for the situation of women, however, there are intelligent and responsible people who see it as neither terribly unjust nor deeply in conflict with the interests of society and the interests of women. In other words, the subjection of blacks is in the nature of a structural *failure;* we do not consistently apply our principles. The position of women (whether the term *subjection* would be appropriate is a matter of dispute) is a structural *feature* of Western societies. Not only does it accord with principles that even now, although under serious attack, are widely accepted; to do away with it would require basic alterations in the social order—for example, in the way children are raised and the way work within and outside the home is compensated and divided.

Feminism might be defined summarily as the movement demanding that these alterations be made. The movement contains numerous and diverse currents of thought. These are fed by varying philosophical views, such as Marxism and existentialism, and flow toward varying goals, some highly radical and others relatively conservative. But all types of feminism call into question the institutional order determining the status of women in Western society today. What mainly concerns us here, engaged as we are in philosophical reflection, is the philosophical character of the feminist offensive. In this connection, one fact is particularly worthy of note: in questioning the basic institutional order, feminism challenges the whole Western tradition of political thought, from its beginnings in ancient Greece to the present day. Why is that?

The answer is simply that the tradition of thought has provided the institutional order with philosophical legitimacy. Feminists call attention, for example, to the views of Aristotle, perhaps the most influential of all political philosophers. Aristotle saw no place for women in activities like philosophy and politics, where human potentialities come to their fullest realization. In effect, women could not be fully human, and this seemed so obvious to Aristotle that the matter was not even discussed. Feminists call attention also to the persistence of such views among the great figures in the history of political thought, all of them men. Even so egalitarian a thinker as Rousseau accepted Aristotle's assumption that the most serious human affairs, those affecting nations and history, are to be handled exclusively by men. Not surprisingly, feminist thinkers wonder whether they should try to enter into the twenty-five-hundred year philosophical conversation begun by the ancient Greeks; perhaps they should start a new conversation. In effect, they say, the status of women has *not* been among the perennial questions.

It really has, however, even though most political philosophers have neglected it, for Plato posed the question at the outset when he argued that women should be eligible for the supreme office in his ideal state, that of philosopher-ruler; and John Stuart Mill, in the nineteenth century, posed the question again in his book *The Subjection of Women*—a work still regarded with respect by feminists. So let us assume that men and women are in dialogue together. In challenging the Western tradition of political thought, feminism opens up some of the deepest issues facing human societies. People differ widely in their answers to these issues (and not simply in accordance with differences of gender). Few would deny, however, that feminism forces us to face the issues afresh. Let us try to do this here.

1. First of all is the issue of equality itself. What does equality mean? Presumably not uniformity, since it would manifestly be impossible to treat men and women always and in all ways precisely the same. But is it possible to treat people differently without favoring anyone? For example, if it were possible for women to bear children and tend young infants but to suffer no setback in their careers on account of the time thus taken, would that be unfair to men by providing women with a fuller and richer life experience than men have? How can we distinguish between differential and prejudicial treatment?

Another issue here is social necessity. As already noted, some argue that the early years of a child's life require the full-time attention of the mother. This implies that, for women, a fairly prolonged withdrawal from the public world into the home is a social necessity. But is it? Can we know what is socially necessary without extensive experimentation? Have we any right to experiment with the well-being of children? Even with experimentation, can our judgments of social necessity ever attain a validity unaffected by cultural, economic, and social conditions that are constantly changing? But suppose it were demonstrated that, in all circumstances whatsoever, children are better off if cared for full-time by their mothers. How much better off must they be to justify the sacrifice of a mother's independent life? Even the most persuasive arguments for the advantages of slavery would not lead us to reinstitute slavery. Sometimes moral necessity transcends social necessity. Does that apply to the liberation of women from child care and housework?

Finally, feminism may prompt us to ask again what may be the hardest and deepest question of all: what makes the principle of equality so compelling? As we have seen, in ancient times highly civilized people often candidly thought of most human beings, women among them, much as we think today of machines—as things to be used and if not usable forgotten about or junked. Few today can think this way. Why not? Is this mere sentimentality? Or have we somehow keener eyes for human dignity than so preeminent a mind as Aristotle had? How could that be?

2. Feminism also forces us to think about the relative authority of nature and convention. It challenges customs and practices sanctioned by centuries of social experience, thus assaulting convention in its most enduring, and for some people most precious, parts. How much respect does convention (whether in the form of a single custom or in the form of the whole network of customs structuring a society) deserve? Does the fact that by definition it is *not* natural condemn it? Does its very existence, indicating that in some sense it "works," entitle it to authority? If it has lasted for many centuries does that add to its authority, showing that many generations have tried it and found it of value, or does it show simply that it has never been rationally examined? If convention is destroyed, what remains? Nature? Is there such a thing, or is nature—*human* nature—merely what convention makes it? If there is such a thing as nature, can it be known? In pondering questions of this kind, it may help to be more specific. Is the family natural, or merely conventional? And what about the traditional roles of men and women: do those accord with masculine and feminine nature, or are they merely habitual and convenient? Here we reach an exceptionally fundamental and fascinating question: are masculinity and femininity—concepts charged with subtlety and emotional power—natural, or only conventional? The question deserves separate treatment, for it concerns that foundation stone of political theory—human nature.

3. Earlier I referred to psychological studies indicating that men and women, and indeed boys and girls, perceive human situations differently—men legalistically, women intuitively; men typically look for relevant rules, women for the possibilities inherent in particular situations. This difference goes with others. For example, men are greatly concerned with personal autonomy and tend to regard relationships as threatening; women are apt to think of themselves as involved in relationships by virtue of their essential being. When conflict arises, accordingly, men think first of their rights and women (although feminism heavily stresses women's rights) of their responsibilities. The highest standard for women may be that of helping, for men that of not interfering. Such differences, of course, vary among

individuals, and they represent tendencies rather than absolute laws. Nevertheless, it seems hardly excessive to say that men and women differ in character—a hypothesis to which common sense, as well as psychological research, lends credence.

Thus arises an absolutely fundamental question for political thinking: are there any universal qualities defining a human being? If so, what are they? I pointed out earlier that political ideas almost always rest on concepts of human nature. But the feminist critique of traditional society forces us to think about human nature anew. If such a thing as human nature exists, is it roughly the same as masculine nature (implying either that women can never become fully human, and equal with men, or, if they can, that to do so they must become like men)? Or if human nature exists, is it the same as feminine nature (suggesting that full equality for women would dramatically improve the character of society)? Or is human nature something that has been buried and forgotten, with men and women so far representing mere fragments of humanity?

4. One of the main characteristics of modern Western society is the division between public and private life; activities like politics and business are carried on out in the world and are in various ways and degrees open to all, while the home is closed to all but those its inhabitants choose to admit. Feminism requires us to examine this division. Today, and traditionally, women have primary responsibility for the private sphere, with the public sphere reserved mainly for men. But this strikes many people as highly prejudicial to women. The public sphere, many assume, is the sphere of full participation in the affairs of the human race, whereas the private sphere is constricting and demeaning. But is this true, one can wonder, in view of the fact that realities like personal love, religious devotion, and reasoned conversation seem to be centered in (although not confined to) the private sphere.

For the ancient Greeks, public life and life in essence were largely synonymous; subsequent developments, such as the rise of Christianity, have made it possible to doubt this equation. But assuming the equation is accepted, what can be done? Must the division between public and private be abolished? One hesitates to say that it must, for that would mean doing away with private life and, one fears, with liberty itself. On the other hand, to say (given a desire to respond to feminist demands) that we need only open both spheres fully to men and women alike sounds too easy. For men and women to have absolutely equal access to the public realm, there would have to be absolutely equal sharing in the duties of the private realm. But in view of the possibility that women possess maternal capacities that men—regardless of their willingness to take on the tasks of child-rearing and home care—do not have, such sharing is not clearly desirable. Nor is it clearly practical. It would require for both partners time away from work, which the exigencies of business and professional life may make it hard to arrange; it would require as well a degree of mutual cooperation in the home that, current divorce statistics suggest, is anything but common. These are rather mundane matters, but they concern a philosophically sweeping issue: the proper structure of the social order.

5. The basis of the social order is also an issue feminism places before us. Many women have felt that society imposes obligations on them that they ought not to have to shoulder. What gives society the right to do this? What gives it the right to interfere with individual freedom? In feminist literature, the issue sometimes appears in discussions of social contract doctrine, which holds that society and the state are grounded in the voluntary agreement of their members. This doctrine closely conforms with feminist concerns. Not that many would claim that societies and states ordinarily, if ever, originate in an explicit contractual agreement. The core of the doctrine is in what it says, not about the origin, but about the moral authority of social institutions. It says, in effect, that the obligations society "imposes" must be freely accepted. Social roles must be filled voluntarily or not at all. Many women have felt that their roles as wives, mothers, and home-makers were not only onerous but practically enslaving, even though originating in a freely undertaken contract of marriage. The burdens ahead are not clearly foreseen by naive young brides; and even if they are, society provides them with few alternatives. The social contract doctrine calls into question situations of this kind. Social and political obligations must be rooted in the will of the individual. This sounds reasonable—indeed, vital—to most people today.

But can society be based solely on the unconstrained choice of every individual? Can so mammoth a task as the bearing and raising of a new generation be accomplished if every individual is completely free to stand aside and take no part? Does the standard of voluntary agreement require that any individual, at any time, must be free to abandon any relationship, with the simple declaration: "I did not know what I was getting into"? With questions like these we face again, as have political thinkers in all ages, a moral dilemma inherent in our collective existence.

6. Feminism also leads us to reflect on oppression in general. One cannot think about the status of women without thinking about the status of other groups that are, or feel, oppressed, such as racial minorities and the poor. If the position of women were altered in accordance with feminist ideals, would the end of all forms of exploitation and wretchedness naturally follow? This is to ask, first of all, what the status of women today rests on—on capitalism, which according to some analysts is the major cause also of poverty and economic inequality? Or does the status of women reflect an ancient patriarchal tradition (a tradition, that is, dictating male primacy) independent of capitalism or even underlying capitalism? Or does it reflect a pride and selfishness that will surface in any system, even in one with absolute equality between men and women? We are asking not just about the status of women, however, but about the sources of injustice. Are all forms of injustice founded on a single, underlying condition, so that correcting one of them is correcting them all? Must they all be attacked simultaneously? Or are they like weeds, diverse and independent, and continually springing up, so that the battle against them is necessarily disorganized and endless?

Questions such as these naturally spawn a great variety of answers. There are many feminist positions; and added to them are the positions of those who reject all feminist positions. The alternatives opened up by the question before us—whether men and women should always and in all ways be treated equally—are bewildering in their number and diversity. How can one avoid drowning intellectually in a sea of questions and answers?

To facilitate reflection—to save us from drowning—I shall mark out four broad alternatives: three types of feminism and one type of antifeminism. Simply for the sake of convenience, I shall give these names. One should remember, however, that these names are the author's; representatives of the corresponding positions do not all use them and some might reject them.

Feminist separatism. For people who hold this position, the aim is not equality for women but rather a separate, or even superior, place for women. In that sense, their answer to the question of whether men and women should be treated equally is negative. While repudiating any form of subordination, they aspire to a distinct women's world, or even to a world ruled by women. Their attitude may be founded on the conviction that women are not merely equal to men, inherently, but are superior to them. For most people, such views are jarring; they seem extreme and unreasonable. But of course they are no more extreme, nor more manifestly unreasonable, than the assumptions of male superiority that have been commonplace for centuries. Representatives of feminist separatism have discussed the possibilities of technological developments allowing fetuses to be conceived and developed outside the womb. The perpetuation of the human race would then no longer impose on women the burdens of pregnancy and childbirth.

Exemplifying feminist separatism is a novel written over fifty years ago by an American feminist, Charlotte Gilman. Entitled *Herland* and valued still by feminist writers, it depicts a society made up entirely of women; the inhabitants had developed a capacity for self-initiated pregnancies—always producing female infants—thus maintaining the population. The society is a female utopia. All relationships are entirely harmonious and cooperative; beauty is everywhere, both in the countryside and in the towns; problems are handled with unfailing practicality and success; the inhabitants are handsome and lithe, and they are serious, inquiring, and cultivated as well. They have achieved a complete and satisfying existence entirely without men. At the end of the novel three men who had found their way into this paradise are accepted by three of the women as mates. Throughout the book, however the men are again and again comically thrown off balance by the superior competence and discernment of the women. And it is made clear that the women who accepted them as mates were in no way dependent on them for their well-being.

Radical Feminism. In contrast, radical feminists are very much concerned with equality. Their answer to the question before us—whether men and women should always and in all ways be treated equally—is yes. But they attach a major condition: that society be radically changed. They seek access, not to the present world of men, but to a transformed world—one more worthy of being shared than the one men have created. Patriarchal society is degraded by conditions like competition and violence, and imperialism and war. And not only do radical feminists call for social transformation; they are apt to believe that women can make a decisive contribution to the needed transformation through a spirit more personal and compassionate than men ordinarily evince. As one might infer, radical feminists are far less respectful of convention than of nature—that is, of human nature—where they see potentialities that, with the liberation of women, could come to reality in a world profoundly in need of renewal.

The radical response to some of the issues discussed earlier is interesting. Concerning the dichotomy of public and private spheres, radical feminists do not necessarily call for its abolition. Some of them call rather for its reinterpretation. The private sphere would become a place into which one may rightfully withdraw but where one cannot be forcibly confined. The public sphere, on the other hand, would be opened up to emotions and concerns hitherto treated as private; it would become more personal and more of a dialogue, less legalistic. As for the roots of injustice in general, it is common for radical feminists to see the liberation of women as the key to general human liberation. The patriarchal subjection of women is organically connected with, or even the basis of, all major forms of injustice, such as racial discrimination and class oppression. Thus a world renewed by the liberation of women would be new not only for women but for everyone.

Liberal feminism. In their comments on the present status of women and the patriarchal attitudes of political thinkers of the past, liberal feminists sound much like radical feminists. How they differ from them might be summarily indicated by saying that they do not find the general structure of liberal democracies, that is, of most contemporary Western societies, to be completely unacceptable. While affirming the natural equality of the sexes, they are apt to be less sure than radical feminists that children can be well reared outside the home and away from the mother; and they are more open to the possiblity that biology may impose unique obligations on women. Hence they are friendlier to the family than are radical feminists. Also, they are less hostile to the public world as presently constituted and consequently more apt to be satisfied if women gain equal access to that world and men share more fully in the tasks of the home. Above all, as the term *liberal feminism* suggests, they wish for liberty—the liberty institutionalized in most Western societies and enjoyed more or less fully by men (at least by white, middle-class men) but partially withheld, feminists believe, from women. Indeed, real liberty would suffice. Society does not need to be transformed but only to be made fully accessible to women and fairly administered.

Patriarchal conservatism. This is the camp of those who answer no to the question of whether men and women should always and in all ways be treated equally. They are not necessarily men; many women share this view. And if they are men, they are not necessarily what feminists call "male chauvinists." But they do accept prevailing arrangements, arrangements undeniably granting a certain primacy to men. To anyone conscious of the intelligence, learning, and passion characterizing much feminist literature, to accept the society so scorned in such literature may seem peculiarly backward and blind. But probably far more people occupy this position than any of the others we have discussed; and it would be hard to show that they all are lacking in intelligence and humane feelings.

The more moderate of the patriarchal conservatives would probably rest their case on the complementary character of men and of women. They would insist that men and women are different and that their differences are enduring and natural, not just products of convention. Whether they are absolutely equal would not greatly concern them. What would concern them far more would be the way typical male and female characteristics fit together in the working of society. They would hold, for example, that men tend to be aggressive and thus are suited for posts of large-scale management and leadership; that women are attentive and compassionate and thus good at creating harmony and warmth among small numbers, as in families; that there is a certain correspondence, in short, between the male temperament and the public world and between the female temperament and the private world. To be mindful of this correspondence is vital alike to the conduct of public affairs and to the care of the family. To ignore it is to neglect the very structure of civilization.

The more moderate of patriarchal conservatives might also offer certain practical observations. For example, social order depends on degrees of authority and degrees of subordination. To insist mindlessly on absolute equality is to tamper with the basic conditions of a workable society. Men may sometimes, even often, lack the inherent qualities justifying their present primacy. But primacy has to be held by someone; to insist on its being held by someone demonstrably superior to everyone beneath reflects perfectionism of a kind that fits very badly into the actual world. Another of these practical observations might be that the present order is not oppressive for most women. Once the tasks of child-rearing are completed, women have extensive liberty and leisure, and through voluntary organizations, such as churches and public-interest pressure groups, have a multitude of opportuntities for entering into the affairs of the larger world.

In sketching these positions, I have tried to show that none is absurd, none indefensible. On the other hand, it must be noted that none is free of serious weaknesses. A serious weakness in feminist separatism, for example, is that it fractures community. It rejects a major premise of this book, the ideal of unrestricted dialogue, with men and women equally taking part. As for radical feminism, its gravest weakness may lie simply in its revolutionary cast; it calls for immediate and sweeping social changes. But history comes close to proving (although events beginning in 1989 in Eastern Europe may require that this conclusion be reconsidered) that human beings cannot quickly and completely transform society. In trying to do so, they release uncontrollable human forces and create unmanageable situations.

Is liberal feminism, then, the answer? Not beyond all question, certainly. The weightiest argument against it, perhaps, is not that it is flawed as an answer but rather that, *from a feminist perspective,* it is no answer at all. It fails effectively to address feminist concerns. In accepting the present order of society, along with male definitions of liberty, and of public and private life, it leaves women with unjust handicaps and leaves society degraded by competition and violence. So, at least, radical feminists would be very apt to argue. As for patriarchal conservatism, finally, despite an appearance of sobriety and good sense—an appearance far from wholly deceptive—it can be charged with skirting the issue of equality and thus leaving unchallenged institutions and practices violating the supreme standard of justice.

Readers who feel bewildered—not only by issues concerning the subordination of women but by issues concerning inequality and equality generally—should not be discouraged, for these are truly bewildering issues. This is one reason they have never been settled. If reflecting on them were a game, we might prefer not to play. But convictions concerning equality and inequality determine how society should be organized. And these convictions are explosive, having caused countless revolutions from the time of the early Greek city-states to the present. Hence, again and again we are compelled to reflect on the troubling realities of inequality and on the enthralling visions of equality. We have little choice but to take on the bewilderment we naturally feel as we approach those things that "thought cannot think."

■ Suggested Readings

Plato. *The Republic*
Aristotle. *Politics,* Books I and III–VI
Locke, John. *The Second Treatise of Government*
Rousseau, Jean Jacques. *Discourse on the Origin of Inequality*
Kant, Immanuel. *Critique of Practical Reason*
Paine, Thomas. *The Rights of Man*
Tocqueville, Alexis de. *Democracy in America,* 2 vols.
Kierkegaard, Søren. *The Present Age*
Mill, John Stuart. *The Subjection of Women*
Marx, Karl. *Capital,* Vol. I
Nietzsche, Friedrich. *Thus Spake Zarathustra*
Ortega y Gasset, José. *The Revolt of the Masses*
Camus, Albert. *The Plague*
Orwell, George. *The Road to Wigan Pier*
Okin, Susan Moller. *Women in Western Political Thought*
Elshtain, Jean Bethke. *Public Man, Private Woman: Women in Social and Political Thought*
Benhabib, Seyla, and Cornell, Drucilla (eds.). *Feminism as Critique: On the Politics of Gender*
Coole, Diana H. *Women in Political Theory: From Ancient Misogyny to Contemporary Feminism*

CHAPTER 4

■ Power and Its Possessors

The discussions of unity and disunity and of equality and inequality put us in an advantageous position from which to begin exploring the main subject of political science, power. Because people are disunited, power seems necessary for ensuring order; because they are unequal, power seems justified as a way of placing everyone under the rule of the best human qualities. Many of the controversies of politics, moreover, have to do with the impact of power on unity and disunity and on equality and inequality. Power may be used to separate human beings and to bring them together, as is exemplified in policies of racial segregation and integration in America; it may support inequality, as when special tax benefits are accorded to the wealthy; and it may support equality, as is done in many countries through systems of national health care. Perhaps it would be impossible to use power so that it would neither divide nor unite, neither discriminate nor equalize. It is because of these interconnections that the preceding two chapters have prepared us to reflect on power.

Some of the most basic and difficult questions about power arise from its moral dubiousness. Perhaps power is evil in essence. Certainly the use of power normally involves much evil; it tends to make those who possess it arrogant and it presupposes evil, as is evident in the conflicts that render order dependent on power. That human relations are pervaded by power is an unmistakable sign of the radical imperfection of human beings.

Have even these few assertions, however, carried us too far by expressing certainty about matters that in fact are far from certain? Is it true that human beings are radically imperfect? Is power really indispensable? Some of the greatest idealists, such as the Russian novelist Leo Tolstoy, have answered both questions negatively and have called for the drastic curtailment or even the total elimination of power.

Here we have encountered a question that we must answer before we go any further. If politics is the use of power, one of the first questions of political thought is clearly whether power is really necessary.

13   Is power the only source of order?

The argument that it is not has been based on at least three different ideas. One is that people are good and that consequently order is spontaneous. John Locke, for example, in framing the philosophy of liberal government, assumed that human beings are fundamentally reasonable. For Locke, most people have the sense to see that others have certain rights, such as the right to life, simply because they are human beings; further, most people are disposed to respect these rights. Locke saw people as having both the capacity and the inclination to live according to reason and the laws of nature. As a result, they depend on power only for overcoming certain deficiencies in the order that most of them spontaneously keep. They do not depend on it for creating order. In sum, one source of order, other than power, is the reasonableness and the decency of human beings.

Another principle put forward to show that order is not wholly dependent on power is the idea of natural harmony. The clearest illustration of this principle is probably the theory of the classical economists, who flourished in the nineteenth century and provided what is still the basic rationale for free enterprise. The classical economists did not regard human beings as good. On the contrary, they assumed they were materialistic and self-seeking. But they did not conclude from this that order must be created and sustained with power. They believed that if governments would merely ensure the main conditions of individual economic activity, such as security of property and stability of currency, but otherwise would not curb the freedom of people to seek profits in accordance with their own selfish promptings, good order would come into being naturally. The products most needed by society would be manufactured without forcing anyone to make them; the manufacturers would be justly rewarded by the purchasers. On the other hand, those unable or unwilling to help meet the needs of society would lose out in the market and thus be automatically penalized. In this way, good order would arise from natural economic laws, with only a minimal application of human power. For the classical economists, order was contrived by what one of them called the "invisible hand" of the free market rather than by the visible hand of the government.

Finally, many thinkers have seen order as depending primarily on habit, custom, and tradition. They do not assume either the goodness of humans or the harmony of nature. Order rests rather on the human tendency to do what has always been done, to think what has always been thought, and to respect what is ancient. A society that is given a chance to develop peacefully will gradually build up an intricate structure of customs and traditions. This structure will contain more wisdom than any order deliberately designed and built at a particular time because it will be the work of a number of generations. Obviously, if the principle of human goodness is radical, because it leads naturally to a willingness to abandon established arrangements and restraints, the principle that order arises from habit and from loyalty to tradition is conservative.

Here we have touched again on the views of Edmund Burke, discussed in Question 3. According to Burke, the major source of order is the habit-forming nature of human beings.

Anarchism is the idea that one of these forces—human goodness, natural harmony, or custom and tradition—or a combination of them, is sufficient to ensure order and that government therefore can be abolished. Typically, however, it is human goodness that anarchists count on, for the other sources of order contain an element of coercion. To act under the sway of natural forces or of habit is not to be fully free. Only if human beings are spontaneously orderly can the ancient conflict of order and freedom be resolved without compromise on either side.

A far more common position is that these three sources all produce some order but that they have to be supplemented with power. This is the position of liberals. They usually assume that human beings are reasonable and decent but not perfect, that the laws of supply and demand can efficiently regulate some relationships but not the entire economy, and that custom and tradition contribute to social integration but do not alone ensure it. Thus power is not the only source of order, and government can and must be limited. But no other sources of order, either singly or in combination, are sufficient, and power is therefore indispensable.

At the opposite pole from anarchism and liberalism is the view that humans are irremediably disorderly. Power therefore is the only effective source of order. This view can be found in early Christianity, with its emphasis on original sin. It was the view of Hobbes, a logical outcome of the principle that human beings are essentially estranged. Its most notorious representative, however, is Niccolò Machiavelli (1469–1527), the Florentine statesman, exile, and writer who formulated many of the basic rules of power politics.

Contrary to his lurid reputation, Machiavelli probably had a somewhat less pessimistic view of humankind than either Augustine or Hobbes. He wrote often of the virtue and corruption of politics, showing that he did not consider human beings as wholly and incurably evil. Machiavelli saw virtue as consisting in qualities, such as loyalty and honesty, that predispose people to uphold order voluntarily; only when such qualities are lost is absolute rule inevitable. Nevertheless, Machiavelli regarded all uncoerced and uncontrived order as highly unstable, and this was the heart of "Machiavellianism." Human beings tend always to be fickle and selfish, and are ingenious and tireless sources of chaos. Hence, order depends on the resoluteness and skill of political leaders. Machiavelli's two main works, *The Prince* and *The Discourses,* are reflections on the techniques and devices of political and military art. Machiavelli's central teaching is inherent in his pessimistic appraisal of human nature: order, hence civilization, rests not on human goodness but on the political sagacity of rulers.

Let me suggest another way of thinking about the question of whether there is any source of order other than power by asking whether society determines the character of government, or vice versa. Currently, in university classes, government is ordinarily looked at in the context of larger totalities, such as societies and historical eras. As one institution among many, government appears to be merely one element in an encompassing order and to be determined, in its character and policies, by that order. It is possible to reverse this relationship, however, and to see government as the center of thought and action from which the general character of society is determined. Those who desire swiftly to bring about some radical transformation of life are apt to look at things in this way.

From the first point of view, it is clear that power, or at any rate political power, is not the sole source of order; human beings create order spontaneously. From the second point of view, however, political artifice or force keeps society from falling either into some lower form of order or into complete disorder. In this sense, political power underlies the highest forms of order, if not order itself.

The way in which your view of human nature shapes your political ideas can be clearly seen in connection with this question. If people are innocent and benign, order is not problematic; human nature itself is the source of order. On the other hand, if people are selfish and cruel, they are naturally disorderly, and you have to ask how this tendency can be counteracted.

These matters are not so simple, however, that we can merely deduce political conclusions from psychological premises. True, the notion that people are selfish and cruel must prompt us to consider government as a possible source of order; at the same time, it must prompt us to fear what people, in their selfishness and cruelty, may do when armed with the power of government. Easy deductions are barred and simple patterns of thought are untenable. We are compelled to ask, for example, whether any human beings are exceptions to the general depravity of human nature, and, if so, whether it would be possible or desirable to give them limitless power. If we answer either question negatively, then we must ask, more realistically, whether the consequences of human depravity in those who govern can be somehow rendered less dangerous.

The point, however, is that such reasoning is ordinarily carried out under the dominating influence of a concept of human nature. That concept may of course be altered in the course of one's reflections. But it remains a touchstone of political doctrine.

The issue marked out by anarchism, liberalism, and Machiavellianism is forced on us today by the disorder in the world and in American society. The hatred and confusion filling Africa, Asia, and Latin America and the high crime rates in American cities indicate that order cannot be taken for granted. Does order among nations today depend on the prodigiously expensive and destructive armed forces of the United States? Does order within the United States require that the police be freed from procedural rules that safeguard individuals but perhaps inhibit the suppression of crime?

As these questions indicate, in asking whether there can be any order aside from that created and sustained with power, we are asking to what degree life can be free and cooperative. This is a difficult but important question. Still, it is only one of several such questions put before us by the fact of power. The most controversial of these questions, both among political leaders and among philosophers, is probably who the possessors of power should be: landed aristocrats? agents of the bourgeoisie? champions of the people? scientists? philosophers? priests? some combination of these? Many of the tensions of politics center on this issue. Civil wars and revolutions are occasioned by opposing answers to it. And philosophers, since the beginnings of political thought, have tried to discover the final and unchanging principles in accordance with which power should be distributed.

To be precise, however, the question is not merely who should have power of any kind—who, for example, should be a father or a teacher—but who should have power of the kind that is over all other power.

14 Who should rule?

"Anyone" and "no one" are among the answers that have been given to this question, as implausible as both may seem.

The answer "anyone" is implicit in the philosophy of Hobbes. One reason Hobbes was willing that anyone should rule lay in his cynical egalitarianism. Hobbes had no faith in "great men" or in aristocracies; no one was exempted from his pessimistic appraisal of human nature. Therefore, he did not feel that it much mattered who ruled. Looking at things so pessimistically, however, could he not just as well have argued that no one should rule? No, for he thought this would result in intolerable chaos. This position makes sense if human beings, as Hobbes believed, are essentially estranged.

Still, we may ask whether intolerable chaos might not also result from giving command to a specimen of Hobbesian humanity—a person invariably and uncompromisingly egotistical, who is merely a complex material object governed like the rest of reality by the laws of cause and effect. Hobbes thought not. His reasoning went roughly as follows: What each in his egotism desires above everything else is self-preservation; self-preservation can be gained only where there is peace; and peace is the product of a strong, well-ordered state. Such a state is a primary goal of the subjects of a ruler. What does the ruler desire? Like everyone else, self-preservation. In the ruler's case, however, the primary condition for fulfilling this desire is power. How is power to be obtained? Through organizing a strong, well-ordered state—the same end sought by the subjects. There is thus a fundamental identity of interest between government and people.

On these grounds Hobbes thought that anyone in command of a state would be about as effective as anyone else and would try to further, albeit for personal advantage, the interest of the governed.

Mistrust of power, of course, is common. But only a few thinkers, and those relatively obscure, have taken the extreme view that no one should be entrusted with power. These thinkers are anarchists, whom we discussed in Question 13. They are pessimistic in their conviction that power will inevitably be misused, but optimistic in believing that it can be dispensed with and that order and peace can be securely established without any coercion at all. To them, every form of power is both intolerable and useless. How can intelligent people affirm so self-contradictory a theory?

They affirm it by maintaining, as we have noted, that the misdeeds of those who govern do not reflect the essential nature of human beings. People in essence are cooperative and unselfish. This will be revealed when governments have been destroyed or perhaps when civilization has further evolved. On such suppositions anarchists have based, in compensation for the terrors many of them have experienced in their own lives, a daring hope: oppression and government itself will die away and humanity will become a perfect community. This hope may strike one as strange and implausible. But it has generated a doctrine whose moral purity and philosophical audacity command respect.

When we consider the answers lying in between these two extremes we cross a path we followed in the preceding chapter—we encounter issues connected with inequality and equality. The question of who should rule has been thrashed out by two broad political and philosophical parties. These are the supporters of the few and the supporters of the many. A reasonable decision in favor of one side or the other can be made only after reflecting on whether human beings are essentially equal or not.

Are there certain virtues, attainable by a few but not by the majority, that render those possessing them deserving of power? It has frequently been claimed that there are. Philosophical wisdom was such a virtue according to Plato; the sanctity supposedly inherent in ordination has occasionally been so regarded among both Roman Catholics and Protestants; and unique political capacities have often been attributed to some minority distinguished by family background, military achievement, or business success. Human beings show a surprisingly strong inclination to exalt some minority or other. Medieval priests and kings may have fallen, but the twentieth century has raised up its own priestly and royal authorities, as is evident in the trust that has been placed in Communist and Nazi elites as well as in scientists, technicians, and managers.

The idea of popular rule has received less support in the history of political thought than we might expect. It is true that twenty-five hundred years ago in Greece many people believed in participatory democarcy, for a number of the city-states were direct (rather than representative) democracies, but the great Greek thinkers either scorned democracy or had serious reservations about it. The conquests of Alexander the Great, several centuries before the time of Christ, largely extinguished democracy, which has revived only in recent times. In the interim there were democratic movements, and people here and there believed in democracy. But political thinkers, while in theory often granting a significant measure of authority to the people, assumed that in practice this authority would be severely limited. Rarely did they advocate popular rule.

Whether the dearth of democratic thought was owing to the class bias of those who had the leisure to think and write, to a wisdom that discerned the insufficiencies of democracy, to the difficulties of organizing popular rule prior to the development of technological media of communication, or to some other cause is uncertain. In any case it was not until the seventeenth and eighteenth centuries that the idea of democracy was uncompromisingly affirmed. Rousseau was the first great thinker in whose writings this occurred.

For Rousseau, we are deprived of our humanity by having to live under a government in which we have no part. This diminution of humanity would take place even if the government were benevolent and wise. However, if a great many people were excluded from participation, the government would almost certainly be selfish and oppressive. Only government by the people can be truly and steadily devoted to the common good. Insofar as the people are neither corrupted by modern urban civilization nor frustrated by defective political arrangements, Rousseau thought they possessed what amounts to a kind of sanctity.

Is it really any more sensible, however, to rest confidence in great numbers than in some select minority? Do the doubts that most political philosophers have had about popular rule constitute a consensus of the wise, which we should hesitate to contradict? The modern experience with democracy and socialism, through which the people have gained more, if not total, power has prompted many misgivings. Numerous observers have judged the cultural tastes of the people to be crude and their political opinions to be based on ignorance and prejudice.

Some reply that in reality the people have gained little power and that their failings reflect the irresponsible influence still wielded by minorities, such as the commercial interests dominating television and the press.

Obviously it is hard to decide between the few and the many. This is why numerous thinkers, from the earliest periods of political thought, have refused to take either side and have argued that aristocracy and democracy should be combined in some fashion. Aristotle thought that this could be accomplished by granting power to a large middle class. Rule by this class, he held, was likely to be more moderate and sensible than rule by either the few or the many.

Where a strong middle class does not exist, Aristotle's advice is inapplicable, for such a class cannot be created easily or quickly and perhaps cannot be created at all. Also, some people feel that while neither the upper nor the lower class should govern alone, each should share in power. Accordingly, political thinkers have given much attention to organizational devices whereby the few and the many might govern together. Some suggest, for example, that the executive should be reserved for persons of special distinction while the legislature should express the will of the people.

A list of the great thinkers who have urged a combination of aristocracy and democracy would be an impressive collection of names. This fact and the arguments already discussed suggest that the idea has wisdom. There is one objection to it, however, that for some will be conclusive: it contains little promise of the radical social and political renewal that many call for. If all classes share in governing, nothing is likely to be done that seriously jeopardizes the interests of any class. Hence, the ideal of government that is neither by the few nor the many, but is mixed, is apt to appeal mainly to those who are satisfied with things as they are.

It is the unsatisfied who often pose most dramatically the question of who should rule. They are the ones most likely to claim that some particular group is not merely the best alternative as a repository of power, but that is can redeem humanity from the vicissitudes and agonies of history. Plato made this claim for philosophers, Marx for the proletariat, and Lenin for the Communist party. When faced with such claims, we have to ask how much can reasonably be expected of rulers. Should we be satisfied with prudence on the part of our leaders and with a conduct of affairs that avoids disaster? Or should we look for redeeming wisdom, for a Moses to lead us out of our captivity within commonplace life and mediocre visions?

A final question concerning power deserves our attention. The modern answer to the question of who should rule is, on the whole, that the many should rule. The prestige of certain aristocratic institutions, like the Supreme Court in the United States, indicates that the answer is not unqualified, but most defenders of minority powers and privileges see such institutions as merely prudent restraints on what is predominantly and properly government by the people. Few openly attack the basic principle of popular rule. It is appropriate, therefore, to consider how popular government can best be carried on.

15 If the people rule, should they do so themselves or through representatives?

Idealists are apt to believe that direct (or "participatory") democracy is far superior to representative democracy. They feel, as did Rousseau, that "sovereignty ... cannot be represented," and they agree with his famous animadversion on the English political system: "The people of England regards itself as free: but it is grossly mistaken: it is free only during the election of members of parliament. As soon as they are elected, slavery overtakes it, and it is nothing."[1]

Perhaps this view is correct. In view of the fervor and frequency with which the case for participatory democracy is made, however, we should remember that the arguments for representative democracy are not insubstantial. Consider the following.

1. The representative system makes it possible, while allowing the people as a whole to have the final word, to empower those who stand out for their intelligence, experience, and interest in political matters. Direct democracy tends to submerge such minorities in the masses.

2. Representatives can devote all of their time to government, whereas the people as a whole cannot. The consequence, since government must be carried on continuously, is that representative democracy can provide steadier popular control of day-to-day government than direct democracy can. Even in a very small state, the entire populace could not be expected to assemble more often than once every few weeks. Thus most of the time government must be carried on by unsupervised minorities.

3. A representative body provides better opportunities for leisured, unemotional deliberation than a great popular assembly does. Representatives are in daily, face-to-face contact, so that their antipathies toward one another may be tempered by personal understanding; also, because representatives are few in number and meet frequently, their relationships can readily be structured by formalities that protect the spirit and the processes of deliberation. Members of large multitudes, on the other hand, cannot for the most part be personally acquainted; the

---

[1] Jean Jacques Rousseau, *The Social Contract and Discourses,* trans. with an introduction by G.D.H. Cole (New York: Dutton, 1950), p. 139.

mere existence of a crowd is incompatible with deliberation and is an incitement to inflammatory speech; and great numbers are more likely than the few making up a representative body to be carried away by some momentary emotion.

4. Direct democracy is workable only in polities that are very small in population and area; otherwise, frequent assemblies of the people are impossible. Representative democracy opens the way to large-scale, even global, political integration. Not only are there military, economic, and cultural advantages to linking together large numbers of people, but there is political safety in numbers. As James Madison (though not a proponent of universal suffrage) argued in the famous "Federalist No. 10," a polity may embrace such a great variety of interests that it would be difficult for a single faction, such as a racial or economic minority, to gain ascendancy and act in opposition to the public interest.

These four points constitute a sober and sensible case for representative democracy. Indeed, it is doubtful that proponents of direct democarcy can present an equally sober and sensible one. This is not to say, however, that their position is weaker; rather, it is a position of another kind. Proponents of representative democracy usually stand on the ground of common sense; this means, among other things, that they expect people in the future to be what they have ordinarily been in the past, beings who en masse rarely manifest either acute intelligence or a firm sense of responsibility. On the other hand, proponents of direct democracy commonly rely more on hope than on experience, on what people might become than on what they have usually been. At least two compelling visions inspire the ideal of direct democracy and it is unlikely that either will be much weakened by the objections of common sense.

First, there is a vision of human beings as governing their own lives not merely in the negative and partial sense of having a sphere in which to behave according to personal preferences, but in the positive and complete sense of deliberating upon and deciding the whole order of life. The individual alone cannot be sovereign in this way, but a populace can. Direct democracy allows the individual to share in sovereignty, and where a large measure of agreement binds together the governing populace, the individual may feel that the decisions of the people are in effect personal decisions. In contrast, representative democarcy means passive citizenship. As Rousseau asserted, you are free when you vote, but at other times you are a subject rather than a sovereign.

Beyond this, there is a vision of community that cannot be accommodated within the concept of representative democracy. Representation modifies but does not overcome the deep division between those who have power and those who do not, between government and governed. Few other circumstances so alienate human beings from one another. An enduring appeal of direct democracy is that it promises to bridge this chasm; no longer will humankind be divided between rulers and ruled. All will be rulers together and all together will rule. A direct democracy could be, fully and literally, a community.

Thus, matching the practicality of one side is the imagination of the other. How can you choose? Pondering the following questions might help you in defining your position:

1. How much of your time is politics worth? Rousseau asserted that "the better the constitution of a State is, the more do public affairs encroach on private in the minds of citizens."[2] But is it necessarily good for public affairs to encroach on your own private affairs? Rousseau thought it was, as must any whole-hearted supporter of direct democracy. But the private affairs crowded out by public activities might be the reading of literary masterpieces, the creation of works of art, the enjoyment of the company of friends and loved ones, the cultivation of personal skill in a sport or a craft, or the pursuit of scholarly or scientific research. Are these all less important than public affairs? Not everyone, certainly, will think so. Direct democracy places heavy demands on the time and attention of everyone, and it is doubtful that you can logically favor this system unless you believe that we fully realize our humanity only in politics and public life.

2. Is it possible for industrial societies to function without bureaucracy, that is, without a highly organized corps of professional administrators? If so (as Marx, for example, apparently believed), direct democracy may one day work. If not, the ideal of direct democracy is probably an illusion, for a bureaucracy is a kind of latter-day aristocracy, a more or less settled and privileged ruling group. Where bureaucracy exists, only lim-

[2] *Social Contract,* p. 93.

ited, indirect democracy is possible, and even that is possible only if the bureaucracy is held strictly responsible to the people. Arguably, such responsibility is more likely to be achieved through representatives who possess a measure of expertise and meet continuously, than by a vast, miscellaneous assemblage of citizens who can meet only occasionally.

3. On what human qualities does the solution of political problems depend? If above all on expertise, that of engineers and social scientists, for example, direct democracy is a dubious ideal. Citizens cannot all be experts in all areas. As everyone knows, however, we live in an era of science and technology, and of complex and large-scale social phenomena, so it may seem that experts must rule. Are there any human qualities, attainable by ordinary men and women, to which expertise should be subordinate? It might be claimed that there are: character and common sense. But do common people really possess these qualities? And are they in fact relevant to the problems facing the modern state?

The whole issue reflects our efforts to reconcile power and personal dignity. The general idea of democracy is that to do this, sovereignty or ultimate power must be in the hands of the people. But how is this possible? Government by the people, literally, would not be government. The concepts of representative and direct democracy are two different ways of grappling with this problem. Representative democracy is the "realistic" solution in that it acquiesces in the inevitability of government, of concentrated power, and merely subjects those who exercise this power to periodic approval by the people. Direct democracy is the "idealistic" solution. It moves a long way toward anarchism; it reduces government to a subordinate administrative apparatus and calls on the people themselves to pass laws. Representative democracy does not overcome the alienation of government and governed, but in its realism does not try to. Direct democracy imaginatively attacks this alienation; the question is whether in the complex, industrial world of the twentieth century it is a real alternative.

These various disputes about the proper location of power are not, as everyone knows, ordinarily carried on in a spirit of detachment. On the contrary, they are acrimonious and impassioned. One of the main reasons for this is that power is something many people avidly desire. For such people, power is equivalent to life, and the prospect of powerlessness is dismaying. But is power really good for its possessors? Does it make for happiness, or is it, in fact, a burden? Does it enhance the humanity of the powerful—for example, by enabling them better to serve others—or does it make them arrogant and callous?

16   Is it good to have power?

Two ancient and diametrically opposed answers dramatize the issue. For Aristotle, politics constituted a particularly favorable sphere for the realization of one's full humanity. When Aristotle said that "man is a political being," he meant in part that through political activity we can actualize our major potentialities. We are essentially united, in the sense that our essence, as expressed in virtues like courage, pride, and truthfulness, can be realized only by means of human relationships. The sum of all relationships is the state (or, more precisely, the *polis*) in that the state embraces and harmonizes all lesser groups. To become completely related to our fellow human beings requires conscious participation in the affairs of state, that is, in politics. In fine, Aristotle saw the possession of power, in company with other citizens, as providing an incomparable amplitude of life.

Aristotle was thinking both of virtue and of happiness. In modern times many people have regarded these as antithetical. For Aristotle, they were indivisible: political activity was at once duty and fulfillment.

Aristotle's views, however, apply only to political activity carried on in a good state. Aristotle saw no virtue or happiness in being, or supporting, a tyrant. True political activity is possible only in the environment of self-government and the rule of law.

A completely different position from Aristotle's was taken by another great thinker of antiquity, Epicurus (342?–270 B.C.). Having seen the downfall of the city-state, Epicurus sought serenity in a life of gentle pleasure and minimal pain. His viewpoint was summed up in the injunction "Live unknown." Epicurus was trying to deal with a general disorientation of life (not unlike the alienation of the present time), resulting from the passing of the city-state as a viable form of human life. In a world suddenly vast and strange, Epicurus wished to discover how a person might attain self-sufficiency and tranquillity. He was led, in his search, to repudiate the notion that "man is a political being." Politics means the very opposite of the good life; it means continuous vexation and dependence on others. Only in private life—a kind of tomb in the eyes of Aristotle—can a person find happiness and independence.

Today, an Epicurean observer of American life would say that those who seek political office, climbing perhaps from local and state posts to the summits of power in Washington, are foolish, for they will find only annoyance and anguish. He would equally condemn radical militants and activists, however, for they violate the rule of detachment no less than do the members of the governing groups they attack. An Epicurean would be unlikely to sympathize even with exhortations to vote. You might better concentrate on maintaining balance and peace in your own personal life, regardless of prevailing political conditions.

Aristotle and Epicurus stand at either end of a wide range of possible answers to the question of whether it is good to have power. Most Americans today would probably be unwilling to endorse either position. Many would probably say that wielding power may not improve a person's life in the sense of bringing fulfillment and happiness; it is a duty, however, and so must at least improve a person morally. A position close to this was developed by the Stoics a century or more after the time of Epicurus and contributed to the political resoluteness needed to administer and defend the Roman Empire.

The Stoic conception of the universe as a divine order dictated the conscientious performance of the duties of one's station; each person should play a part, whatever it might be. Political office should not be sought, but it should be accepted by anyone led thereto by the normal course of affairs. A slave should accept a slave's lot, realizing that one's humanity cannot be destroyed by enslavement by only by failure to fulfill one's duties with a rational and imperturbable consciousness of taking part in the divine order of the cosmos. And once faced with political tasks, a person should perform them without being swayed by the uncertainties and discouragements that assail a conscientious person in a position of power; whatever the consequences, all is as it should be.

Whether or not this outlook is correct, we must admit that so austere an emphasis on duty might well prove useful in times of political trouble. Rome found it so, and perhaps the time is coming when America will as well.

These three attitudes, the Aristotelian, the Epicurean, and the Stoic, all are relatively hopeful and constructive. The Epicurean and Stoic attitudes reflect disillusionment but tell us how to live well in spite of the evils surrounding us. There is a more cynical view, however, and in times as disturbed as ours, it is likely to have numerous adherents. According to this view, power may not be morally or socially beneficial but it is eminently worth having, either for the opportunities it provides for a ruthless person to satisfy personal interests or merely for the pleasure and exhilaration of wielding it. We do not expect to find this attitude argued by philosophers but rather reflected in the lives of those too fully occupied with gaining and using power to have time for thinking and writing. To find it in the writings of a great thinker we must look beneath the surface.

Machiavelli was not indifferent either to the ends sought by rulers or to the inherent morality of the means they employed. Success was not everything for Machiavelli. He was, however, deeply fascinated with power, so much so that he often evinced satisfaction with an adroit political maneuver and showed relatively little concern with either its utlimate consequences or its inherent morality. Moreover, the charm of power seems to have been enhanced, in Machiavelli's eyes, when it assumed some of its more violent and terrifying forms. While he did not explicitly defend the idea that power is an end in itself, much less the idea that it is a means for satisfying the private interests of the one who wields it, his writings do sometimes express the feeling that power is in some measure justified simply by the glory and excitement of political virtuosity.

Whether power is good for its possessors is a pertinent question today. The politics of the twentieth century has been filled with confusion and violence. It is far from clear that power is beneficial in any era to those who wield it. The possession of power in our era appears, at least so far as happiness and morality are concerned, a particularly dubious privilege. Politics is likely to repel sensitive and honorable people and attract the insensitive and unscrupulous. Clearly this situation constitutes a crisis in the political order. And this demoralization, by repelling the best and attracting the worst, will produce further demoralization. How far these remarks apply to various present-day societies can be disputed; that they have some application, however, seems undeniable. This is why the question before us is significant. If the best people spurn the political order, is it not reasonable to suppose that the political order is doomed?

At any rate, let us assume that we have become convinced both of the practical necessity of power and of the moral legitimacy of wielding it. What about those subject to power? Why should they submit?

17 Why obey?

To possess power is at least superficially honorable and glorious. To be without power and subject to the power of others is at least superficially degrading. Why should a person accept such a position? This is one of the central questions in political thought; if it cannot be answered, then the entire political order, with all of its offices, laws, and dignities, is indefensible.

Another way of posing the question is to ask what makes power legitimate or what turns it from naked force into authority. Throughout history human beings have been offended by stark power, by a demand for obedience unsupported by any reference to moral right. But not very much has been required to overcome this feeling of offense; disobedience is dangerous, and a fragile claim to legitimacy may suffice to reconcile most people to subordination. Nevertheless, it is not just a handful of radicals or peculiarly conscientious people, such as Quakers, who ask why obedience is owed to a government. The self-respect of practically all human beings depends on assurance that the government they obey has a moral right to be obeyed.

Probably the oldest and most durable answer to this question is one that today seems absurd: the divine right of kings. Until just a few centuries ago most governments claimed their power was given them by God. This claim was made well before the rise of Christian societies. "From the beginning of history," writes the historian Christopher Dawson, "the king has been distinguished from the tyrant, the magistrate or the official by the possession of a *charisma* or divine mandate which sets him apart from other men."[3] One inference drawn from this principle was, of course, the requirement of absolute obedience. Political resistance was rebellion against the divine.

The concept of the divine right of kings, however, may seem an effort not to answer the question but to stifle it. Power entails an immense moral strain for those subject to it, and it is not surprising that in religious ages people relieved this strain by conceiving of power as divinely sanctioned. The idea of divine right, nevertheless, is thoroughly irrational, not primarily because it is based on a religious premise, but because the premise—that God is—does not justify the conclusion. The idea that God has sanctified every government is no more necessitated by religious faith than is the idea that God has sanctified every revolution. One element in the durability of the idea that kings rule by divine right may well be the desire of governing classes to suppress an explosive question. Certainly the idea was not reached by open-minded inquiry and could not long withstand such inquiry.

A complete change of mind has apparently occurred in recent centuries. Worldiness and religious skepticism have rendered the principle of divine right wholly implausible, and the ideal of personal freedom has shifted the burden of proof, in questions of obedience, to the side of the government. At the same time, the rising self-confidence and political awareness of the people have given disobedience history-making potentialities. Thus the question *Why obey?* has been asked with mounting and ominous insistence.

The simplest defense of obedience, aside from the theory of divine right, may be that contained in the idea of consent. As Locke put it, "Men being . . . by Nature, all free, equal and independent, no one can be put out of this Estate, and subjected to the Political Power of another, without his own *Consent.*"[4] A person is not obliged to obey unless he has voluntarily agreed to do so. At one point, at least, Locke seems to imply that not only does the founding of a government require consent but that every governmental act significantly affecting a person's life or rights requires consent, for he writes that "the *Supream Power*

---

[3]Christopher Dawson, *Religion and Culture* (New York: Meridian Books, 1948), p. 109. The italics are Dawson's.

[4]John Locke. *Two Treaties of Government,* ed. Peter Laslett (Cambridge: Cambridge University Press, 1960), p. 348. The italics are Locke's.

cannot take from any Man any part of his *Property* without his own consent."[5] If this injunction were followed literally, payment of taxes would be voluntary. Indeed, if we are under no obligation to obey unless we consent to do so in each particular case, then strictly speaking we are under no obligation to obey at all.

The theory that political obligation is based on consent subordinates government to freedom. Even assuming that Locke did not mean to go so far as to require consent for every particular governmental act, his general point is that nothing can be rightfully demanded of us that does not accord with each one's uncoerced and conscious will. Not surprisingly, some political thinkers sought to formulate a doctrine of obedience with less anarchistic overtones. One result is the theory of the "general will," which was definitively formulated by Rousseau, although it had been implicit in other political philosophies, such as those of Plato and Aristotle.

According to this theory, the obligation to obey does not depend on a prior act of consent (although it happens that Rosseau did incorporate the idea of consent into his political theory). A government deserves obedience if its commands conform to what Rosseau called the general will. What is the general will? Or, to put the question in a more convenient form, what qualities make a will general? Not simply its being the will of everyone, for this would make the theory of the general will only another form of the theory of consent.

Rousseau explicitly distinguished between "the will of all" and the general will, and asserted that they often differ greatly. The will of all, he wrote, is "no more than a sum of particular wills."[6] The distinctive quality of the general will, according to Rousseau, is that it "considers only the common interest."[7] For a will to be general, then, it must be directed toward the good of everyone. It is not necessary to ask now whether there can be a truly common good, a value shared equally by every member of society. This depends on whether, in answer to Question 1, human beings are essentially united. The point is that the theory of the general will tells us that a government has a legitimate

---

[5]*Two Treaties,* p. 378. The italics are Locke's (as is the spelling of "supreme")
[6]*Social Contract.* p. 26.
[7]*Social Contract.* p. 26.

claim to obedience only when its commands represent the true, ultimate interest of all the people.

Rousseau acknowledged that the people are subject to error, so that the will of all is not necessarily the general will, which has led to the idea that a single ruling person, even an absolute dictator, might represent the general will. Accordingly, some writers have claimed to see in regimes such as Lenin's and Hitler's a Rousseauean spirit. This, however, is based on a misreading of Rousseau. In spite of all the complexities of *The Social Contract,* Rousseau's own words seem quite conclusive. "The general will," he wrote, "to be really such, must be general in its object as well as it essence . . . it must both come from all and apply to all."[8] Thus, while the will of the people may be mistaken, a will directed toward the common good is not the general will unless it also is the will of the people.

Rousseau was not so unrealistic as to demand unanimity in every decision, however. He did not mean it literally when he said that the general will must "come from all." He was willing to accept a majority, with the size depending on circumstances, as a surrogate for "all." This seems reasonable enough. However, the whole idea of the general will introduces a possibility that is startling but quite important. This is, that in obeying the general will, even under duress, you are free. Obedience and freedom, usually assumed to be opposites, in these circumstances are identical. How can this be? The answer is logical. You are free, presumably, when you do what you really want to do; in turn, what you really want to do is realize your own ultimate good. If you live in a just society, however, your own good is identical with the common good; and the common good is the object of the general will. Hence you follow your own real will—you do what you *really* want to do—when you obey the general will. The conclusion is inescapable: in obeying the general will you are free. This would be true even if you felt threatened or crushed by that will.

This inference is stated so starkly in order to make the basic theory clear, not to induce the reader to reject it. If the theory be rejected, it should be only after careful reflection, for Rousseau's view is not absurd. It is a restatement of the ancient conviction that we are essentially united and hence are human—

[8] *Social Contract,* p. 29.

and in that sense free—not in following some wayward individual impulse but in playing the part of active and loyal citizens. And this is true even if we are imprisoned, so long as we are justly imprisoned; and it is true even if some great sacrifice, such as life, lost perhaps in battle, is required of us, so long as the requirement accords with the will and the good of the whole people.

The main problem presented by the question of obedience is the reconciliation of obedience with liberty. "To renounce liberty," as Rousseau asserted, "is to renounce being a man."[9] But it is the essence of government to demand obedience and thus, apparently, a renunciation of liberty. How then can even the best government mean anything but the destruction of the humanity of those living under it? Anarchists claim that it cannot. The theories of consent and the general will, on the other hand, both attempt to justify government by showing how a person can obey and still be free. The principal difference between the two theories is this: one conceives of freedom only in terms of conscious will and tries to legitimize obedience by tracing it back to an act of consent; the other conceives of freedom in terms of a will that may not be fully conscious, since in willing my own welfare I may not know what political measures will promote it. The theory of the general will maintains that even though a law does not rest on explicit consent, it may yet command what contributes to one's real good and thus may enhance one's freedom.

Both theories involve serious difficulties. The theory of consent is simple and comprehensible on the surface, but it is hard to see how it could be put into practice. It cannot mean that the legitimacy of every governmental command depends on a separate act of consent; this would be incompatible with stable, effective government. Thus, it must mean that the legitimacy of each governmental command follows from some prior act of consent. The trouble is that a command rarely has this kind of consent behind it; people do not normally give their clear and specific consent to the government over them. In reading Locke, one can sense the embarrassment this difficulty causes him. In a passage on taxation, he asserts that when property is taken from a citizen, it must be "with his own Consent, *i.e.,* the Consent of the Majority."[10] Thus, individual consent is equated

[9] *Social Contract,* p. 9.
[10] *Two Treaties,* p. 380.

with majority consent. But there is no manifest justification for doing this, and it merely sharpens the question of obedience: why obey the majority? In another passage, Locke asserts that a person gives tacit consent to a government merely by traveling freely on its roads or simply by being within its territory.[11] Judged by this standard, however, the most despised tyrannies have rested on the consent of the governed.

A further question is this: is a person bound by consent that was given in ignorance or confusion? Was a young German who swore allegiance to Hitler when he first came to power morally obliged to obey every command of the Nazi government? These are a few of the questions provoked by the theory of consent.

The theory of the general will implies, on the other hand, that a person might, as stated in a notorious phrase of Rousseau's, be "forced to be free." You might be free in doing, under the supervision of the police, something that you do not at all want to do. You might even be free in prison. Hegel argued that criminals really will their own punishment, which suggests that a government wisely and justly carrying out its penal responsibilities liberates people by locking them up. This idea is not at all nonsensical, any more than it is nonsensical to speak of a criminal as being enslaved by an evil will. But it is an idea that gives one pause. Is there perhaps some dangerous sophistry concealed in the equation of force and freedom?

Another difficulty involved in the theory of the general will is somewhat like the difficulty just pointed out in the theory of consent; it cannot be readily applied. True, government in accordance with the general will is not as far beyond the realm of possibility as government literally by consent. Nevertheless, the theory of the general will, as Rousseau conceived it, requires active and continuous popular participation in a process of legislation that produces just laws and a just order of society. None of the Western democracies can come close to meeting this standard.

This fact makes it apparent that the major theories of obedience do not set our minds at rest and enable us to obey the governments over us with good conscience. On the contrary, they cast the legitimacy of these governments into doubt. In telling us when to obey, the theories of consent and the general will

[11]*Two Treaties,* p. 366.

also tell us when not to obey; and the standards they set are very demanding. Hence they are doctrines not only of obedience, but also of revolution. They have proved this in practice; Locke's philosophy played an important role in the American Revolution and Rousseau's in the French Revolution. Today for these philosophies to be applied rigorously and seriously would be destabilizing. Why, then, aren't the Western nations, condemned by the major theories of legitimacy, seething with revolutionary fervor?

The primary reasons, of course, are that revolution is an extremely dangerous and difficult act and that most people in the Western nations are (whether they should be or not) reasonably contented. Popular contentment is due above all to material abundance; flatly contradicting the predictions of Marx, the progress of industrialism has undermined revolutionary will. In nations like the United States and Great Britain, exceedingly few desire revolution; and with the governments commanding highly sophisticated administrative and police organizations, revolutionary efforts have scarcely the slightest chance of success. It is not just stark impracticality, however, that stands in the way of revolution. For the time being, at least, revolution has been discredited. This has happened because the most dramatic revolutions witnessed in the twentieth century all have ended tragically. All have brought into power tyrannical governments. There has arisen in response a widespread feeling that revolution transcends human capacities, that it expresses the kind of arrogance the Greeks called *hubris* and considered a forerunner of disaster. This feeling may be ill-founded, but there is little doubt that it exists, and it reinforces the stability brought by industrial prosperity.

The prevailing indifference and skepticism concerning revolution, however defensible or indefensible in general, leave the whole issue of obedience unresolved and place us in a dubious relationship with government. Most people in the Western nations are normally acquiescent, but their acquiescence is habitual rather than thoughtful and reflects little respect for their governments. If they think about the matter, they are more or less conscious that the governments over them do not measure up to the highest standards of legitimacy, but for all of the reasons cited earlier they do not contemplate revolution or, indeed, any form of principled, as distinguished from personally expedient, disobedience. But this is a morally unsatisfactory situation. Obeying always and as a matter of course means nothing less than abandoning selfhood; the center of choice and responsibility is shifted from the self to those who command. Moreover, one is implicated morally is the injustices done by government and society, for obedience is support; only through obedience do governments and societies stand. Such considerations are probably not as far from the minds of ordinary citizens as one might suppose. A vague sense that the moral stakes are high is what makes most people desire some assurance that the government they obey is legitimate.

Domestic attitudes reverbrate abroad. The unthinking acquiescence that prevails among Americans is matched by a foreign policy that frequently opposes revolution in other nations. It is true that this policy is based on calculations of national interest rather than on ideological evaluations of revolution. But those calculations are not indisputably realistic, and the antirevolutionary calculus would not prevail so consistently were it not supported by a general antipathy to revolution among American citizens. Thus Americans, although unsupported by a considered and relevant doctrine of obedience, bolster obedience throughout the world.

Is there any way we might recover and affirm a sense of responsibility in matters of obedience and disobedience? It is doubtful that this should be done by trying to reanimate the revolutionary spirit of 1776 (America) and 1789 (France); the contemporary sense that a revolution is usually a tragedy has much to commend it. And to advocate casual and persistent disobedience, even without revolutionary intentions, would be irresponsible. Civilization depends on obedience being normal and disobedience exceptional; otherwise, the fundamental order undergirding a cultivated life would break down. Nevertheless, obeying is a serious responsibility, and it bears on every human being, even on those—the majority—who never think of it. A revolutionary spirit carries a consciousness of that responsibility, and the passing of the revolutionary spirit, however realistic, is not without a moral price. The question, *Why obey?* occurs only to human beings, not to beasts. Hence, never to ask the question is literally bestial.

These reflections drive us irresistibly to the idea of civil disobedience. Does that idea tell us how we might recover and affirm a full sense of political responsibility? Civil disobedience can be contrasted both with casual and with criminal disobedience. Unlike casual disobedience, it is selective and purposeful. One disobeys a law that is considered unjust or symbolic of an unjust condition; and one disobeys in the hope of furthering a political purpose, such as changing the law. Unlike criminal disobedience, civil disobedience aims at a public, not merely personal, value, and it affirms the principle of law by acquiescing in the penalities attached to disobedience. Practicing civil disobedience requires not only courage but political sophistication—a knowledge of techniques and strategies. A solitary individual is not likely to possess the requisite knowledge, and a significant measure of civil disobedience is therefore not likely to emerge merely from scattered personal decisions. A movement, or some kind of collective effort, is needed. Should a civil disobedience movement be mounted? Should thoughful people begin mastering and spreading the knowledge on which civil disobedience depends? Would this help to revitalize the question *Why obey?* and thus render the state of obedience—which is no doubt normally incumbent on us—more thoughtful, responsible, and fully human than it is at present?

■ Suggested Readings

Plato. *Apology*
——. *Crito*
——. *The Republic*
Aristotle. *Politics,* Books I–IV
Marcus Aurelius. *Meditations*
Saint Augustine. *The Political Writings of St. Augustine,* ed. by Henry Paolucci, Chapters 1–3
Machiavelli, Niccolò. *The Prince*
Hobbes, Thomas. *Leviathan,* First and Second Parts
Rousseau, Jean Jacques. *The Social Contract*
Paine, Thomas. *The Rights of Man*
Mill, John Stuart. *Representative Government*
Marx, Karl. *The Civil War in France*
Green, Thomas Hill. *Lectures on the Principles of Political Obligation*
Tolstoy, Leo. *Resurrection*
Niebuhr, Reinhold. *Moral Man and Immoral Society*
——. *The Children of Light and the Children of Darkness*

Tillich, Paul. *Love, Power, and Justice*
Arendt, Hannah. *The Origins of Totalitarianism*
————. *The Human Condition*
Márquez, Gabriel Garcia. *The Autumn of the Patriarch*
Kundera, Milan. *The Unbearable Lightness of Being*

CHAPTER 5

■ Limits on Power

Because all power is morally dubious—hard to justify and likely to corrupt—the confinement of power to its proper bounds is a central problem of civilization. Power constantly tends to become arbitrary and limitless, and tyranny is one of the ancient afflictions of our collective existence. But never in history has power been so boundless and destructive as in the totalitarian dictatorships of the twentieth century. These regimes have made it plain that, contrary to Hobbes, not only the lack but the lawlessness of a central power renders life "solitary, poor, nasty, brutish, and short." To ask about the proper limits on power and how these limits can be enforced is to inquire how life can be made decent and civilized.

Limits on power are basically of two kinds: moral and constitutional. Moral limits are those deriving from moral law, or from what is believed to be moral law; their efficacy depends solely on moral convictions. For a government to refrain from using murder as an instrument of foreign policy, even when murder is within the scope of its legal powers, would exemplify respect for a moral limit. Constitutional limits may derive ultimately from moral law, but what makes them constitutional is their embodiment in a basic written law—a law that takes precedence over all others and is upheld by society and enforced in the courts. This law may be represented by one supreme document, as in America, or it may be merely the content of a body of customs, statutes, court decisions, and historical documents, as in Great Britain. A constitutional government is one that is limited by such a law.

We shall discuss both moral and constitutional limits, beginning with moral limits because they must in some sense underlie constitutional limits. First we shall consider what may be the oldest, most fundamental question concerning the relationship of morals and politics.

18 Should governments be under the same moral limits as individuals?

One great political thinker, Machiavelli, has become notorious for arguing that they should not, because they cannot. We have already noted Machiavelli's belief that there can be no order among human beings and nothing accomplished in human affairs without power. A companion belief is that effective use of power is incompatible with strict observance of the moral law. No ideals can be realized without doing evil. To perceive the somewhat tragic coloring of Machiavelli's argument, it is necessary to understand that Machiavelli never expressed indifference to the moral law and never glorified evil. The greatness of Machiavelli's thought depends on the tension inherent in the idea that there is a moral law but that rulers on occasion must break that law.

No such necessity, however, can be claimed by private individuals. Rulers must sometimes be immoral in order to establish and preserve the state; for the sake of the same end, subjects must always be moral. Social order would collapse if private individuals considered themselves free to break the moral law when their interests require it. The political universe thus is morally unique.

By setting forth this point of view, Machiavelli gained one of the most unsavory reputations in the history of thought. Shakespeare referred to him as "the murderous Machiavel," and among the synonyms of "Machiavellian" in Roget's *Thesaurus* are "false," "crafty," and "dishonest." What is most striking about the opposing arguments, however, is how faint and infrequent they are. So far as I am aware, the chief works of political thought contain no argument, answering to Machiavelli's, for the same uncompromising morality among rulers that is expected of private individuals. One great thinker who disagreed with Machiavelli was Immanuel Kant (1724–1804), but in none of his major works does he systematically take issue with the Machiavellian argument. Many thinkers have believed that the health of the political order depends on the moral rectitude of its members. But Machiavelli too believed this; his writings abound in expressions of admiration for the honor and probity of the ancient Romans.

Where Machiavelli differs from the others is in saying explicitly what they seldom deny: while political order depends on respect for moral standards, it depends also on the capacity of rulers occasionally to violate those standards. In view of the silence of the great political thinkers concerning so unsettling an idea, one wonders whether it is Machiavelli's chief distinction to have divulged a shameful truth (one writer speaks of his "appalling sincerity")—a truth others have been too discrete to acknowledge.

Opposition to Machiavelli, then, comes less from political philosophy than from common moral convictions. But can people with these convictions hold their ground in the face of political reality? Let us consider lying as an example. Anyone who is repelled by the evasive and deceptive speech common in the political world might consider these two questions: (1) Could a government operate successfully without often concealing its plans and withholding much of the information at its disposal? (2) Should a government refuse to lie even if it might thus gain some great good like ending a war or helping an underprivileged group? It is possible to answer both questions affirmatively, but that is not the side of plausibility and common sense. Rather, these questions lead to the Machiavellian conclusion that we cannot demand from rulers the same candor and truthfulness we expect of personal associates.

But having moved this far toward Machiavelli, we should ask whether *every* moral limit is conditional on political circumstances. If rulers may lie to reach political goals, may they kill? Machiavelli said yes, defending not only political deceit but also political murder. But if we go this far, what is left of ideals and conscience? Is it in the nature of things that profoundly evil means can be used to attain good ends? The Communist regimes of Russia and China have been willing to engage in large-scale killing for the sake of community, but neither has attained its goal.

Underlying this question is an issue concerning the nature of the moral law. We may here employ the distinction made in Question 3 between moral absolutism and moral relativism. Moral absolutism is the theory that there is a moral law, usually said to derive from nature or from God and independent of the interests and opinions both of individuals and of societies. Moral relativism is the theory that morality is relative to some variable circumstance, such as the desires of the individual or the needs of society. At first glance it may seem that the choice between these alternatives would decide your answer to the question of whether governments should be under the same moral restraints as private individuals. Absolutism would seem to bar all exemptions and relativism to admit exemptions without limit.

Issues in the field of political theory can seldom be conclusively settled, however, merely by making a direct inference from some philosophical principle. So it is in this instance. We may argue that a moral law must be broken, but that it is nevertheless in some sense absolute. For example, we may say that "Thou shalt not kill" is an absolute law even though under certain conditions, as in war, killing is unavoidable. You can object that absolute means unconditional, and thus should not be applied to a law that must sometimes be broken. But is it not possible that evil acts, such as lying or killing, remain evil regardless of the circumstances in which they are committed? Is it not possible to be in some sense guilty for doing something that circumstances made it necessary to do?

On the other side, whether relativism opens the way for an affirmative answer to the question of the right of rulers to ignore moral limits depends on exactly what the moral law is relative to. If it is relative to each individual's desires and circumstances, then those who possess power are not subject to the same moral restraints as those who do not; but if morality is relative to the culture or the species, then both rulers and ruled may logically be subject to identical laws.

These remarks are intended as warnings against oversimplification, not as indications of the ways people usually look at things. There is no doubt that absolutism tends to bar any distinction between the morality of politics and the morality of private life. This implication can be avoided only by establishing two principles: necessity bars full adherence to the moral law, and a person is morally bound to pay some regard to necessity. In other words, it must be shown that perfect morality is a practical and moral impossibility—owing not to the weaknesses of human nature but to the conditions of human life. It may be possible to do this. But moral absolutism affirms a single, all-embracing moral order, thus placing governments under the same moral restraints that are incumbent on private individuals, so that any violation of these restraints requires a particular justification if it is to be in any sense legitimate. Even such a justification may not relieve from all guilt those who violate the moral law. From this standpoint, politics may be viewed as a sphere of moral tension and even of moral tragedy.

Relativism allows the argument that political leaders and private citizens inhabit two different moral universes or that political leaders are not within any moral universe at all. For example, if morality were held to concern only relationships among citizens of the same nation, then international relations would not be subject to any moral rules; political leaders would be free, in diplomatic and military activities, to act as they please, responsible only to the moral bonds uniting them to their own subjects. Moral relativism might also take the form of the argument that the possession of power entails liberation from all moral rules whatever. In this situation, political leaders would not be morally restrained even in relation to their own subjects. They would live not in a separate and unique moral universe but in a moral void.

In a sense, moral relativism clears the air. It does not subject political leaders to the strain of acknowledging the authority of moral rules they are forced to break. They can act with clear conscience under their own separate rules. The shadows of moral tragedy that are cast over political life by moral absolutism are dispelled.

This relief from tension may strike the reader as wholesome. But there are serious risks inherent in allowing rulers such liberty. These risks are particularly great when we completely abandon the idea that governments and private individuals inhabit a single moral universe. If "power tends to corrupt" under the best circumstances, then surely this tendency is enhanced where power means liberation from moral limits. Further, if government is exempt from the moral standards that apply to ordinary citizens, must government not be beyond their moral judgment? And if government is beyond their moral judgment, is it not beyond their political judgment as well? And if this is so, is it not unchecked and irresponsible? Of course, moral absolutism does not eliminate these risks either, but it does draw attention to them.

Can you perhaps circumvent a host of moral dangers and philosophical difficulties by simply insisting on the same moral standards for everyone and refusing to grant any exceptions? Perhaps you can. But this possibility may invite an idealistic distortion of reality. The political scene in the twentieth century has displayed so many paradoxes and terrors that we are bound to doubt that political realities can be dealt with as unequivocally as the moral law, in its majesty and its simplicity, seems to demand.

Today, the question of whether governments should be under the same moral limits as individuals is put forcefully to Americans by their role as citizens of a superpower in a world of war and brutal international rivalry. There is, for example, the issue of assassination. Amid the conflicts and tensions of power politics, a nation often has an interest in the death of a foreign figure—a leader, perhaps, or a secret agent. The ax-murder of Trotsky, who had been exiled by the Soviet government and was living in Mexico, by a Stalinist agent is only the most spectacular example from recent times of official assassination. It is public knowledge that the United States has attempted, and carried out, acts of assassination in recent decades. How should Americans feel about this fact? Relativists will perhaps be undisturbed, for in their minds there may be no moral laws governing the relations of one nation with another. Machiavellians may be disturbed but will nevertheless consent in principle (in principle only, since any particular act of assassination would have to be politically necessary in order to be justified). But anyone who believes in absolute moral laws will be tempted to say that a nation should in no circumstances whatever engage in murder. Would an absolute ban of that kind make sense? Would it make sense in all circumstances whatever, for example, even if the very safety of the nation were in peril? If a nation is willing to kill enemy soldiers in battle, as every nation must be, is it logical for it to recoil from killing, however it can, foreign civilians who seriously threaten its interests?

An issue weighing more heavily on many minds today than the morality of assassination is the morality of nuclear war. Americans have a personal interest in this issue, since they are the only people who have ever used nuclear weapons in combat. The bombs dropped on Hiroshima and Nagasaki took over two hundred thousand lives, most of them civilian lives. Is America's use of the bombs morally defensible? The argument over Hiroshima and Nagasaki begins with the question of necessity. Couldn't the bombs have been dropped on an uninhabited area? If it was not necessary that cities be the targets, few would defend the President's act. But suppose that devastation in uninhabited areas would not have swayed the Japanese leaders, and that hundreds of thousands of lives—both American and Japanese—would have been lost in the invasion of the Japanese home islands. One might argue on those grounds that it was necessary to bomb Hiroshima and Nagasaki. Might one argue, in response, that on moral grounds that "necessity" should have been rejected?—that the bombing was mass murder and unjustifiable on any grounds? If so, then shouldn't the United States have refrained from countless other acts of violence committed during the war with ordinary weapons: the bombing of Tokyo and Berlin, for example? Would you say yes even if such restraint would have prevented the United States from winning the war? On the other hand, if you sanction the bombing of Hiroshima and Nagasaki, aren't you accepting the principle that governments may rightfully employ terror against civilians? It is not easy either to affirm or to deny the subordination of governments to moral law.

Stated broadly, the question is whether waging nuclear war can under any circumstances be a moral act. During the Middle Ages, political thinkers developed the concept of the "just war." It was argued that war was just when it met certain conditions, such as having a reasonable purpose and having prospects of attaining that purpose without inordinate destruction. The principal thrust of the concept was that war can be moral. It is often asked today whether the concept of just war hasn't been nullified by nuclear weapons. How can a nuclear war be moral? It seems that a nuclear war would have to be purposeless, since at the end nothing would remain—no civilization, perhaps no human beings at all. What ends could justify such means? What moral calculus could justify universal annihilation? The legitimacy of nuclear war must appear doubtful even in the eyes of Machiavellians and relativists.

If the legitimacy of nuclear war is doubtful, however, so is the legitimacy of the policy of deterrence that the United States has followed almost from the beginning of the nuclear age, for a policy of deterrence involves readiness to wage nuclear war. Can such a policy possibly be moral? But what alternative is there to deterrence? Would a policy of deterrence be moral if practiced by presidents who pretended to be ready to strike yet were secretly resolved never to do so—not even in response to a nuclear attack on the United States? Or is so paradoxical, hidden, and restrained an attitude impossible for human beings to maintain for very long?

Such questions do not lead immediately to clear answers. If they did, the world would not be embroiled in bitter controversy concerning nuclear policies. These questions do, however, make clear the urgency of moral reflection. In the unparalleled crisis of civilization to which nuclear arms have brought us, one is not seriously tempted to abandon all moral considerations. That would be like abandoning the helm and all navigational aids during a storm at sea. To understand the relationship of governments to moral law may literally be a matter of life and death.

Pondering the moral limits on power leads to the matter of constitutional limits. These are different, as we have seen, in that the former rest on moral consciousness, the latter on law. Both, however, give rise to similar doubts when imposed on the possessors of power—doubts about the wisdom of subjecting governments to invariable limits without regard to variable circumstances. Hence the question that follows.

19 Should governments in all circumstances be under constitutional limits?

The issue has been forcefully posed by the twentieth-century conflict between democratic and totalitarian nations. During World War II and the early stages of the Cold War, it was tempting to see the democracies as altogther good and the dictatorships as altogether bad. But there came a realization that good and evil are not so neatly distributed; not only is there much evil in those countries where government is restrained by constitutional limitations, but the evil may be in some measure protected by the limitations. For example, in the United States, the richest country in history, many people are hungry and undernourished. Would this be so if the government were not severely inhibited by a variety of substantive and procedural limitations laid down in the Constitution?

No political idea in the West has greater authority than constitutionalism. For more than two thousand years there has been a remarkably wide and stable consensus that government ought to be carried on within publicly known and enforceable restraints. Perhaps the most influential modern expression of this consensus is found in the writings of John Locke. But Locke is only one of several great modern thinkers who have been firmly committed constitutionalists. Locke's views, moreover, were drawn from a solidly established medieval tradition, itself the outgrowth of an ancient Greek and Roman constitutionalist tradition. Few other ideas can claim so impressive a background. Time after time, from the beginning of political thought, lawless government has been condemned as monstrous and unnatural.

The opposition to this tradition, however, is substantial—in the quality of those representing it, at least, if not in their numbers. No great thinkers have actually advocated totalitarianism, that is, governmental control of every detail of life, but several have been enemies of constitutionalism. Four stand out in the history of thought, and each represents a different motive.

1. Plato opposed constitutionalism because of his faith in the wisdom of a few. Later in life, when he faced the improbability that the wise could ever gain power, he endorsed constitutionalism. But earlier, when he believed that philosophers might become rulers, he opposed the subjection of government to preestablished limitations. He did this on the logical grounds that perfect wisdom is quite competent to decide for itself how far its power should reach. Plato likened the philosopher-ruler to a doctor, who is not hampered by prior rules but in each particular case can prescribe precisely what the health of the patient requires.

Today we do not have Plato's faith in philosophers. But we do accept the Platonic ideal in a somewhat different form; we assume, or many of us do, that our social problems can be solved by experts. It is scientific and technological intelligence, rather than philosophical, that commands our trust. Thus we may logically ask whether America, with a government confined by limitations established in the eighteenth century, can attack such problems as poverty and urban disorder with the full resources of twentieth-century social and physical science. The American Constitution makes it next to impossible for a scientific plan to be uncompromisingly applied to any major social problem. This is partly owing to the procedural forms for decision making that are inherent in constitutionalism and that the American Constitution imposes. These forms ensure that every measure finally decided upon embodies a great number of compromises; these compromises may render the measure acceptable to the various interests affected by it, but they inevitably rob it of scientific integrity. But beyond procedural limitations are substantive limitations. Under a constitutional government, people cannot be forced to move, alter their living habits, take certain jobs, or do any number of things that science might deem necessary for solving social problems.

It is not too much to say that constitutionalism and scientific government are incompatible. Which is of greater importance? This is the question Plato puts before us.

2. Hobbes opposed constitutionalism because of his pessimistic appraisal of human nature. Many passages in Hobbes's writings show that he did not desire or even envision the possibility of anything like modern totalitarianism. Nevertheless, he regarded human beings as far too restless and selfish, too inherently chaotic, to afford governments that were barred absolutely from certain areas of life. Hobbes's views on religious toleration exemplify this attitude. While being far from an ideologue wishing to impose a single set of beliefs on everyone, he thought that government must have the power to regulate religious creeds and forms of worship. An inviolable rule of toleration would invite a reopening of "the war of all against all."

In quiet American suburbs today Hobbes may seem a mere doctrinaire pessimist. But look beyond the suburbs: are not the cities, with their poverty and racial tensions, Hobbesian worlds? Is not the whole globe Hobbesian, divided as it is among suspicious, heavily armed nations?

The impact of such conditions on constitutional government is apparent in society today. Some people, looking to safety of life and property, demand that police be allowed to deal with criminal suspects with whatever harshness and guile seem necessary for uncovering and suppressing crime; certainly they should not be bound by every rule a careful judge might find implicit in the Constitution. A very Hobbesian demand! Hobbesian sentiments are also behind the willingness of many people to set aside constitutional limits in foreign affairs. The principles applied to domestic crime and to international conflict are the same: order is prior to all other values, and in some circumstances order depends on authoritarian rule.

3. If Plato opposed constitutionalism out of faith in the few, Rousseau did so out of faith in the many. Granted, such a statement must be severely qualified. Rousseau never explicitly attacked constitional government. Moreover, he was passionately committed to one aspect of constitutionalism—the principle of government by law. He held that no command of the sovereign populace was valid unless it took the form of law. (The idea of government by law is constitutional because it implies a certain limitation on government—it must always adhere to the form of law. It is only one aspect of constitutionalism, however, because, while adhering to the form of law, a government might regulate religion, speech, and every other individual activity.) Nevertheless, the example of Rousseau demonstrates that government by the people can take on a totalitarian flavor. Just as Plato assumed that no human agency had the wisdom or right to restrain the philosopher-rulers, so Rousseau held that no human agency could properly impose limitations on the people except the people themselves. Rousseau seems to envision a commonwealth in which the lives of individuals are absorbed into the common life and regulated in every detail by the popular will. Rousseau calls for a "civil religion," for example, "a civil profession of faith of which the Sovereign should fix the articles, not exactly as religious dogmas, but as social sentiments without which a man cannot be a good citizen or a faithful subject."[1] Rousseau declares that anyone refusing to sub-

---

[1] Jean Jacques Rousseau. *The Social Contract and Discourses,* trans. with an introduction by G. D. H. Cole (New York: Dutton, 1950), p. 139.

scribe to the articles of this faith be banished and that anyone who does subscribe to them and then "behaves as if he does not believe them" should be put to death.

Democratic totalitarianism is remote from the spirit and the structure of the American Constitution, but during the sixties the actions of militant students showed signs of it. In campus uprisings the normal proceedings of universities were disrupted, opponents were shouted down, and "nonnegotiable demands" were the order of the day. Student gatherings were often characterized by an impassioned unanimity that may have been in some sense democratic but, in its intolerance of disagreement and its lack of restraint, was far from constitutional.

Social critics have often asserted that the established pattern of restraints, both within universities and in society at large, is designed to preserve the status quo, along with the inequalities and injustices that it is imperative to destroy. Perhaps this is so. However, the assertion raises questions of utmost seriousness. Is constitutionalism harmful, rather than valuable, when unaccompanied by justice? Is constitutionalism a lesser value than justice?

4. In asking these questions, we have come upon a fourth possible reason for opposing constitutionalism: it stands in the way of justice. A great many powerful people in our time have thought this. Perhaps the most influential and gifted of them was Vladimir Ilyich Lenin (1870–1924), the principal creator (with Trotsky) of the 1917 Bolshevik Revolution and of the modern Soviet state. Lenin had studied thoroughly, and he accepted unreservedly, the doctrines of Marx. Hence his basic principles were democratic; the very purpose of overthrowing capitalism was to give liberty and power to the people. But Lenin had inherited Marx's cynical view of Western constitutionalism (it only masked the limitless power of the ruling class), and, in addition, he discovered something Marx had not seen: working people did not spontaneously become revolutionary as capitalism advanced, but rather, they developed an inclination to compromise with the upper classes and to accept the continuance of capitalism so long as they benefited from occasional improvements in wages and working conditions. In Lenin's words, they developed "trade-union consciousness" rather than revolutionary determination. The conclusion that Lenin

drew was simple and daring, and it was fateful for modern civilization. The working class could not be allowed to develop spontaneously. It had to be aroused and disciplined by an absolutely dedicated and united elite of revolutionaries. This elite, "the vanguard of the proletariat," would lead the working class first in overthrowing capitalism and then in forcibly suppressing the last remnants of capitalism, thus laying the foundations for universal liberty and authentic democracy. This was the philosophy of the Communist party, which Lenin founded and led.

Lenin's outlook is reminiscent in some ways of both Plato's and Rousseau's. Lenin's elite, like Plato's, is scientific. True, Lenin's conception of science, derived from dialectical materialism, was very different from Plato's; but Communist revolutionaries, like philosopher-rulers, were assumed to understand perfectly the determining forces and the final ends of human existence. Although Lenin was an active revolutionary during all of his adult life, he always applied himself to theoretical questions with intense earnestness. Lenin's outlook is reminiscent of Rousseau's in that the ultimate aim was democracy. Indeed, Lenin's vision of democracy was more sweeping than Rousseau's: government itself would finally disappear and the people would rule without the relatively slight restraints inherent in the very existence of government. This expectation, however, signals one way in which Lenin differed from both Plato and Rousseau—that he did not believe in government at all; he was an anarchist (despite the ironic fact that he was also the founder of the modern totalitarian state).

Lenin dramatically represents, and did much to create, or at least to spread, a view widely accepted in the twentieth century—a view that prevails far beyond the boundaries of Marxism. This is the view that constitutionalism (and democracy as well) depends on a certain degree of industrial development and distributive justice; it is futile to ask for constitutional safeguards in countries that are nonindustrial, poor, and governed by oppressive landowning oligarchies. The conclusion usually drawn is that agrarian nations must pass through a transitional period during which the ruling oligarchy is overthrown and eradicated, some degree of industrialization is effected, and wealth is redistributed. While these things are occurring, it is not only appropriate, but necessary, to dispense with constitutionalism. Countless scholars and students—many of them not Marxists or Leninists—share these assumptions.

Given the strength and prevalence of Leninist assumptions, it may be that Lenin offers many readers the most convenient center for their reflections on the question of how important constitutionalism really is. Are we, perhaps unconsciously, being condescending in assuming that poor and illiterate peasants neither understand nor care about constitutionalism? After all, constitutionalism is, in some measure at least, liberty—a matter of universal interest. Further, are we being naive in supposing that a generation or so of revolutionary tyranny will pave the way for constitutionalism? It is hard to see that anything of the sort has happened in the Soviet Union. Dostoevsky foresaw a hundred years ago that in times to come "sages" would proclaim that there is no crime and no sin, but only hunger; that is, antisocial behavior would be attributed to economic circumstances. Therefore, Dostoevsky said, reformers would write on their banners: "Feed men, and then ask of them virtue!"[2] Lenin fulfilled Dostoevsky's prophecy, as do the multitudes who consciously and unconsciously follow him. Dostoevsky believed that postponing "virtue"—moral standards, decency in human relations, and above all liberty—would be catastrophic; it would threaten the permanent loss not only of liberty, but of the very qualities that make us human.

Considering the importance of the question before us, let us look at it briefly from a different vantage point. There is a broad consensus among political thinkers that power can be kept within constitutional limits only by being divided. Hence, supporters of constitutionalism are almost invariably supporters of divided power; on the other hand, those who favor power wholly responsive to the will of those wielding it, unrestrained by constitutional limits, practically always favor concentrated power. Thus we may rephrase the original question so that it reads: should there be more than one main center of power in society? From this angle, we may see things that were not apparent in the preceding discussion.

The idea that power should be divided among two or more independent centers rests on a tradition no less ancient than that of the idea of constitutional government. When Plato faced the improbability that philosophers would ever gain power, he

[2]Fyodor Dostoevsky, *The Brothers Karamazov,* trans. Constance Garnett (New York: Modern Library, n.d.), p. 262.

concluded that it would be wise to avoid concentrating power in any single group; instead, power should be divided between those with characteristics indicative of wisdom (such as age) and those chosen by lot, thus representing the populace as a whole. This idea, touched upon briefly in our consideration of the question *Who should rule?* is usually referred to as "the mixed state." It was probably old, as common sense if not as political philosophy, even when Plato was writing, and it has endured both in common sense and in political philosophy to the present day. It has assumed a great many different forms, including the form prescribed in the American Constitution. Throughout its long history and in all of its varieties, it has been rooted in one primary conviction: totally concentrated power menaces civilized existence.

Even Christian orthodoxy, which might be expected to dictate priestly sovereignty, contains its own unique version of the principle of divided power. This is the "doctrine of the two swords," set forth by Pope Gelasius I near the end of the fifth century and followed in some form by almost every succeeding Christian thinker. According to this doctrine, not all power should rest in the same hands, not even in the hands of the Pope. Human beings should not be under the exclusive control of a single sword. True, most Christian thinkers, not only during the Middle Ages but well into modern times, held that there should be only a single church. However, most did not argue that this one church itself should govern or totally control those who govern. The task of ensuring temporal order, distinct from that of guiding people toward salvation, should be under a separate authority.

Protestant and atheistic critics are quick to point out that Christian thinkers of earlier times were rarely tolerant, and that the doctrine of the two swords was often construed in a way that set the Church over the state so decisively that it denied the spirit of the doctrine although not its letter. All of this must be admitted. Nevertheless, the tenacity of the doctrine of the two swords remains impressive. It shows that even devout Christians, certain as most of them were that God had authorized a particular human organization to interpret and guard his word, shared the traditional Western mistrust of concentrated power.

American institutions, it can be seen, derive from ideas many times older than America itself. The separation of powers among the three branches of government is a variation on a theme that can be traced back at least as far as Plato and the Greeks. The separation of church and state is a version of the medieval principle that even authority derived from God does not justify undivided power.

Thus one can hardly help feeling that there should be more than one main center of power in a society. Perhaps, however, there are other things of greater importance, such as achieving scientific government, order and peace, complete democracy, or justice. It is striking that every thinker just cited as an opponent of constitutionalism was an opponent also of divided power. For Plato, philosopher-rulers would not check one another, even when sharing power, for all possessed perfect understanding and therefore could not disagree; and for people of lesser understanding to check them would be intolerable. For Hobbes, any division of power was an invitation to chaos. Rousseau regarded the dispersal of power among separate centers as undesirable since it meant limiting the sovereignty of the people. Lenin opposed all checks on Communist rulers.

As pointed out in discussing the constitutional limits on power, these thinkers are not out of date. They represent attitudes that are still powerful in the twentieth century. Plato calls for the comprehensive and organized use of knowledge in solving social problems, Hobbes for the utmost efficiency in keeping order, Rousseau for the unchecked ascendancy of the people, and Lenin for absolute justice. All these demands are insistently voiced in our time, and all, at least implicitly, are demands for concentrated power. Are there good grounds for resisting them?

The issue before us is where and how to mark out the boundaries of power. We have reflected on the moral and constitutional boundaries. These are like disputed borders between nations, the scenes of many battles. There is a third boundary, perhaps even more fiercely contested—the economic. The issue here is whether the economic system ought to be free of governmental intervention. Does it work according to laws of its own ("the laws of supply and demand") that will only be thrown askew by governmental tampering? Does it tend naturally toward a more just and efficient order than governmental planning can achieve? The issue is whether government should keep its hands off the main centers of economic power.

20 Should governments ordinarily leave the ownership and control of industry in private hands?

This question is broader than it looks. The word *industry* is used as shorthand for all major means of production—land, mines, electrical power, communications, and so forth, as well as factories. Nor is the question concerned with production only, apart from distribution; whoever controls production controls distribution as well. In sum, this question asks about our responsibility for the earth—for the whole physical setting of human life and for all of the materials that can be used for the maintenance and improvement of life.

An old idea, accepted by both Locke and Marx, the fathers respectively of "free enterprise" and of socialism, is that the earth is the common possession of humankind. By some primal right, established by God or inhering in the nature of things, it belongs to all. But how can humankind actually take the earth into its possession and use it—by allowing individuals freely to appropriate parts of it, or by placing it in the custody of governments?

The answer endorsed in one way or another by all defenders of capitalism was given by Locke when he asserted that "the Condition of Humane life, which requires Labour and Materials to work on, necessarily introduces *private Possessions.*"[3] While the earth *belongs* to the entire human race, it can be *used* only by individuals; and for individuals effectively to use things, they must own them. Hence the government's responsibility for the earth is fulfilled in protecting the rights of property. Thus ran Locke's argument.

Is it true, however, that efficient use of the earth requires individual appropriation? Does not the history of industrialism indicate, on the contrary, that our exploitation of the earth depends on immense economic organizations and that the individual alone can do almost nothing? Locke asserts that a person has a right to keep "the Acorns he picks up under an Oak, or the Apples he gathered from the Trees in the Wood."[4] What rel-

---

[3] John Locke, *Two Treaties of Government,* ed. Peter Laslett (Cambridge: Cambridge University Press, 1960), p. 310. The italics are Locke's.
[4] *Two Treatises,* p. 306.

evance have such examples to the industrial systems of the twentieth century? Today in America hardly a single item in daily use is the product of individual labor. Our cars, clothing, food, and household utensils are produced by large, complex business organizations, and these organizations in turn are integrated into vast national and international economic systems.

Furthermore, doesn't the history of capitalism indicate that free appropriation by some brings deprivation to others? It has been urged, of course, that those who are able to appropriate a great deal vindicate by this very ability their right to all they appropriate, while those who have little thus prove how little they deserve. We may well be suspicious, however, of a logic that begins with the principle of our common ownership of the earth and ends with the principle that a few can rightfully take most of it for themselves. Not surprisingly, this logic has failed to achieve universal acceptance.

It has also been urged, of course, that individual appropriation is not only just, whatever the inequalities that result, but also beneficial for everyone. The few who gain wealth for themselves, it is said, also create wealth for society. America, with its vast concentrations of private wealth along with the historically unparalled prosperity enjoyed by the majority, is evidence in favor of this argument. But not conclusive evidence. Given America's natural advantages, an economic system other than capitalism might have produced goods just as abundantly while distributing them more equitably. Further, as has often been noted in recent years, while great numbers in America are prosperous, a sizable minority is not. In view of the ugliness and squalor of the inner cities, America's poor today may be more wretched than the poor in most other societies, either of the present or of the past.

The major idea underlying the case for individual appropriation—the idea on which thinking might be advantageously focused—is that of the natural harmony of the free market. This idea was briefly explained in connection with Question 18. The gist of it is that where people are free to produce, sell, and buy as their own economic interests dictate, the economic system will perform efficiently and justly. The things people want will be produced, because that is in the interest of the producers; they will be sold at prices acceptable to both sellers and buyers, for otherwise the two parties will not deal with one another. The myriad daily decisions involved in the working of a vast economic system will be made, not by a distant government board trying in vain to comprehend the infinite complexity of a nation's economic life, but by multitudes of private individuals, each one impelled by self-interest to be realistic and rational. This, of course, is what Americans know as "free enterprise." It is one of the most attractive ideas ever formulated, for it promises material abundance, fairly distributed, without any sacrifice of individual liberty. But does it, realistically, make sense?

Surprisingly (in view of the somewhat utopian flavor of the idea), it does; at least most people nowadays believe that it does. Not that so many political leaders and writers and scholars would trust an entirely unfettered market. But there is widespread recognition, even in Communist nations, that many economic problems are better resolved through free competition than through bureaucratic control. The chief issue now is not whether to rely on the free market at all, but how far to rely on it—almost entirely (the view of those often called "conservatives") or only guardedly (the typical position of "liberals").

This issue no longer stirs the ideological passions it once did; many people, both on the right and the left, agree that the extent of governmental intervention is a matter to be decided experimentally. It should be noted, however, that the issue will never be allowed to rest entirely on practical grounds. The greatest weakness of "free enterprise" is probably that it violates the Western moral tradition. It sanctions selfishness and materialism. It tells us to concentrate on personal advantage and to interpret personal advantage in terms of money. It tells us to forget about the welfare of others and the public interest; let others take care of themselves and let the market take care of the public interest. It has nothing to say about values (wisdom? serenity? beauty?) that cannot be translated into market prices. There are always people, many of them taking pride in their "hardheadedness," who can follow such a doctrine with untroubled consciences. But there are always others, viewed as "soft" and "sentimental" by the realists of the free market, whose allegiance to such values as equality, the common good, and cooperation, will lead them in another direction.

It is understandable, then, that a number of thinkers have sought altenatives to individual appropriation. These alternatives all amount to socialism of one kind or another.

Socialism in the broadest sense stands for the idea that humankind must assert its primal right to the earth by actually taking the earth into its possession and using it cooperatively. Socialists have not agreed whether this should be done through governmental action or in some other way. But they are united in their unwillingness to tolerate private appropriation of the earth.

Socialism has drawn much of its moral force from the democratic tradition, according to which government should be carried on only with the consent, if not the active involvement, of the governed. Power belongs to the people. But property, of course, is power; thus, large concentrations of private property are by democratic standards suspect. Most socialists think democracy and capitalism are flatly contradictory. Socialists often see themselves as extending to the economic sphere the democratic principles already widely accepted within the political sphere.

A contrary opinion, of course, is often heard in America, where democracy in politics and capitalism in economics are widely regarded as natural allies. Democracy is thought to be threatened more by concentrations of governmental power than by concentrations of private property.

One of the most serious questions about socialism is whether *common* appropriation can, in practice, mean anything but *governmental* appropriation. Most socialists would refuse to assent to any such equation. Socialist literature is filled with ideas for voluntary cooperation. Many socialists are scarcely more trustful of government than are typical capitalists, and Communists of course go so far as to anticipate "the withering away of the state."

In practice, however, common appropriation has nearly always meant governmental appropriation; and communism, as everyone knows, has led to something very different from the withering away of the state. Do we see here signs of an insuperable difficulty in socialism? Perhaps if all of us together are to appropriate the earth, this must be done through the one agency that represents all of us together, namely, the government. An economic enterprise might be taken over by a cooperative group smaller than the whole society; a factory, for example,

might be run by its workers. But this is not common ownership, and a worker-run factory might behave no more responsibly in relation to society as a whole than a capitalist-run
factory. Government may be a socialist's only recourse.

The trouble is that government ownership and common ownership are not at all the same. It never occurs to Americans, for
example, to think of the postal service, with all its buildings and
equipment, as common property; it belongs to the government
and that is a different matter altogether. This is not to suggest
that governmental ownership is necessarily a bad thing. It might
in some circumstances contribute both to efficiency and to public responsibility. But such advantages cannot be taken for
granted; even if they are realized, governmental direction of the
economy, with the powerful officialdom and pervasive red tape
that would inevitably evolve, is far from the ideal of common
appropriation that is the inspiration of socialism.

There is one way, indeed, in which governmental control of
the economy may be even further from common ownership
than is private ownership. Governmental control unites the political and economic centers of power. Thus, these do not check
one another, as they occasionally do in a capitalist system. This
would not matter if the government were fully responsible to
the people. But governmental responsibility is imperfectly realized even in the most democratic countries, and as government
becomes larger and more complex, popular understanding
and control may grow weaker; bureaucrats may overshadow
the people and their representatives. In this way socialism
could mean, contrary to its intent, that power is more concentrated and uncontrolled than it would be under a system of private ownership.

If the signal weakness in the case for individual appropriation is the amorality of the market, that in the case for common
appropriation is bureaucracy and all it has come to stand for:
impersonality, inefficiency, uncontrollability. Not, of course,
that such adjectives describe bureaucracy altogether. The administrative branches of the federal and state governments in
America help citizens in innumerable ways, and they help many
who are greatly in need—the retarded, handicapped, and unem-
ployed; the poor, sick, and old. They employ countless able and
conscientious people. And they are checked in diverse ways to
assure their responsibility to the public—by legislatures, elected

executives, courts, interest groups, and citizen's lobbies. Still, governmental bureaucracy (and in some measure the smaller bureaucracies in business and elsewhere) is an ominous presence in twentieth-century industrial nations. A bureaucracy is a kind of human machine, so far as such a thing is possible, and is designed to carry out efficiently (and regardless of the political opinions of the bureaucrats themselves) the directives of top officials. Hence set functions and prearranged relationships (as in the design of a machine) belong to the essence of bureaucracy. It seems to follow that impersonality, as well as the kind of inefficiency associated with red tape, are bound to characterize a bureaucratic organization. And while a bureaucracy can be reasonably responsive to elected officials and to public feelings, it is hard to see how a nation under a large bureaucracy could realize the degree of popular political involvement called for by the ideal of democracy.

One of the most disquieting characteristics of bureaucracy is that it tends continually to grow. Ideally, of course, a bureaucracy would be merely as large as is needed, growing at some times and shrinking at others. But once a bureaucratic agency is established, those who staff it and those whom it serves have a vested interest in its continuance and are usually able to exert strong political pressure in furtherance of that interest. The result is that bureaucracy rarely shrinks, although it often grows.

Hence, just as proponents of individual appropriation and market economics may properly be challenged with the query, What about cooperation and public service? so proponents of common appropriation may fairly be asked about bureaucracy. It is said that a competitive market interferes with cooperation among citizens and common devotion to the public good. Does not a bureaucracy do the same thing? It is charged against the market that it brings about gross and unjust inequalities. But will not a bureaucracy inevitably be a privileged group, enjoying a level of remuneration and degree of security far higher than do ordinary citizens? A free market supposedly leads to concentrations of economic power that are incompatible with democracy. Does not a bureaucracy involve concentrations of managerial power that are also undemocratic? Such questions might be multiplied indefinitely.

In this kind of impasse, common sense immediately suggests that the truth is somewhere between the two extremes. And indeed such a suggestion is not without weight. In the history of political thought it is probably Thomas Aquinas (1225–1274), the author of what has since become the official philosophy of Roman Catholicism, who has most clearly delineated a theory that sanctions neither unrestrained individual appropriation nor total governmental control. Aquinas argued that property should be held by individuals but regulated by law and custom to ensure its being used in the common interest. He maintained, as an American in business might, that one will look more carefully after what is one's own than what is held in common, and that the economy will, therefore, be better managed under a system of private property than under any other. At the same time, Aquinas condemned the use of property primarily for personal profit; it should be used for the common good, and society has a right to see that it is. On this side of his thought, Aquinas seems less like an American businessperson than like the kind of socialist the businessperson would excoriate as a dangerous radical.

Is the issue thus resolved? Not necessarily. In political practice, it is often sagacious to profess a middle position; in political theory, however, such a tactic is often only a way of avoiding issues. Thus one must ask whether the Thomist position resolves the dilemma of private versus governmental ownership or merely obscures it.

Does the right of individual ownership, according to the middle position, mean that an individual can appropriate and use some significant part of the earth according to purely personal desires and contrary to the will of society? If so, then what is ostensibly an intermediate position turns out to be, in essence, an individualism like that made explicit by Locke. If it does not mean this, however, and the individual's use of personal property can be supervised and controlled by society, then one might question how significant the right of individual ownership actually is. In substance, the theory would seem to be one of common ownership. If, finally, sometimes the individual and sometimes society is responsible for the earth, where should the line between the two be drawn, and how should disputes between them be decided? Unless those questions are answered, what is offered is less a theory of property than an argument to the effect that property questions cannot be decided in a general theory. That may, of course, be the truth.

The question of whether individuals should be free to appropriate the earth has always been important but never as momentous as it is today, because technology has placed the earth much more fully at our disposal than it has ever been before. The right of individual appropriation is a far more sweeping power than it was in the days of Locke. Private persons have used the earth in ways that have affected whole nations. In the twentieth century, for example, the lives of the American people have probably been shaped as much by General Motors as by the Supreme Court. Is it right, then, that General Motors is private property? On the other hand, if you mistrust government, then the immense power of private property may be just what makes you oppose any scheme of public ownership or control, for that would greatly increase the power of government.

Is there any way, then, of fulfilling the spirit of the biblical assertion that "the heaven, even the heavens, are the Lord's: but the earth hath he given to the children of men?"[5] Is there any way humanity can possess the earth without being possessed in turn by the powerful?

Power is so dangerous that the quest for limits has been a quest for firm and unchanging limits—for eternal moral laws, understood by all; for constitutional rules impervious to the shifting sentiments of rulers and peoples; for a clear and lasting knowledge of where governments must stop when tempted to intervene in the economic system. The quest for limits has been for *preestablished* limits, for boundary lines not subject to continual reconsideration and change. And that is where much of the trouble lies.

The idea of government under preestablished limits and the idea of government without such limits are equally unsatisfactory. The former implies that good rulers will be hindered; the latter, that bad rulers will not. The former means compromise and delay in carrying out the best of plans; the latter, expeditious accomplishments of the worst. It is not surprising that people have long sought to avoid both horns of the dilemma by finding ways to keep governments from doing evil but not from doing good. Several possible solutions might come to mind— for example, arranging matters so that the interests of rulers and ruled are identical. One solution, however, stands out from

---

[5] Psalm 115:16.

the others for its simplicity and appeal. Governments might be restrained from doing what they ought not to do, but not from doing what they ought to do, by placing them in the hands of persons with perfect understanding and wisdom. In short, constitutions might be replaced by complete philosophical understanding, religious revelation, or scientific comprehension. Is there any validity in such a notion?

21   Can political power and perfect knowledge ever be joined?

Flawless, all-encompassing knowledge has been the object of perennial hope. Plato powerfully expressed this hope in his ideal of the philosopher, a man or woman who had ascended from the cave of ignorance into the light of "the Good." Many Christians have believed that perfect understanding has been given to us through Christ, although we could never have found our way to such understanding through reason. In modern times, faith in Christ has declined, but faith in reason, comparable in intensity to Plato's although based on a different concept of reason, has reawakened with the progress of science.

Can government ever be made the servant of such knowledge? The idea that it can has naturally accompanied the hope that perfect knowledge might be attained. As we have seen, Plato thought that philosophers should be rulers. Medieval Christians, in spite of the doctrine of the two swords, were continually tempted to grant the Pope a power as limitless and unified as they believed Christian revelation to be. The modern political imagination has long been fascinated by the idea of technocracy, government carried on by masters of technology and science.

The idea of joining power and perfect knowledge may have serious flaws, but at the very least it is noble and attractive. It represents the ineradicable feeling noted in connection with constitutionalism; one of the greatest of all evils is to be helplessly subject to the blind and selfish will of another human being. The idea of constitutionalism is that rulers should be compelled to stay within certain legal boundaries. The idea of subordinating government to perfect knowledge is much more radical. It proposes to eliminate the very willfulness and ignorance that necessitate legal boundaries. It envisions doing away with arbitrary government by cutting its roots in human nature.

What constitutionalism would merely check—capriciousness and stupidity—perfect knowledge would wholly abolish.

The notion that this is possible, however, rests on two assumptions: that perfect knowledge is available, at least to some; and that this knowledge has the power of determining the behavior of its possessors, of transmitting to them, as it were, its own perfection. Both assumptions have frequently been challenged.

As for the first, a widespread attitude of the last century or two has been what might be called "epistemological discouragement," that is, discouragement over the possibility of gaining sure and comprehensive knowledge (*epistēmē*, in Greek). In the past, especially in the Middle Ages, it was widely believed that such knowledge, comprehending humanity's origin, nature, and end, had been given to us by God; reason might help us lay hold of it, but ultimately it rested on a divine guarantee. Now, however, that faith is alive only in the minds of a few. Church leaders may cite figures showing widespread religious belief, but even they are more likely to study human nature by reading social science than by pondering the New Testament.

It is often assumed that faith has been defeated by science. That is an oversimplification. It is an ominous fact that we have lost faith not only in Christian revelation but in science as well. Of course, everyone would agree that scientists have made striking discoveries. The question is whether there is any absolute truth contained in these discoveries. Do they concern reality itself or only our perceptions of reality?

David Hume (1711–1776), a skeptical philosopher, a lucid writer, and a major figure of the Enlightenment, argued that neither observation nor reasoning can validate the universal and invariable physical laws that scientists claim to establish. At the center of Hume's argument was the contention that there is no necessary connection between cause and effect—not, at least, so far as we can *know*. We see that an experience of one sort, say, the rising of the sun, is usually or always followed by an experience of another sort, in this case the spread of daylight. But we do not see any necessity binding together these two experiences. If tomorrow the rising of the sun were accompained by the spread of several feet of water over all the earth while darkness continued, that would provide a *different* experience than we had ever had before, but not one in conflict with any law established by preceding experiences. Nor would it be in conflict with reason. We are able by reason to infer that Socrates is mortal if Socrates is human and if humans, by definition, are mortal. We are not, however, able to infer that light will spread over all the earth when the sun rises; all we *know* is that we have seen it happen that way in the past. (Likewise, we cannot know that all humans are mortal, only that all humans have been observed to die; the conclusion that Socrates is mortal depends on the *assumption* that all humans are mortal). Hume did not deny that our "laws" are convenient generalizations and very useful for everyday living. But the universality and necessity that make them laws in the strict sense of the term cannot be verified and are not, therefore, matters of scientific knowledge. By virtue of this argument, and similar arguments concerning other elements of "knowledge," Hume was one of the major sources of our "epistemological discouragement."

The most profound and influential attempt to answer Hume and to show that true and certain knowledge is possible was made by Immanuel Kant (1724–1804), regarded as among the greatest philosophers of all time. Kant's *Critique of Pure Reason,* a classic in philosophical literature, has as its immediate intent a defense of science. A crucial point in Kant's response to Hume was that the concept of causal necessity is a precondition of coherent experience. With that and other concepts, we link together our sensations and form the things around us and the world in which we live. Without it, we would fall into a chaos of sounds and colors, without form or stability. This implies, however, that scientific laws derive their universal and invariable character from the structure of the human mind rather than from the structure of reality itself. Reality is unknowable; indeed, it is unwarranted to think that reality itself even has a structure. Thus Kant's defense of science is highly equivocal. It offers assurance that scientific laws can have absolute validity. But this validity consists only in telling us how reality must appear to us if our faculties are properly used; in telling us only how reality must appear to us, and not what it is in itself, scientific laws are purely relative.

Thus Kant, too, became a source of epistemological discouragement, contrary to his own intentions. A dramatic sign of Kant's influence today and of the weakness of our faith in science is existentialism. Many different philosophies and attitudes have been referred to as existentialist. If any single theme is common to them all, it is probably the idea, deriving ultimately from Kant, that a human being in not an object of knowledge—at least not that and nothing more. A human being is a subject—one who may *have* knowledge but who is not included within that knowledge. A person may gain understanding of humanity by looking inward, but not by objective analysis.

If this is so, the changeless, all-inclusive knowledge envisioned by Plato and by many admirers of modern science cannot be obtained. The ideal government, dedicated to the service of such knowledge, is no better than a noble dream.

Many do not agree with these critics of reason; not everyone is totally discouraged about the possibilities of knowledge. Few would deny, however, that the critics have done much to set the mood of our time—a mood in striking contrast both with the confident faith of the Middle Ages and with the rationalistic self-confidence of antiquity. Today it is hard not to wonder whether we can know anything at all except, perhaps, that we inhabit an impenetrable darkness.

The possibility of perfect knowledge, however, is not all we have to consider. In asking whether governments can ever become servants of perfect knowledge we must also ask whether, if such knowledge were gained, people would be disposed to respect it. They might not; they might know all things, yet behave impulsively and foolishly. The human race might finally fill out and perfect the physical and social sciences, yet still be stupidly and brutally governed. It is not obvious that perfect knowledge means perfect virtue.

Some thinkers have held that while the equation of perfect knowledge with perfect virtue may not be obvious, it is nevertheless valid. Socrates apparently believed that full moral knowledge—that is, knowledge of human nature and needs, and knowledge of what is really good—leads inevitably to moral excellence. A person who knows, fully and certainly, what is good is bound to choose it; an evil person must be an ignorant one. It follows that knowledge—full and profound knowledge—cannot be misused.

Socrates' identification of knowledge and virtue has been a powerful influence in history. It underlay Plato's concept of the philosopher-ruler and antiquity's long-sustained commitment to the cultivation of reason. It has no doubt also contributed substantially, albeit indirectly, to the unhesitating enthusiam with which most of us, in modern times, have supported the advance of science. We have assumed rather casually that the progress of science is bound to mean the improvement of life.

In recent decades this assumption has appeared increasingly dubious. We have gained vast quantities of knowledge through the physical and social sciences, but we seem as likely to use this knowledge for evil ends, like nuclear warfare and brainwashing, as for good ends, like peace and the elimination of poverty. We now feel menaced, rather than saved, by our knowledge.

Why is this so? Is it because our knowledge is still imperfect and incomplete? Or was Socrates wrong and is it possible to understand all things and still be selfish and cruel?

During the past century or two, the most resolute defenders of the ideal of joining power and perfect knowledge have probably been social scientists. This is not to say that every social scientist is a utopian, without reservations about the possible perfection or social utility of the knowledge being sought by sociologists, psychologists, and political scientists. Such reservations, nonetheless, have not been prominent in the writings of social scientists. On the contrary, the effort to establish social sciences comparable to the physical sciences in precision and certainty has been pressed so aggressively that those favoring intuitive or philosophical approaches have had to fight for survival.

Few would deny that social scientists speak with a certain moral force. They seek an end to the guesses, approximations, biased opinions, and unsupported sentiments that compose much of the content of present-day political discourse. They also want to provide governments with the capacity for effective action. These aims go back to the time of Plato and have an indisputable moral dignity. Few would deny, moreover, that they are in some measure realizable. That we can gain precise, objective knowledge of society and that this knowledge has practical uses has already been demonstrated. The question is, How far does such knowledge extend? Can all major social problems be solved scientifically? This question comprises two subordinate questions.

1. Can all social realities be understood scientifically? Social scientists must assume that all realities, including human beings, are in the nature of "things," that is, subject to the laws of cause and effect and accessible in their entirety to observation by anyone with normal faculties and the necessary training in

scientific procedures. If this is so, then precise statements about human behavior can be formulated and tested, and a science of human behavior is a reasonable goal. Doubters are apt to have a different impression of the nature of reality. They may, for example, be unwilling to set aside as illusory our strong conviction that when faced with alternatives we are able to choose; they may believe that freedom is a reality. If they are right, then our glaring inability always to foresee what human beings are going to do is owing to something essential and enduring in human beings—their freedom—and not to a temporary defect in our knowledge. In addition, some human qualities may not be observable in the same way something under a microscope is observable. A physical scientist does not need to (and cannot) identify with an object under a microscope, but a student of social phenomena may be unable to understand human emotions without experiencing them or at least vividly imagining them. Perhaps no one can understand terror, hatred, the lust for power, and the other passions of the political universe without actually feeling and being moved by them. In short, whereas effective observation of the physical universe seems to require detachment, effective observation of the social and political universe may require involvement—at least, the involvement of empathy. If there is substance in these conjectures, then novelists and philosophers will often understand society better than social scientists do.

2. Is the scientific understanding of society always beneficial? If governments know what is good for society and how to attain it, will they necessarily choose it? Social scientists are practically always silently or outspokenly Socratic; they assume that all the knowledge we can gain will be good for us. They do not often, like nuclear scientists, envision with apprehension or horror the ultimate consequences of their research. Their critics, however, have not been so confident. Many have granted that although a scientific knowledge of human beings may be possible, governments are not reasonable and responsible enough to be counted on to use this knowledge for the best purposes. For example, if everything a human being feels, thinks, and does is a product of objective social and psychological forces, and we can understand those forces scientifically, then we are potential masters of human consciousness and behavior. And who is "we"? Presumably, teams of social scientists

and civil servants. Possessed of powers of manipulation such as human beings have never had before, might they not make slaves of us, *even if they made us happy?*

The Western tradition provides a weighty alternative to the Socratic viewpoint. While Socrates apparently believed that every effort should be centered on knowing good and evil, the Book of Genesis seems to say, in the form of a great myth, that such knowing is the very essence of iniquity. Adam and Eve were cast out of paradise for tasting, contrary to God's command, fruit from "the tree of the knowledge of good and evil."

The myth of the Fall is not something anyone can confidently interpret. It suggests, however, that the state in which we were intended to live was one of such complete unity with the good that we did not know anything *about* the good because we did not in any degree stand apart from it; and we did not *choose* the good because we were not conscious of any alternative to it. The destruction of this state was an act of deliberate self-estrangement. We deliberately set ourselves apart from reality. And we did so arrogantly; the motive was pride, sheer self-assertion. Our objectifying and calculating minds, then, and our consciousness of good and evil, come from sin; but they are also punishment, and a curse, for they make us aliens in the universe. Such a view sounds extreme, but it is not entertained solely by religious believers. Many American students in recent decades, not to speak of poets and writers in earlier times, have sought a spontaneity of life and immediacy of experience precluded by the Socratic premises underlying Western institutions such as universities.

The dilemma of our civilization may be symbolized in terms of these two great sources of understanding: the Greek and the Hebraic. One exalts the human mind and leads logically to the idea of government simultaneously directed and restrained by a knowledge comprehending all needs and all means to their satisfaction. The other humbles us and tells us that as long as we seek to be "as gods, knowing good and evil," we will suffer the anguish of labor, estrangement, and mortality.

Here we can hardly help feeling that we are in the presence of the mystery of being—of the things that "thought cannot think." This is why the biblical view is set forth not as a theory but as a mythical event in the lives of the first human beings. We are trying to think about something that is not accessible to observation and is not even an event except in a metaphorical sense. We are trying to think about the roots of the human situation. In doing this most of us find it impossible to choose one side or the other, as we might in dealing with a question of fact. We find ourselves drawn toward the paradox that both interpretations are somehow true.

We must remember, however, that the very function of a paradox is to keep thought alive. Anyone who simply says that both Socrates and the author of the Genesis myth are probably right, and then comfortably sets the whole question aside, has misused the concept of paradox. Any truth contained in a paradox is hidden; it cannot be reached by accepting the paradox in the same way we accept a statement of demonstrable fact. It is of the essence of a paradox that formal acknowledgment of the kind we accord a demonstrable fact is nonsensical. A paradox is true not in itself but in the understanding it impels us to seek.

We must try to understand *how* the Socratic and biblical views might both be valid. We might ask, for example, why Socrates was habitually ironical, as though what he said and what he meant were—paradoxically—quite different. Was he hinting that the theoretical inquiries he pressed so indefatigably could not possibly succeed, or rather that they could succeed only through failing—disclosing truths of a kind that no theoretical conclusions could embody? Pursuing this line of thought, we might ask whether the Genesis myth can be interpreted so that it yields a similar idea. Is it a condemnation only of the presumption of thinking that good and evil can be completely and securely known? Does it allow for the strange wisdom that Socrates seems to exemplify—a wisdom that is not found at the end of a search but in the search itself?

■ Suggested Readings

Plato. *The Republic*
Cicero, Marcus Tullius. *On the Commonwealth*
Saint Thomas Aquinas on Politics and Ethics, ed. and trans. Paul E. Sigmund
Machiavelli, Niccolò. *The Discourses*
Hobbes, Thomas. *Leviathan,* Second Part

Locke, John. *The Second Treatise of Government*
Rousseau, Jean Jacques. *The Social Contract*
Hamilton, Alexander; Jay, John; and Madison, James. *The Federalist*
Hegel, G. W. F. *Philosophy of Right*
Mill, John Stuart. *On Liberty*
Koestler, Arthur. *Darkness at Noon*
Orwell, George. *1984*
Strauss, Leo. *Natural Right and History*
Lippman, Walter. *The Public Philosophy*
Friedman, Milton. *Capitalism and Freedom*
Berlin, Isaiah. *Four Essays on Liberty*
Rawls, John. *A Theory of Justice*

CHAPTER **6**

■ The Ends of Power

Power must be used as well as restrained. In carrying on political thinking, therefore, we must consider the ends of power. This is no easy undertaking; it incorporates two large and refractory problems. First, what are the ends of human life? Clearly it is impossible to understand anything about the purpose of government without understanding something about the purpose of life itself. But this has been an enigma for every generation. Some of the thinkers of our own day—Jean-Paul Sartre, the French existentialist, is perhaps the greatest—have reached the seemingly despairing conclusion that human life has no purpose whatever. But once we have identified the ends of life, we must estimate what power can do to help us reach them. Power cannot do everything; it cannot, for example, make one person love another. Thus, thought about the ends of power can go astray in two ways—by misconstruing the ends of life and by misunderstanding the capacities of power.

The difficulty of thinking about the ends of power, however, is matched by the importance of doing so, especially now, when we are deeply confused about the proper activities of people and governments. Our confusion no doubt has many sources; the ceaseless, unplanned rearranging of our lives by technology and the permeation of thought and feeling by the fads cultivated by commercial television may disorient us far more deeply than we realize. Whatever the causes of our confusion, the political consequences are likely to be significant. Lacking wise and settled purposes, we devote our resources and attention to secondary problems—exploring space, rather than eliminating poverty, is a possible example—and we will be fortunate if we do nothing worse than that. The time may come when we will be sorely tempted to escape the burden of discord and uncertainty by placing absolute power in the hands of some leader or party claiming superhuman insight. In one way or another, if we sink unprotestingly into doubt and indifference regarding the ends of power, those ends are likely to be set by the irresponsible and insensitive.

For these reasons, reflecting on the ends of power is not a leisurely diversion but an urgent and practical duty. But with so difficult a task, where should we begin?

A person's first response, when asked what government should do, is likely to be that whatever the value pursued, it should be one that all can share. The good at which power aims should be a common good. This may seem elementary. But is it? Is there any such thing as a value all can share? And do not those who have power always pursue their own good in preference to the good of others, even when their intentions are idealistic? Let us ask at the outset whether every government does not necessarily pursue the good of only the few, the few who control the government.

22 Does every government serve merely "the interest of the stronger"?

The phrase, "the interest of the stronger," and the argument that it describes the goal of every government are attributed in *The Republic* to a contemporary of Socrates, Thrasymachus. In effect, Thrasymachus held that human beings are estranged in essence; hence it is meaningless to speak of the common good or the general welfare. The ends of each person are purely personal, and they are likely to be in conflict with the ends of others. People with power, consequently, seek their own good alone and sacrifice the welfare of others to attain it. It follows that every social and political order, the most ancient and venerated and the most carefully designed, is fraudulent. Governments usually claim the sanction of both God and the people; but that is false, because what they actually do, and are intended to do, according to Thrasymachus, is to further "the interest of the stronger," of those who have power.

No great thinker has wholly agreed with Thrasymachus. Some, though, have been so deeply suspicious of established governments that they have assumed that most do, in fact, serve only "the interest of the stronger," although they may believe that under some exceptional condition, like philosophers becoming rulers, the case would be otherwise. Karl Marx, for example, had this attitude.

Marx, of course, believed that the working class was destined to seize all power for itself. With this event, government would come to serve the interest of all so completely and so obviously that it would no longer even be coercive; the state would "wither away." Until that time, however, governments would inevitably betray the interests of most of the people. Marx saw the liberal democracies of his time as little better than disguised dictatorships carried on in the interest of the upper classes. Such devices as written constitutions, representative assemblies, and popular elections, which supposedly compel governments to serve the welfare of their subjects, were instruments of fraud, elaborate devices for veiling the tyranny of landowners, industrialists, and financiers.

Marx's view stemmed partly from his conviction that the decisive power in any society was in the hands of those owning the means of production. Less decisive were the various governmental instruments of power, such as legislatures and police. In certain circumstances governments might gain independence from class control, but they usually were agents of the dominant economic groups. Thus, governments were simply in no position to serve the common good. But a more crucial point for Marx was that in a society divided among warring classes there could be no common good; the interest of one class was necessarily the oppression or destruction of another class. Even a philosopher-ruler, in a Marxist universe, could not devise a formula to unite the bourgeoisie and the proletariat.

These considerations placed Marx provisionally on the side of Thrasymachus. Marx qualified Thrasymachus's position by adding "until the Communist revolution"; otherwise, he agreed that the "justice" maintained by governments is nothing but the "interest of the stronger."

It would hardly be too much to say that refuting Thrasymachus has been the principal aim of political thought. Plato devoted the whole of *The Republic* to this task. Of course, not all thinkers have had Thrasymachus consciously in mind, but most have tried to show that government can further some state of affairs that is not merely in the interest of the stronger but in the interest of all. Even so cynical a thinker as Hobbes argued emphatically that peace is needed by everyone. Rousseau and Marx, who thought that governments rarely if ever sought a common good, concentrated on showing how the reign of selfishness might be overcome. When liberalism, in response to Marxist criticism, tried to show that liberal and democratic regimes could act in the interest of workers as well as of owners, they were simply renewing the ancient effort to refute Thrasymachus.

Can he be refuted? Your answer will depend on whether you believe that people are in essence estranged or united. Even in a just society some members must get less—leisure, job satisfaction, wealth, and so forth—than they desire and than others get. This is strikingly true of soldiers who lose their lives in battle, of workers who perform indispensable but stultifying jobs, and of criminals who are punished. The problem is to show that these people are not being sacrificed to the interest of the strong, but are somehow contributing to a common good. This can be done, thus refuting Thrasymachus, only if all are essentially united and society so organized that those who, voluntarily or under compulsion, sacrifice conscious desires for the good of others actually make those sacrifices for a common good, thus for their own highest good, and are not merely means to the ends of others.

This idea may seem far-fetched, but in actuality it is not distant from common sense. We do not generally think of a soldier who has died in war (unless, perhaps, unjustly drafted or in an unjust war) as having been victimized by the strong. Nor do we ordinarily think that of a criminal in prison. We feel the fate of each to be in some way justified. How? We think it serves some end, such as the survival of the nation or the maintenance of justice, which is assumed to be more important to each person even than life. People do not always feel this way, but they usually do; otherwise the governments over them would depend purely on force to survive.

But rather than facing such complicated questions, can we not simply say that each person has interests that here and there coincide with the interests of others, thus making society possible? In this way we avoid speaking of such mysterious things as a "highest good" that is also a "common good" and that may be completely unknown to the individual. But unfortunately we cannot resort to so attractively simple an expedient. The reason is that the *conscious* interests of millions of people rarely, if ever, do coincide. Not even such elemental values as order and peace are desired by absolutely everyone; revolutions and wars always produce examples of people who profit from chaos. Social order therefore depends on a degree of coercion. This usually takes the form of peaceful pressure, although no society can avoid the occasional use of open force. This coercion is simply an assertion of the "interest of the stronger" unless it is exercised in behalf of a common good. And if the good is truly common, it must be the good of those coerced, but it must also be unperceived by them or else they would not have to be coerced. In short, since people cannot be united in their *conscious* interests, they must be united in their *real,* but often unrecognized, interests. Otherwise, every government serves merely "the interest of the stronger."

The issue of moral absolutism versus moral relativism is closely linked with this question. If there are absolute moral laws or absolute values, they must in some way define a common good, otherwise they would not be both good and absolute. Thus a moral absolutist might regard justice as a good to which every purely individual interest is properly subordinate; the imprisonment suffered by a criminal would then be demanded by the criminal's own essential nature.

On the other hand, if all moral rules and values are relative to circumstances or persons—if they merely represent someone's idea of what is good and not good in itself—then it is questionable whether the idea of a truly common good makes sense. A moral relativist may be logically bound to side with Thrasymachus; certainly, Plato's attack on Thrasymachus was an attack on moral relativism in general. But the paths of thought are intricate enough to make the assertion of an invariable rule in this matter inadvisable. Many relativists have been as hostile toward the outlook of Thrasymachus as Plato was.

In speculating on this question, we are traversing the most rugged and uninviting terrain in the whole realm of political theory. But there is no way of avoiding it. A political system is essentially a set of arrangements by which some people dominate others. How can this be made morally tolerable? Civilization is carried on under a great moral shadow. We must assume that all civilized life rests on the exploitation of the weak unless we can show that Thrasymachus was wrong and that government can serve the interest of all.

At this point let us assume that governments can and should serve the common good. What is this good?

Out of the din of modern history, one answer comes clearly to our ears: liberty—the ideal of individuals being able to live as they choose. The cry of liberty is heard in the French and American revolutions; liberty is the central value in liberalism, the rise of which can be traced back to the Renaissance and which has dominated European and American political life for almost two centuries. This is not a unanimous answer, as is shown by communism, which accords equality and community priority over liberty. But communism is a conscious revolt against the liberal tradition that has hitherto been dominant. The same is true of other antiliberal movements, such as conservatism and fascism; their rebellious temper testifies to the ascendancy of the liberalism they reject.

It seems appropriate, therefore, to reflect on the ends of government by reflecting on liberty. Buffeted by the ideological hurricanes sweeping through our century, we are bound to seek, as a refuge from confusion, the true purpose of government. Can we find this refuge in the liberal tradition?

23 Is the final goal of government simply to enable individuals to live as they choose?

An affirmative answer to this question is apt to sound plausible to anyone living in the latter part of the twentieth century. Such an answer calls for no leap of faith, it commits one to no grandiose ideals. It suits a time that has seen faith take the form of terrorism and ideals fade. The idea that governments should strive simply to enable individuals to live as they choose is credible to a disillusioned generation—to people who are not sure of much except the self and its momentary pleasures and the consequent desirability of freedom from interference. Such people (that is, most of us living at the present time) are drawn to a minimal politics, a politics that makes no large assumptions about our concern for one another or our common ideals and that places few demands on us; it could even be called a politics of narcissism, or self-absorption. It is bound to be, at least implicitly, contractual; one obeys the law not because the law comprises the demands of justice or a great common purpose but because the law is a condition of one's own security. Citizenship is premised on self-interest. The functions of government are narrowly conceived; the main thing is protecting each individual against physical harm inflicted by others.

To ask merely to be able to live as you choose may seem to be a rock-bottom political demand, as though one could hardly ask less of a government. Before discussing some of the greater demands that might be made and that constitute alternative answers to the question before us, we may gain perspective by noting an even more minimal demand, one widely asserted at the present time. That is survival. It is the enormous nuclear arsenals of the superpowers that provoke this demand. All of us now live as though held at every moment in the sights of the gun of someone whose only absolutely reliable quality is deadly accuracy. This causes many people to feel that the final goal of government is simply peace, or, more precisely, the avoidance of nuclear war. The missiles of the superpowers, it is felt, have reduced political life and thought to an elemental level. The age of grand ideals has passed—even the age of ideals no grander than that of living as you choose. Mere living, the continuance of the human species, has become the supreme political goal. Is this point of view valid? If it is, then a discussion of traditional political goals is anachronistic and manifests blindness to the urgencies of our time.

It is essential to put the question accurately. If asked whether there is any political goal that would justify our unleashing a nuclear conflict at this very moment, all of us would doubtless say no. But that is not how the question of peace presents itself. What we are asked, rather, is whether there is any political goal that justifies our running a *risk* of nuclear war. It is possible to say there is not. But the implications of such an answer are startling and, for most people, unacceptable. If nothing can justify even the risk of nuclear war, it follows that the American government should adopt any course of action that would eliminate or substantially reduce that risk. The most effective measure probably would be for America to give up its nuclear arsenal immediately and allow some other nuclear power to dominate the world. Although lesser nuclear powers would remain in existence, the threat of an all-consuming nuclear catastrophe would be greatly lessened. The fact that hardly anyone in this country would urge such a measure is evidence that political ideals like liberty are not as anachronistic as apostles of survival sometimes suggest. Something tells us that life becomes meaningless unless it has a goal beyond its own preservation; as Jesus said, those who strive above all to save their lives lose them. Hence even in the face of possible nuclear war, we feel impelled to ask about political ideals.

We are brought back in this way to the original question, made more somber perhaps by the nuclear age, but not invalidated. What ultimate value should government serve? What do we really care about? Is liberty, living as we choose, a high and noble enough ideal to justify our refusing to flee to the safety of a global tyranny and living deliberately under the threat of nuclear annihilation? Let us look briefly at some alternative ideals.

1. *Happiness.* Naming happiness as an alternative to living as you choose may seem like hairsplitting. It is not, however, and the distinction is important. To have the liberty of living as one likes does not necessarily lead to happiness. The trouble lies in the responsibility and doubt such liberty may entail. One may, of course, take refuge in conformity. One who has liberty, however, faces at least occasionally the daunting question, How should I live? And that question brings in its train other daunting questions, such as, What is life for? and What is true? To face such questions may be necessary to our dignity but hardly to our happiness. Indeed, Dostoevsky said that "nothing has ever been more insupportable for a man and a human society than freedom."[1] The importance of recognizing that happiness is a goal different from liberty lies in two facts. One of these is that today happiness powerfully attracts us. As-

---

[1] Fyodor Dostoevsky, *The Brothers Karamazov,* trans. Constance Garnett (New York: Modern Library, n.d.), p. 262.

surance of a life beyond death has faded for many people, and industrialism has made happiness more easily and universally attainable than ever before in history. Conservatives and progressives, capitalists and socialists—all of them promise the people happiness. The other fact that makes the distinction between happiness and liberty important, however, is that these goals are not necessarily harmonious. The pursuit of happiness can lead us away from liberty—not only toward social conformity but toward political totalitarianism, toward a society in which someone else will answer the questions that loom over us when we can live as we choose. Dostoevsky argued in the celebrated "Legend of the Grand Inquisitor" that if happiness is our aim then a benign dictatorship is the system that best suits us; we can be happy only where we are told authoritatively how to live and what to believe.

2. *Justice.* For many philosophers, justice is the highest political value; it is the central theme, for example, of Plato's greatest dialogue, *The Republic.* For Plato, justice is the proper order not only of society but of the individual soul. Hence it is inseparable from humanity. To give up justice for peace would be to sacrifice humanity for survival—an absurdity. The ideal of justice has an uncommon majesty; in all ages there have been people who valued justice more highly than their lives. If majestic, however, it is also impersonal and demanding. It is a concept of fairness in the apportionment of values such as wealth, status, and power.

Clearly, there can be varying interpretations of fairness. At least one great dividing line runs through the middle of the camp of justice. On one side are those who interpret justice mainly as recognizing the special virtues and achievements of a few. *Excellence* is apt to be the watchword on this side of the line, and justice is conceived as a kind of inequality. On the other side of the line are those less impressed with the differences among human beings than with the similarities. Justice therefore is equality; the watchword is apt to be *compassion.* On both sides of the line, however, justice is uncompromising. It does not go comfortably with liberty and may require the sacrifice of happiness. It tells us that liberty is less important than fairness, that those who are not freely just must be coerced, and that happiness is trivial unless it is found in the true order of human relations and the human soul.

3. *Tradition.* I use this word to designate the complex of customs, institutions, myths, and time-honored beliefs that grow in a society over decades and centuries. A tradition ordinarily embodies concepts of justice and other political ideals and so is not ordinarily affirmed as an exclusive value. Many intelligent people, nonetheless, have felt that tradition is a society's most precious possession. It is the primary condition of our humanity. A human being stripped of everything derived from tradition is no longer human, except in potentialities, but is rather a peculiar kind of beast. At least this is the view often held by admirers of tradition. Thus, for example, our understanding of justice is not a pure prescription of reason but rather is derived from customs and practices that may have been worked out over centuries; this is exemplified in the dependence of the American sense of justice on the Constitution and on the ancient and intricate body of constitutional law developed by the Supreme Court. Wisdom is not the inspiration of philosophers, but the understanding of human ways and needs that is built up in the course of a long period of historical evolution and is deposited bit by bit in the institutions, myths, and other components of tradition. In a sense, a tradition is wiser than any person. For all of its wisdom and majesty, however, tradition is fragile. It can be destroyed not only deliberately, through political revolution, but also negligently, through reckless technological and social change. And once it is destroyed, it cannot be quickly rebuilt. Defenders of tradition are usually called conservatives. In their view, a government has no other end quite as important as safeguarding the inherited decencies and insights that make up a tradition.

4. *Community.* The sovereignty of personal choice is not nearly so old and durable an ideal as someone living in a liberty-minded modern nation like America might assume. From the age of Pericles to the present day many of the greatest minds and most serious reformers have believed that we are all, in our essential being, at one and that the ultimate aim of politics is to make our essential oneness a reality. Thus, personal choices have to be curbed and directed. Arguably, this implies no sacrifice of freedom. If freedom is living according to your true being, and if your true being is essentially united with the true being of others, then freedom in its truest sense is experienced only in community. Nevertheless, if your ideal is community,

you cannot live simply as you choose. You must be formed and led for the sake of a life in common. Both Plato and Aristotle held to such a view, as did practically all medieval philosophers; and in the modern world the ideal of community has been represented by thinkers as profound and diverse as Rousseau, Hegel, and Marx.

Today, one of the more interesting restatements of the communal tradition has come from certain feminists. The ideal of community, conceived and carried forward almost altogether by men, has been more or less rationalistic; the moral authority and integrating power of law, for example, has been stressed repeatedly. Various feminist thinkers, suspicious of male rationalism, have tried to envision community in a more concrete and inclusive fashion. They have brought within the circle of community personal concerns and dialogical relationships which often in the past have been seen as altogether private. The hypothesis, referred to earlier, that women differ significantly from men in their ways of experiencing and approaching the world, has suggested a concept of community warmer and richer than the concepts ordinarily advanced by male philosophers.

The point should not be exaggerated. None of the male philosophers of community referred to earlier were cold legalists, none thought reason and law the sole significant bonds among human beings. And there have been male philosophers, such as the great Jewish thinker Martin Buber, who have formulated unsurpassably warm and personal doctrines of community. Nonetheless, when one remembers Kant's insistence that if a society were disbanding and had one prisoner awaiting execution for a capital offense, it should without fail carry out the execution; and when one remembers that Kant, with his doctrine of the human race as implicitly and ideally a "Kingdom of Ends," was perhaps the major source of the modern concept of community; then one may feel that traditional theories need the injection of less implacably legalistic attitudes. Critics often fault feminists, especially in their organized political activities, for stressing women's rights and ignoring women's obligations; the abortion controversy, for example, has prompted such charges. Whatever their public policies, however, in their writings feminists have frequently shown a sensitivity to the thick web of human relationships, as opposed to the abstract structure of individual rights, that renders community an attractive goal. In comparison, living as you choose will seem to some a thin and unsatisfactory ideal, and justice a cold and incomplete vision of the good society.

Happiness, justice, tradition, and community are not the only conceivable alternatives to the liberty of following one's own desires. They do, however, offer a basis for reflection. The question that arises is simply whether any of them warrant giving up the simple and appealing aim of living as you please. How can one go about tackling this question?

Perhaps it will help somewhat to note that all five ideals are essentially one or the other of two kinds. One kind is based on the principle that values are realized by separate individuals; they are not readily, or at least not necessarily, shared. This is the case with living as you choose and happiness. The other kind of ideal is based on the principle that values are necessarily realized in common with others. This is the case with justice, tradition, and community. For example, if I want to be able always to do as I please, I will hold aloof from others and maintain only loose human connections; but the very act of seeking justice puts me in relationship with my fellow human beings. On one side, human beings are thought of as separate atoms, on the other side, as a single body.

Thus the basic question one faces is the first question asked in this book: Are human beings estranged in essence? Any thinking done in connection with that question can here be turned to account. If your answer was yes (human beings *are* estranged in essence), then you have ruled out justice, tradition, and community as final political ends; if your answer was no, you have ruled out living as you choose and happiness. Admittedly, political theories sometimes contain difficult and even illogical combinations. At the very least, however, if you believe human beings are essentially estranged, then liberty and happiness are the goals most readily affirmed, whereas if you believe human beings to be essentially united, then the ideals of justice, tradition, and community are within easy reach. Very simply, the question is whether governments should aim at something particular to an individual alone—a private value— or at something we can only possess in common.

Another earlier question can be usefully recalled at this point. This is Question 7, which opened the second set of questions. Are human beings unequal in essence? If you think that they are, you are strongly positioned for affirming the kind of justice that recognizes special virtues and achievements. Also, you might easily accept tradition as a political goal, since traditions practically always embody marked inequalities. On the other hand, if you consider human beings essentially equal, you can move easily to the individualistic ideals, for anyone is capable of living by personal choice; and while people are not equal in their capacities for happiness, it would be difficult to discriminate in any meaningful way against the unhappy or to claim that one person's happiness is less important than another's. At the same time, however, the concept of essential equality provides a favorable position in which to affirm at least two of the collective ideals: egalitarian justice, for obvious reasons, and community, since equality does away with differences, such as those of power and social status, that divide people from one another.

Before concluding the discussion, we must briefly take note of something that complicates the issue but that a fair consideration of the ideal of liberty demands. In the preceding discussion I have usually written as though living as you *choose* is the same as living as you *please,* with mere personal preferences and immediate desires governing your conduct. But to assume that liberty is necessarily this and nothing more risks oversimplifying, and perhaps degrading, the concept of liberty. It is possible to assume that living as you choose is very far from making the most *appealing* choices, that rather it involves the onerous task of making the *right* choices. On that assumption, liberty might require wisdom, self-discipline, and even self-sacrifice. The significance of liberty would be, not that it makes room for personal pleasures, but that it is essential to the realization of higher values; for example, community may be held to be real only if it is entered into freely. This points to the fact that affirming one of the four values described earlier as alternatives to living as you choose—happiness, justice, tradition, and community—does not necessarily rule out affirming liberty too. It rules out only a particular concept of liberty (one no doubt widespread in America): that of liberty as simply living as you please.

It can help, in thinking about issues as abstract as these, to resort to concrete examples. And in thinking about the goals of government, some of the most relevant examples are issues concerning governmental coercion. Where are you willing for the state to interfere with force? This question can help you decide what goals you deeply believe government should pursue. The following three topics may serve to bring the question before us.

1. *Suicide.* Suicide is self-murder. Practically everyone supports the right of the state to prevent, and punish where it cannot prevent, the murder of others. Why? Because murder denies the right of people to live as they please? or their right to be happy? If so, perhaps suicide is different from ordinary murder and ought to be permitted. Yet you cannot legally sell yourself into slavery; and if that is a reasonable prohibition, is it not also reasonable to prohibit the complete denial of one's own rights that is entailed by self-destruction? Is it true, moreover, that we sanction the prevention of murder simply to protect individuals from having their freedom or happiness interfered with? Is it perhaps rather that we consider murder to be monstrously wrong? Is suicide less wrong than other kinds of murder? It is noteworthy that people often defend the right of suicide in conversation but rarely do so in concrete instances. When the police use nets and lassoes to prevent someone poised on a high place from jumping, there is never a storm of public protest. Why not? Does an actual attempt at suicide bring momentarily to light a deep, perhaps unrecognized, sense of values that are common and not merely individual? Does it provide a glimmering of a value that transcends even liberty and happiness? Or are we irrational to interfere when someone embarks on so deeply personal an act as suicide?

2. *Abortion.* This is commonly defended on the grounds that whether a woman has a child is her own affair entirely and that government cannot rightly interfere. A permissive view of abortion fits comfortably with the individualistic values—living as you choose and happiness. Feminists have emphatically, and it seems unanimously, or nearly so, claimed the right for each woman to make her own decisions in the matter. Their central contention is a perfect illustration of individualism; if a woman can be forced to bear a child, they maintain, her body and her life in effect can be taken away from her. Those who oppose them on this issue argue that individualism such as this would justify not only abortion but infanticide as well; when it

comes to another life, the life of another human being or potential human being, they assert, then a person's autonomy must be limited in behalf of our common humanity. This stormy issue, then, arises ultimately from the question of whether we are essentially estranged or essentially at one. The flat assertion of feminists that a woman has a right to control her own body jars the conscience of anyone who assumes an essential unity among us; on the other hand, the unqualified claim of their opponents that a fetus is a person, with rights under law, strikes anyone whose view of values is individualistic as strained, for a fetus cannot live as it chooses or enjoy happiness.

3. *Pornography.* Freedom from every kind of censorship is a dominant idea mainly among liberals. The supporting argument usually is based on the presumed right of people to live as they please; the kind of magazines they read or movies they watch in the privacy of their homes is no one's business but their own. This is not a bad argument. If we are essentially estranged, and one's life is entirely one's own and no one else's, then any governmental interference in private life is intrusive and presumptuous. A similar argument might apply to those who take part in producing pornography and supplying it to others. Many who might otherwise accept such arguments, however, have had second thoughts. This is partly because children, even very young children, have increasingly become objects of pornographic attention. It is also because feminists have become sensitive to the ways in which pornography degrades women. As a result, pornography faces serious opposition. The question is what values this opposition presupposes and reveals, although the question cannot be simply answered. Can the disgust most people feel when faced with the pornographic exploitation of children be traced back in some way to self-interest, or does it represent revulsion before the violation of a crucial and common value, such as justice to those who are helpless and dependent? Does the concern felt by women about the degradation they suffer through pornography reflect an instinct of self-protection, or is it an awakening to a great and common evil: an ostensibly private amusement that in fact debases *human beings?*

These issues may help in the task of reflecting on the governmental goals discussed in this chapter. They point, however, to further possible goals. The feelings some people have about suicide and abortion seem to be not so much feelings of injustice as simply of moral wrong. Justice and morality are closely related but not precisely the same. Justice is that part of morality concerning our relations with others. Thus it might be argued that suicide is not unjust, yet is morally wrong. Pornography involves questions not only of morality but also of truth. It is degrading to women, it might be argued, because it presents them falsely, as though they were mere objects to be used for satisfying lust. Thus we are led into a broader field of inquiry. The following question may serve to open the gate leading into this field.

24 Does government have any responsibility for truth and morality?

No one, of course, would deny that people in public office ought to be reasonably truthful and moral. But the question does not concern anything so uncontroversial as the need for trustworthy government officials. What it asks is whether those officials are responsible for upholding truth and cultivating morality in the societies they govern. Have they any proper role in defining what people should believe or how in their personal lives they should behave? Is government concerned merely with maintaining order and protecting personal freedom, or is it concerned with the true and the good? In a word, does government have any *spiritual* responsibilities?

Today one is likely to be surprised that such a question is even asked. Secularism has become axiomatic in Western politics, and secularism means among other things that the relationship of citizens to ultimate matters—such as the true and the good—is not the business of government. If any organization is to be involved in a person's spiritual affairs, that organization is normally the church; and church and state must be strictly separate. And whether the church, or any other organization, or anyone else at all, is in fact to be involved must be left for the individual alone to decide. The individualism once taken for granted in economic matters is now taken for granted in spiritual matters.

This is perhaps a good thing. It is worth noting, however, that some of the greatest thinkers have not been of the same mind as contemporary Americans; they have not shared either our spiritual individualism or our political secularism.

Moreover, aside from what has been thought in the past, isn't it doubtful that so fundamental a question has been absolutely and permanently settled? Perhaps not, if truth and morality fall altogether within the purview of churches. But do they? Are not human beings, whatever their attitudes toward religion, intrinsically spiritual—concerned with the true and the good? And if so, are they not concerned with these values in all of their relationships, beyond as well as within the churches? And surely society and the state cannot be sound if they are unconnected with truth and morality. Clearly we need to think further on this matter.

Let us begin with the first value, truth. Does government have any responsibility for truth, or, to bring the question nearer to the point, for the beliefs of those it governs? The idea that government should be wholly detached in matters of belief, and individual men and women left completely on their own, developed fairly recently, only two or three hundred years ago. Locke defended such a doctrine near the end of the seventeenth century. He was not the first to do so, but he spoke for an idea that was still controversial and generally unacceptable.

Moreover, the reasons earlier thinkers advanced for asserting governmental responsibility for beliefs were not absurd. They may have been inadequate, but they were not incomprehensible or manifestly unreasonable. To begin with, these thinkers thought that we can know with assurance what the truth is. The question "Who is to say?" would have been attributed by most of the great Greek and medieval thinkers to laziness, confusion, or something else that obscured the importance and availability of objective truth about humanity and the universe.

Why not let one discover the truth for oneself? Most of these thinkers would have made the sensible (although possibly erroneous) response that discovery of the truth is difficult even for the greatest minds and altogether beyond the capacity of average minds. Consequently, if government and society do not help the individual decide what to believe, most people will suffer paralyzing uncertainty and, finally, despair. The result for society, since social order depends on common beliefs, will be weakness and disorder.

Most thinkers of the past would not have inferred from these considerations that the government should have an exclusive and unchecked right to proclaim the truth. Nor would they have inferred that the government should try to uphold the truth with violence and terror. Aristotle, for example, held that scientists and philosophers had primary responsibility for finding the truth and making it known, and the typical medieval thinker believed that supervision of belief was the duty primarily of the spiritual power, the Church, rather than the temporal. Even Plato and Augustine, thinkers of a more radical and impassioned temper than many others, were far from desiring that truth be promoted by force. Education was the way taught by Plato; and Augustine sanctioned the use of violence against heretics only after long hesitation and with utmost reluctance.

But none of these thinkers, and few others until recent times, ever entertained the modern idea that government is spiritually neutral. To know the truth was for them one of humanity's principal aims, and government was far too great an influence on human life to be barred from participating and helping in the common pursuit of this aim.

It is noteworthy that Locke based his individualism, in economic and spiritual matters alike, on the same broad principles and that the typical American liberal has rejected these principles in regard to property but clings to them in regard to belief. Locke assumed a certain essential estrangement among human beings. This meant, in economics, that the use one makes of personal property is not the business of anyone else; it meant, spiritually, that the beliefs of one person are of no proper concern to anyone else. Locke also assumed that, despite estrangement (which does not necessarily eventuate in conflict), there is a natural harmony among individuals. Thus, he thought, if each person acquires and uses property according to the dictates of selfish interest, order, and prosperity will naturally ensue; likewise, in the spiritual realm, if each one is left free to seek out and affirm one's own personal truth, universal truth will emerge spontaneously. Finally, Locke conceived of freedom primarily as the absence of governmental restraint. One is economically free, therefore, if not interfered with in acquiring and using property, even though, as a matter of fact, one may have little property and even be starving. Correspondingly, Locke apparently saw people as spiritually free so long as their beliefs were self-chosen, even if those beliefs were false and in some way spiritually destructive.

The typical liberal of the present day has left Locke's economic theory far behind. In considering economic questions, a contemporary liberal is likely to assume (1) that human beings are not essentially estranged, but that each has some responsibility for the welfare of all others; (2) that there is no natural harmony, that unrestrained accumulation of profits by individuals leads to drastic inequalities and to cycles of inflation and depression, and that a just and stable economic order consequently depends on governmental action; and (3) that freedom to starve is not real freedom.

With respect to personal belief, however, the same liberal is likely to remain an unreconstructed follower of Locke. Does some underlying logic hold together this seemingly divided consciousness? It does not seem so.

If you still think government should stay out of personal beliefs, test that idea. Imagine that a belief you detest—for example, that white people constitute a superior race or that America should be organized and governed by the military—has won the allegiance of a large and powerful group in the country. Would you object if the government took steps to ensure that this belief was not taught in the public schools or proclaimed in the nation's press?

Let us turn to another dimension of our spiritual life, morality. During antiquity, people were less concerned than we are with material welfare and less concerned than people of the Middle Ages were with faith. They gave much attention, however, to morality—not as a puritanical discipline denying worldly pleasures for the sake of life beyond death, but as a discipline for living fully within this world. Correspondingly, they viewed government as occupying a position of moral leadership. Thus were the spiritual and the political fused. Is this appropriate? Does government have any responsibility for the moral character of individuals?

For most people today the answer would be an emphatic no. To begin with, it is commonly held, moral theories are very open to doubt. Anyone who presumes to say what is good and what is evil is indulging a mere personal opinion, something that cannot be proved and thus should not be forced on others. The notion that governments should define the good and impose it on people is particularly outrageous, for governments are not wiser than private individuals; on the contrary, they are often uniquely benighted. If morality is the capacity for living well, then one person has as good a claim to being moral as another. Each of us has personal and unique ideas of what it means to live well and should be allowed to practice these ideas without interference. Besides, even if it were right for government to try to make people moral, how could it? A moral action must be freely done, whereas government can only coerce. An act done under governmental command could not possibly be moral.

These statements represent familiar attitudes in twentieth-century America; although sometimes thoughtlessly delivered, they are not baseless or arbitrary. Beneath them lie some of the major principles of modern liberalism, such as individualism, moral relativism, and the idea that government belongs on the periphery of life and not at its center.

However, the notion that government does have some responsibility for the moral character of individuals is represented by thinkers of the stature of Aristotle and Thomas Aquinas and is not as unsound as many Americans would suppose. Aristotle's argument might be reduced to the following chain of principles: living well is not doing just as one pleases but depends on understanding and adhering to a pattern of life that is valid for all human beings; discovery of this pattern requires unusual insight as well as the gradual development of tradition; most people, therefore, need society to provide moral illumination and structure for their lives; government is the principal agent of society and thus is properly involved in the fulfillment of society's moral responsibilities.

This argument would not justify a government's deciding all by itself what is moral and then forcing it on people. Political power should serve a moral consciousness that is the mind and tradition of a whole culture and not something created by a government. Moreover, the moral responsibilities of government should be carried out less through coercion than through example, through education, and through the respect, rather than fear, inspired by the laws.

These two views concerning the moral functions of government (we may call them the liberal and the moralistic) involve two very different conceptions of law and its place in life. In the liberal view, the principal purpose of law is protection; the law should ensure security for persons and property and provide the individual with a sphere in which one can live as one pleases. In the moralistic view, law should prescribe what is right, not merely what serves the convenience of individuals, for the primary purpose of law is to give moral form to life. The liberal must feel on the whole that the less law there is, the better. The moralist, without being totalitarian, feels that the individual should have the law at hand as a guide and monitor.

Most Americans easily see the weaknesses in the moralistic view. It accords government a dangerous eminence and evinces relatively little respect for the freedom and uniqueness of personal life. Because the weaknesses of the liberal view are not so obvious, it seems appropriate to point them out.

For one thing, liberals often rely on the notion that moral rules are purely subjective and personal; this is why they believe governments should not lend their weight to such rules. But are not some rules incumbent on everyone? Presumably those against murder and theft are. If we admit that much, we have given up the casual relativism so often expressed (but perhaps not so often really believed) by liberals and have acknowledged that every human life should be carried on within a common moral structure. Some, of course, claim that we need rules against murder and theft only for the protection of possible victims, not because murder and theft are instrinsically wrong; thus it is said that there should be no law against self-murder, suicide (which, it is assumed, hurts no one except the person committing the act). Here we must probe our feelings carefully and deeply to determine whether we really think murder and theft are morally neutral; if we are candid, we may find a more tenacious moral consciousness in ourselves than we had been willing to acknowledge. But even if we stick to the claim that we care nothing about universal morality but only about harm to others, is the argument saved? Why should we care about harm to others if we are indifferent to morality? A person who is really indifferent to morality would care only about harm to the self and only for selfish reasons would accept social arrangements that protect everyone. This is one form of the social-contract doctrine. Perhaps no argument can forcibly dislodge a person who consistently adheres to this position. But such a person is committed to a grim and lonely redoubt.

Another weakness in the liberal view is that it places a burden of moral discernment on the average individual that may be too heavy to bear. During the last generation or two we have come to realize that the *material* well-being of an individual is decisively affected by conditions prevailing in the whole society and manageable, if at all, only by the whole society; thus in time of severe unemployment an ordinary laborer is likely to suffer severely regardless of personal initiative and ability. But is not the *moral* well-being of an individual also decisively affected by society? An individual's ideas of right and wrong are, by and large, learned from the society. Surely it is inevitable, then, that individuals living in societies that are morally degraded or empty will suffer demoralization, that is, the confusion and apathy that a person must experience when unable to see that any one course of action or way of living is preferable to any other. Does not the individual need moral as well as material help?

Finally, we may ask the liberal whether it is possible, let alone desirable, to place government on the periphery of moral life. Through such influences as personal example, education, and law, government inevitably has a powerful effect on the moral attitudes and practices of its citizens. Would it not be best, then, for political leaders, rather than trying in vain to separate themselves from morality, to acknowledge the influence they inevitably have and exercise it as wisely as possible?

I suggested earlier the possibility of testing one's principles by imagining governmental efforts to suppress beliefs that seem false and dangerous. Here a similar experiment may be in order. Imagine that the government is trying to encourage moral attitudes that are apparently valid and desirable. Imagine, for example, that public education, and the urging and personal example of leaders, are being used to cultivate a sense of fairness toward all races. Would that be objectionable?

The old idea of a wall between church and state obviously does not come near to resolving the issue before us. The relationship of the temporal and spiritual realms, assumed by many to be a problem we have left far behind, appears after all to be among the perennial questions. To establish this, I have presented arguments primarily on one side of the issue.

We should not forget the other side, however. Although we have found the question of a government's spiritual functions more alive than most people today suppose, it would be reckless—and reactionary—to think of government as the major spiritual power in society. The arguments separating the spiritual and the temporal, however commonplace endless repetition and frequent oversimplification may have made them, are weighty.

These arguments are based on the nature of political and spiritual leadership and the differences between them. Political leadership necessarily involves the use of power—molding minds and influencing behavior in order to reach preconceived goals. This fact casts a deep shadow over all political life, for power relationships are inherently base; some people are objectified and used by others. And such relationships tend to become worse in actuality than they necessarily are by nature, since power encourages arrogance among its possessors and irresponsibility among the powerless. Politics is the darkest area of our collective and historical existence, and that is why ancient wisdom tells us to beware of mixing the political and the spiritual. Political leaders are not ordinarily very spiritual people, and the moral precariousness of their position can only be enhanced by spiritual aims and the consequent lure of spiritual pretensions.

Spiritual leadership, on the other hand, is closely linked with powerlessness. It is said of the Messiah depicted in the Book of Isaiah that "he will not cry or lift up his voice, or make it heard in the street" and that "a bruised reed he will not break, and a dimly burning wick he will not quench." Rather than having power, spiritual leaders may have to suffer from the power of others. The Messiah is likened, in another passage in the Book of Isaiah, to "a lamb that is led to the slaughter."[2] The fusion of spirituality with powerlessness and with suffering is consecrated by the New Testament through the image of the Crucifixion. And it is not in Christ alone that this fusion is realized; it becomes an authoritative pattern for all Christians. Paul "boasts" in one of his letters that he has been lashed five times, beaten with rods three times, on one occasion stoned, and three times shipwrecked; that he has been "in danger from rivers, danger from robbers, danger from my own people, danger from Gentiles, danger in the city, danger in the wilderness, danger at sea, danger from false brethren"; and that he has experienced "toil and hardship, through many a sleepless night, in hunger and thirst, often without food, in cold and exposure." "Who," he asks, "is weak, and I am not weak?"[3] Jesus and Paul were anything but men of power. On the contrary, the story of the Cruci-

[2]Isaiah 42:2–3 and 53:7 (Revised Standard Version).
[3]II Corinthians 11:24–29 (Revised Standard Version).

fixion and Paul's account of his own tribulations carry the unmistakable intimation that spirituality and powerlessness are mysteriously conjoined. Spirituality is apt to be impaired, or even destroyed, one may surmise, if mixed with political power. We glimpse here the intuition underlying the doctrine of the two swords.

If the idea of the separation of state and church is worth recalling, so is the idea of tolerance. It bears on both beliefs and morals: individuals should be free to hold and voice their own conceptions of the truth and also to live according to their own visions of the good. The idea of tolerance is easily misused and distorted. Sometimes it represents nothing better than an absence of moral convictions or indifference to others. And it is often pressed too far; not everything can be tolerated. But it rests on a compelling fact—that there can be no genuine life and no true relationships if there is no tolerance. If people have to think and act in conformity with official, or even with merely social, requirements, then everything is falsified. Tolerance thus is one of the primary requisites of life. And tolerance merely for true opinions and right actions will not suffice; there is always and everywhere tolerance of that sort. There must be tolerance for beliefs we consider erroneous and actions we deem immoral. Tolerance must extend far enough to be dangerous. Otherwise it is a mere formality, a courtesy I extend to those who think and act on the whole as I do, and not a policy that accepts important disagreements and differences and does this in an effort to make room for abounding life and serious communication.

The sinister possibilities inherent in joining political and spiritual leadership and denying tolerance are indicated by the totalitarian states of our time. Nazi Germany was at once a political and (in however debased a sense) spiritual organization, and Hitler took responsibility for both the worldly order and the ultimate ends of the German nation. The past intolerance of the Soviet regime has rested on the presupposition that the rulers are responsible for spreading truth and destroying error. It is noteworthy that these exalted conceptions of political responsibility have not simply fallen short of perfect realization; they have led to unprecedented horrors.

Having opened up this question, so seldom seriously discussed in our day, we are in a good position to consider a closely related question. One spiritual function that everyone grants the government (although some might say it is not a spiritual function) is defining and dealing with crime. Let us consider in a very general way how this function should be fulfilled; we may conveniently do this by reflecting on punishment.

25 Is avenging crime a proper aim of government?

This is a question about retribution; it concerns the requirements, not of a thirst for vengeance, but of justice. In spite of similarities of sound and appearance, the word *avenge* has very different connotations from the words *vengeance* and *revenge*. A crime might be *avenged* dispassionately and even regretfully. A crime is *revenged,* however, only in a resentful and vindictive spirit. One is a matter of justice; the other, of *vengeance.* The distinction is important because it is difficult to make out a strong case for revenge or vengeance. There are obviously poisonous passions at work among the vengeful, and there are terrible dangers for society and individuals once the sequence of injury, retaliation, and counterretaliation has been set afoot. But justice is another matter entirely. It is not personal rancor that causes us to care about justice, but a sense of the primal order of being. For a crime to pass unavenged seems, to many at least, like a derangement of the cosmos. Some sort of balancing seems imperative.

But doubts still can arise, hence the following discussion. Is dispassionate justice the highest standard of human relations? What about mercy? Is there not something deeply offensive in the cold and implacable execution of a human being, even when the human being is a murderer and the execution is just?

To reflect on the question as to whether avenging crime is a proper end of government requires giving some thought at the outset to the nature of crime. In our time, crime is probably more often thought of as evidence of sickness than of sin. In fact, even to speak of sin in discussing social problems is sure to raise eyebrows. A student of social problems usually does not accept the kind of moral absolutism the word *sin* suggests and does not regard the law as based on morality so much as on mere social convenience.

The sickness evident in crime is often seen, moreover, as a sickness of society rather than of the criminal. Crime is traced back to social conditions, such as broken families and unemployment. When this is done, the criminal comes to be seen as a victim and society, in a sense, as the criminal.

There is some truth in this way of looking at crime. If the criminal were not in some measure a victim, how could one explain the higher crime rate in slums as compared with suburbs? Indeed, if there were not some statistical correlation between crime rates and either social or psychological conditions, crime would be a thoroughly senseless phenomenon, entirely outside the sphere of reason.

The question of whether crime can be regarded as *altogether* an illness rather than a moral transgression, however, cannot be decided by statistics. And this question is of utmost importance; your answer to it involves your whole conception of the individual and the relations of individuals and society.

The first issue you must decide is whether the individual is wholly comprehensible through causal explanations. Can a person be completely understood in terms of various laws—physical, psychological, and social—or does one stand in some sense above the various causal sequences? In other words, is one free? The view that a person is entirely explicable in terms of causes may be termed *naturalism,* for it sees human beings as belonging completely to the order of nature. Let us call the contrary view *voluntarism,* because it maintains the possibility of free or voluntary acts. Naturalism is the basis of the view that crime is sickness. Presumably sickness is not freely chosen, but caused.

Where does retribution—avenging crime—come into the matter? For naturalism, clearly, it does not at all. If humankind is viewed naturalistically and crime is regarded as illness rather than sin, retribution is senseless. A physician would not punish a patient for contracting pneumonia. From a naturalistic viewpoint, crime presents two problems: the reformation of the criminal and the prevention of future crime. The first is connected primarily with the welfare of the person who committed the crime; the second with the welfare of society. Both, however, are problems of control and management rather than of morality. The criminal must be reshaped in order to be no longer a criminal, and society must be reorganized so that it is no longer a breeding ground of crime.

One question about the naturalistic approach is whether it is possible to control either the criminal or society in a way that

will assure desirable results. Certainly it cannot be done as yet. A more serious question is whether the naturalistic approach, in however benign a fashion, is degrading to human beings. Does it treat them as things that psychiatrists and social planners can mold as they please? Does the dignity of the individual disappear?

Voluntarism obviously offers a very different perspective. Assuming the reality of a moral law, the principle of retribution inevitably takes on a certain amount of authority. First, avenging a crime can be seen as a way of vindicating the moral law. A crime is implicitly an attack on that law (for the sake of simplifying and abbreviating the discussion, we pass by the complicating issues that arise when legality and morality do not correspond). Retributive punishment—eye for eye, tooth for tooth, hand for hand, foot for foot, burning for burning, wound for wound"[4]—is a reassertion of the moral law. It is thus a restoration of true order.

Second, a voluntarist or moralist can think of a criminal as deserving punishment in the sense of having a right to be punished. This idea sounds very strange. Yet if human dignity derives from our being, unlike animals, subject to a moral law, then one suffers an indignity when treated as being exempt from that law—which is apparently what happens if breaking the law does not call forth from others its reassertion. In other words, a person is treated with disrespect if allowed to break the law without being punished. Thus Hegel declared that an individual "does not receive . . . due honour . . . if he is treated either as a harmful animal who has to be made harmless, or with a view to deterring or reforming him."[5]

The principle of retribution, then, does not threaten the dignity of the individual, as the naturalistic approach to crime seemed to do. It is, nevertheless, surrounded by difficulties, some arising from the side of nature and some from the side of morality. The former result from the unquestionable fact that a person is at least in part a natural being and crime—at least in part—is an illness. Crime can in some measure be treated and cured. In some cases retribution and therapy can be combined,

---

[4] Exodus 21:24–25.
[5] Georg Wilhelm Friedrich Hegel, *Philosophy of Right,* trans. T. M. Knox (Oxford: Clarendon Press, 1952), p. 71.

but not always. For example, retributive standards might call for a long prison sentence, which would perhaps complete the moral destruction of the criminal; therapeutic standards might call for a period of hospitalization that would not be particularly punitive. The principle of retribution provides no way out of this dilemma.

A similar difficulty, also rooted ultimately in our natural being, arises from the standpoint of the interest of society. The dilemma is that the prevention of crime is imperative yet is not necessarily accomplished through retribution. For example, crimes might best be prevented by executing everyone who commits any crime whatever, but by the standard of retribution, this would be grossly unjust. The problem of prevention, like that of individual therapy, must be addressed, but the principle of retribution provides no way of doing so.

Yet another difficulty involved in the idea that avenging crime is a proper end of government is that it presupposes powers of judging human character and motives that we do not very clearly possess. Let us assume that we have determined with certainty (although this is not always easy) that a particular person has perpetrated a particular crime. Can we determine with certainty the moral gravity of the perpetrator's offense? To do that, would we not have to know every detail of the criminal's life and be able to weigh with absolute accuracy every extenuating circumstance from the moment of birth to the moment of the crime? Would we not have to be able to enter into the mind of the criminal and understand even better than the criminal the motives of the crime? Often people unthinkingly convert the horror they feel at a particular crime into horror at the criminal and then unhesitatingly prescribe savage punishments. It can be argued, however, that the gravity of a crime does not always accurately indicate the moral fault of the criminal, and that justly avenging a crime requires a knowledge of the latter as well as the former.

Our inability to judge the moral fault behind a crime—assuming we suffer from such an inability—is both natural and moral. It is natural because it stems in part from the mere fact of our finitude; our knowledge of the past and of other persons is always limited. It is moral in that our misjudgments are worse than they have to be. We are often prejudiced and we are persistently unwilling to admit how limited our knowledge

really is. We love to judge because we love to assume the lofty position of one righteous and wise enough to pronounce upon the sins of others. That is, we love to forget our fallible humanity and act like God. Hence the command and warning of Jesus: "Judge not, that you be not judged."[6]

Finally, in assessing the principle of retribution, we need to consider the matter of forgiveness. Owing largely to the influence of Christianity (although Christianity is not the only religion calling for forgiveness), we feel that we stand on a higher moral plane when we are merciful than when we are punitive. To exercise mercy is presumably to withhold punishment. Some theologians have denied this, but it is hard to see it as just that a criminal might receive a fitting punishment and yet remain guilty, with forgiveness still necessary for "clearing the books." On the other hand, it is hard to see what forgiveness can mean if it is not an alternative to punishment. It is necessary, therefore, to ask whether crimes should be forgiven rather than punished. If so, when? Should crimes sometimes be punished, but with less than the commensurate penalty and with forgiveness, as it were, "making up the difference"?

In the Christian view, forgiveness manifests the height of human moral consciousness. The principle of retribution, therefore, is seriously in question. Nevertheless, forgiveness is difficult to understand. It expresses a willingness to pass over legitimate grievances. That is not only beyond the capacity of most of us; it can be asked whether it is reasonable and prudent. Does it not mean that people can get away with anything? Is not chaos and rampant unfairness the inevitable result? It must also be asked whether there are preconditions of forgiveness. Must someone repent? How can we judge the degree and sincerity of repentance? The biggest question about forgiveness, however, derives from the standard of justice. Is it not unjust to refrain from punishing someone who has committed a wrong?

Such questions become even sharper in the realm of politics. Can forgiveness be a *political* virtue? Could a person gain and hold power, even in a constitutional and democratic state, without judging and retaliating against opponents? Could a government manitain order if it closed its prisons and practiced forgiveness? Could a nation assure its security if, in place

[6]Matthew 7:1.

of power politics, it followed a policy of universal mercy? It would be a mistake to regard such questions as purely rhetorical, refuting the idea of forgiveness. The figure of Abraham Lincoln shows that. Lincoln was severely realistic and highly effective as a politician; yet he was much given to forgiveness. This was expressed in his attitudes toward both deserters from the Union Army and the rebellious Southern states. There is another matter in the world of political realities that may serve even better than the example of Lincoln, however, to show that the principle of forgiveness cannot be barred from the realm of political thinking. This is the issue of capital punishment.

The proposition that avenging crime is a proper end of government leads inevitably, if practiced, to executions. Anyone who has illegally killed someone else must, in turn, be killed. And perhaps there are worse crimes than murder, such as treason; if murder is a capital crime, then these presumably would also be capital crimes. The argument in favor of capital punishment is often based on the claim that it constitutes a deterrent. That, however, is an impossible argument (even if it *is* a deterrent), for we cannot sacrifice lives merely for law and order. The argument from deterrence would collapse in a moment were it not for the unspoken assumption that executions will be carried out only in conformity with the standard of retribution: only those will die who deserve to die. No one suggests capital punishment for stockmarket swindlers or corrupt politicians or tax evaders, although such people may do more harm to society at large than murderers do. The principle of capital punishment has weight for one simple reason alone: apparently it is just.

Opponents of capital punishment, like those on the other side, often stray onto misconceived grounds of contention. It is said, for example, that "two wrongs do not make a right." But that is not obviously true; it is contradicted by the concept of retribution, which represents one of the oldest and most tenacious of human instincts. More precisely, a "wrong" visited on the perpetrator of a wrong is not clearly a wrong; the standard of justice seems to say that it is right. Opponents of capital punishment often conjure the horror experienced by someone awaiting execution; it is far worse, it is said, than the horror experienced by a murderer's victim. But that is a highly conjectural argument, and no doubt the truth varies from instance to instance; little is accomplished by speculating on the feelings of criminals and their victims. And even if it could be established that being executed is more painful than being murdered, does that make capital punishment wrong? It is not clear that feelings alone decide the issue. Opponents of capital punishment have also gone seriously astray owing to their concern with race. They have demonstrated that in America the penalty of death is not imposed in a racially equitable fashion. That is a serious criticism of our penal practices. But it is not a serious criticism of capital punishment; the death penalty would have to be accepted if the racial inequities were eliminated.

I suggest that there are only two strong (although not necessarily conclusive) arguments against capital punishment, and these are the main arguments against the principle of retribution itself. The first is that we can never appraise the character and motives of a person surely and finally enough to warrant our deciding that the person deserves to die. Sentences other than death are alterable (a prisoner may be paroled or have a prior sentence reduced) and flexible (a prison term may be anything from a month to life); but death is irrevocable and has no degrees. Human beings do not have the wisdom, it can be argued, to deal in such penalties. The other strong argument against capital punishment rests on the principle of forgiveness. We should be merciful enough to let people live, it is claimed, even people who have committed grave crimes. We need not refrain altogether from punishing them (for example, with life terms in prison) but only from killing them. While guarding society and doing justice, we should leave room for mercy.

Broadly, the issue here is between law, in its impersonal and majestic generality, and, to speak boldly, love, in its personal perceptiveness and adaptability. The studies indicating that women have a distinctive moral sense, more intuitive and situational than that of men, suggest that the issue might be construed in terms of gender. Resolute enforcement of the law, and fair but unrelenting retribution for every crime, would be a male version of social harmony; a female version would allow for more personal spontaneity and would season justice with forgiveness. But this is obviously too simple. Numerous men have taken the side of love, and women at times (as in cases of rape) have upheld law and retribution. It may be that the issue is rooted in the existence of two different temperaments or minds, a legalistic and a personalistic. Or perhaps it stems from the fact that some have power and some do not, with the former (predominantly men) inclined to insist on implacable enforcement of the law and the latter (including both men and women) more sensitive to the nuances of situation and person and more sympathetic toward the powerless. No doubt one should be cautious in employing dichotomies of this kind. Without question, however, there is a deep divide, both personal and philosophical, between those in whom the word "crime" immediately arouses thoughts of law and punishment and those who think first of understanding and mercy.

We have now reflected rather extensively on the uses of power—on its ultimate purposes as well as on its limits. We may appropriately bring these reflections to a close by asking how great a role, in general, government should have in human life.

26 Should governments try to create societies that fulfill all needs and desires?

This question brings us to a position overlooking one of the great chasms in the Western political mind. On one side lies what can be called "the politics of redemption." Some of the greatest thinkers in history—Plato, Rousseau, Marx—represent this general outlook, which is that the goal of politics and of political thought is a life on earth that is altogether good. There are no great, unconquerable evils in human nature or in the essential structure of earthly life. Felicity is not a gift of God, nor is it reserved for a heavenly existence or a time after death. It can be attained through human wisdom and planning here on earth.

Exponents of this view are not generally bland optimists; they have often deeply hated the social and political world about them. But their mood has not been the resigned disenchantment of those who take it for granted that worldly happiness is unstable and unsatisfying. Rather, it has been tinged with the impatience and digust of those who feel that we have betrayed our potentialities. Finding themselves in hell, they have called for the creation of heaven. The Communist vision of vital, universal community, arising from the conquest of all poverty, injustice, and enmity, exemplifies the politics of redemption.

On the other side of the chasm lies what I shall call "the politics of convenience." This is a politics based either on skepticism about the capacities of human beings and the possibilities of life on earth, as in much Christian thought, or on satisfaction with things as they are. Both attitudes prompt a politics of low expectations and low demands, since the world either cannot or need not be much improved. Government is not called upon to bring salvation but only to enhance the convenience of life.

Locke exemplifies the politics of convenience based on satisfaction with things as they are. He did not assert that life without government would be terrible or impossible. He would not have dreamt of saying what Rousseau said, that when "man" founds a government and enters into the civil state, "his faculties are so stimulated and developed, his ideas so extended, his feelings so enobled, and his whole soul so uplifted, that, did not the abuses of this new condition often degrade him below that which he left, he would be bound to bless continually the happy moment which took him from it forever, and, instead of a stupid and unimaginative animal, made him an intelligent being and a man."[7] That is the voice of redemptive politics. For Locke, a government may save time and annoyance by doing for its citizens what they otherwise would have to do for themselves. But that is all; it cannot turn hell into heaven.

A chasm, not a mere line, divides these two concepts of power, because each has allied concepts and attitudes; each, therefore, is the center point of a whole political philosophy. Those who speak for the politics of redemption are often preoccupied with the state of the human soul—for example, with one's relationship to the true and the good (Plato) or one's moral perfection (Rousseau); those who speak for the politics of convenience are usually concerned primarily with external arrangements and with their efficient and orderly control.

Again, on one side all attention is given to the public realm—logically, since politics can redeem us only if private life is completely subordinate to public life. On the other side, the greatest concern is the security of the private realm, with the public realm seen primarily as a threat. Further, those thinkers who are engrossed in the state of the soul and the possibility of

---

[7] Jean Jacques Rousseau, *The Social Contract and Discourses,* trans. with an introduction by G. D. H. Cole (New York: Dutton, 1950), pp. 18–19.

its renewal through reformation of the public world generally view the earth as the possession of all human beings in common and wish either to regulate severely or to abolish private property; Plato, Rousseau, and Marx were all, in differing ways and degrees, enemies of private property. On the other hand, those thinkers who are concerned mainly with external arrangements and with protection of private life will usually, like Locke, be strong defenders of private property.

Finally, the politics of redemption is likely to be a politics of concentrated and unlimited power. Admittedly, this is not true of Marx, for whom the final redemptive act in history, the proletarian revolution, prepared for the disappearance of the state. But the man who first put Marxism into practice, Lenin, was an exponent of unlimited, highly centralized power, and both Plato and Rousseau were more or less opposed to dividing or limiting power. On the other hand, the politics of convenience is typically embodied in ideals such as constitutionalism and the mixed state. It is easy to understand why. To divide power, and draw consitutional bounds around it, is obviously prudent (unless one shares Hobbes's view of human nature) when one's aim is merely to eliminate some of the inconveniences of daily existence and to ensure the safety of life and property. It is prudent, but it is no way to bring about "new heavens and a new earth"; if that is the aim, there must be a new political order as well.

Not that everyone must be on one side or the other. It would be hard, for example, to know where to place Hobbes; and some readers may, in developing their own political ideas, discover ways of combining redemption and convenience—or, perhaps, of choosing neither one. But I do suggest that we encounter here a profound and dangerous issue for modern society.

At this stage of history, having seen both the Soviet and Chinese revolutions eventuate in tyranny, the politics of redemption arouses misgivings among most of us. It seems to express self-deification on the part of its practitioners. Political leaders claim the power that the Old Testament attributes to God alone—that of erasing and avenging all injustice and of guiding humanity to its destined fulfillment. The politics of redemption seems also—since human beings do not in fact possess the power of redemption—certain to bring severe disappointments. Thus it prepares the way for disillusionment and political apathy.

Perhaps the most troublesome thing about the politics of redemption, for many, is that its means seem likely to be as boundless as its ends. Political leaders who conceive of themselves as redeemers are not apt to be careful about moral and constitutional limits. Can the niceties prescribed by conscience and constitutions be allowed to inhibit the attainment of justice and community for all humankind? Magnificent ends may justify atrocious means, and a politics of redemption may turn out to be also a politics of treachery and terrorism. In contrast, the politics of convenience goes naturally with sobriety and moderation in the choice of means. The ends are not so glorious as to justify limitless violence. The politics of convenience is founded on a temperate estimate of human virtues and powers; its practitioners will naturally be disposed to mistrust intemperate means.

Albert Camus (1913–1960), a French essayist and novelist who was swayed by his humane and poetic disposition toward a redemptive politics yet was checked by a stubborn streak of sanity, devoted much attention to this issue. He brought many of his concerns to a focus on the issue of political murder. As a participant in the French Resistance during World War II, he was in contact with many Communists during the Stalinist era, and he felt acutely that he was living in murderous times. Politics, he said (obviously not thinking of all politics, but of the politics of extreme situations, which includes all redemptive politics), involves killing; therefore, to meet our political responsibilities, we must know when and by what right we can kill. He was concerned especially with limits. How can there be a political murder that does not immediately shatter all limits and open the way to unrestrained terror? His answer was that you have a right to kill for political reasons only if you are willing immediately to give up your own life in reparation. You can rightfully sacrifice the life of another in a great political cause only by accepting the sacrifice of your own life at the same time.

Camus's thesis has a look of justice, yet it is not entirely satisfactory. How do you show forth and prove—even for yourself, indeed especially for yourself—your willingness to give up your life? It is easy to think that you are willing to give up your life if you do not actually have to do so, and Camus did not assert that anyone carrying out a political murder must at the same time commit suicide. Moreover, some of the most violent men in politics are fanatics who unhesitatingly sacrifice their own lives. That does not legitimate their terrorism, as Camus well knew. Hence Camus here provided only an inner check for people of conscience but no clear, objective limit on the violence inherent in redemptive politics.

It is not surprising, then, that he went further and repudiated redemptive politics altogether. This meant to repudiate communism, which was widely supported in French intellectual circles in the aftermath of World War II, and Camus was bitterly denounced. Camus did not take a conservative position; on the contrary, his impulses were strongly reformist. He was concerned especially with the poor and the oppressed. But he insisted on our remembering that we are finite. We cannot know society comprehensively and exhaustively, but only portions of it. Therefore, we cannot know the final source of the evils that afflict society. Camus was not tolerant of these evils. He considered resisting them necessary to our very humanity. But to discover their ultimate cause and by attacking that cause to eradicate them once and for all is beyond our powers. In short, redemptive politics is impossible. Social evils will always exist, and it is our part as human beings, living in solidarity with one another, to attack these evils unceasingly. Yet we know all the while that we can never completely destroy them.

Camus criticized various aspects of the politics of redemption. For example, it is characteristic of political redeemers to affirm a pattern of history and claim that their own purposes are furthered and made inevitable by historical destiny. This, Camus held, encourages the abandonment of moral limits and the resort to unrestrained murder. It is, moreover, an illusion; if we cannot comprehend society, neither can we comprehend history. Our minds cannot reach to the beginning or the end. History as a totality, Camus declared, is nonexistent for human beings. It is also characteristic of political redeemers to single out a particular group, such as the working class, as a unique and infallible source of redemptive insight and power. For Camus, human beings are finite without exception. No group is a predestined agent of redemption. Camus attacked Marxist deification of the workers, although he himself came from a working-class family and regarded workers with great sympathy and respect.

Camus was thoroughly political; through politics we struggle against injustice and realize our solidarity as human beings. Yet politics lures us into limitless crime. This is often due, ironically, to redemptive intentions; those who seek the complete eradication of evil become monstrously evil themselves. It is essential, then, to be at once humane and moderate. What Camus offers is an eloquent version of the politics of convenience.

Americans are apt to be easily won over. The politics of convenience, combined with our vast resources, has served most of us fairly well. It might be well to note, therefore, that the politics of convenience is not without weaknesses.

For one thing, the politics of convenience has not served all of us equally well. There are minorities that it has served, and continues to serve, very badly. It was often "convenient" for the colonists in early America to enslave blacks, and it is still "convenient," in the sense of being less expensive and troublesome than a determined effort to bring about racial integration and justice, to abandon the majority of blacks to the squalor and lawlessness of urban ghettos. Also, it has been convenient for men to assign women the tasks of keeping their homes and raising their children while they themselves tended to the affairs of the world at large. Here the convenience involved has had unique force: to raise their children to adulthood is one of the most demanding and inescapable obligations of human societies; and because women must bear the children, and are able to nurse them, it is easy (although perhaps entirely erroneous) to infer that they are best-fitted to raise them. In view of such examples, it is hard not to wonder whether one who concentrates on convenience thereby suffers a deprivation of moral imagination. Is the concern for convenience more or less indifferent, by its very nature, to justice and compassion? Will it arise primarily among the comfortable and powerful?

This outlook may have another weakness, equally serious. Convenience, even very great convenience, enjoyed equally by all classes and races, and by both men and women, may not long satisfy human beings. A "sensible" person would say that political redemption is a pipe dream and that we should be satisfied if we can merely enhance the ease and comfort of life. Most people are not sensible, however, at least not in the long run. Nor is it obvious that they should be. From the time of

Isaiah to that of Marx, people have imagined an era when "the eyes of the blind shall be opened, and the ears of the deaf unstopped," when "the burning sand shall become a pool, and the thirsty ground springs of water."[8] Will we be nobler and better when we cease to have such thoughts? Yet into how much terror and disappointment will they lead us?

■ Suggested Readings

Plato. *Gorgias*
———. *The Republic*
Aristotle. *Nicomachean Ethics*
Saint Augustine. *The Political Writings of St. Augustine,* ed. Henry Paolucci
Saint Thomas Aquinas on Politics and Ethics, ed. and trans. Paul E. Sigmund
Locke, John. *A Letter Concerning Toleration*
———. *The Second Treatise of Government*
Mill, John Stuart. *On Liberty*
———. *Utilitarianism*
Dostoevsky, Fyodor. *Crime and Punishment*
Green, Thomas Hill. *Lectures on the Principles of Political Obligation*
Troeltsch, Ernst. *The Social Teaching of the Christian Churches,* 2 vols.
Buber, Martin. *Paths in Utopia*
Berdyaev, Nicolas. *The Destiny of Man*
Lippman, Walter. *The Good Society*
Eliot, T. S. *The Idea of a Christian Society*
Schumpeter, Joseph. *Capitalism, Socialism, and Democracy*
Dewey, John. *Liberalism and Social Action*
Niebuhr, H. Richard. *Christ and Culture*
Voegelin, Eric. *The New Science of Politics*
Galbraith, John Kenneth. *The Affluent Society*
Arendt, Hannah. *The Human Condition*
Wolff, Robert Paul. *The Poverty of Liberalism*
MacIntyre, Alasdair. *After Virtue: A Study of Moral Theory*
Kariel, Henry. *The Desperate Politics of Postmodernism*

---

[8]Isaiah 35:5 and 7 (Revised Standard Version).

CHAPTER 7

▉ Historical Change

"To ask earnestly the question of the ultimate meaning of history takes one's breath away; it transports us into a vacuum which only hope and faith can fill." Anyone who tries to think philosophically about history, immediately realizes the truth of this observation by a leading historian of ideas.[1] And it applies not only to questions about the ultimate meaning of history but to many other questions about history—the extent to which we can control it, the means of effective control, and the significance and natural direction of historical change. Because they arise only when inquiry is pushed to its ultimate limits, all philosophical questions can give us the feeling of being on the edge of a precipice, but philosophical questions about history seem particularly dizzying. How can we possibly speak with assurance about the nature and course of the whole stream of human events?

Yet anyone who reflects on politics with seriousness and persistence is inevitably led to try. This is largely, I think, because of the imperfection and failure that attend all political undertakings. Even relatively modest undertakings like Woodrow Wilson's effort to link the United States to a global association of nations are often blocked. Exalted ideals, like those ascendant in France in 1789 and in Russia in 1917, usually lead to vio-

---

[1] Karl Löwith, *Meaning in History* (Chicago: University of Chicago Press, 1949), p. 4.

lence and tyranny. Are all great political ideals and efforts futile? If not, which ones may bear fruit and under what conditions? If so, is there anything enduring, is there any refuge from historical change? Such questions force themselves even on those who would prefer to ignore them.

It is not political failure alone, however, that gives rise to the philosophy of history. Even when the prospects of immediate success are good, one may be unexpectedly faced with an insidious little question. What then? Just as the present will give way to the immediate future, so that in turn will give way to the distant future. If world peace and perfect justice are achieved, what then? The answer is that the person asking this question and all of the person's contemporaries will die. Any paradise they create will be left to generations unborn. Finally, too, any such paradise will itself decay and disappear. Ultimately the very earth will become uninhabitable. Many people ignore these certainties, but we cannot with philosophical good conscience suppress the sense of ultimate pointlessness they provoke. Awareness that the human pathway leads to a final abyss has prompted some of the most breathtaking questions about history.

While we reflect on history, we must remember the mystery of things and the ultimate irresolvability of our questions. Asking about the meaning of history "transports us into a vacuum which only faith and hope can fill" because it confronts us forcibly with one of those realities thought cannot grasp. History as whole is not an object before us. This is partly because it is unfinished and partly because what is finished—the past—is made up of human experiences that are not, in their incalculable depths and subtleties, accessible to an outside observer. We cannot speak of history as we can of the chemical composition of water or of the rate at which physical objects fall. Yet thought and speech inevitably objectify the things they touch upon. Hence we can hardly avoid looking on history *as if* it were an object before us. To speak of something that is not an object as if it were an object, however, is to speak paradoxically.

But suppose we cease to be paradoxical and begin speaking of history as something surely and fully known. Then we may fall prey to serious, and even murderous, illusions. Some of the most majestic and compelling visions human beings have attained concern the goal and meaning of history. This is illustrated by the prophets of ancient Israel and, in the modern

world, by Karl Marx. Such is the power of these visions, however, that they are often taken as objectively true. When that
happens, they may produce totalitarianism and violence, for
some people then will feel that the secret of all things is in their
possession and the future of the human race is under their command. The philosophy of history is a dangerous discipline, and
humane and sensible people often urge us to forsake it and confine ourselves to questions not so likely to arouse our arrogance.

To forsake the philosophy of history, however, would be to
foresake the effort to understand our possibilities and goals
comprehensively. Hence we must think about history, but in
such a way as to keep alive the consciousness that we are inquiring into a reality that our minds cannot encompass. We
must think of our questions as ones that our humanity compels
us to ask, even though they are finally unanswerable. A state of
mind so balanced and restrained, yet patient and determined,
is not easily attained. It is possible, however, and it is the only
way to historical understanding.

We shall restrict ourselves to some of the more manageable
queries. Let us begin with one that arises naturally from the
disappointments of our time. So much has happened in defi-
ance not merely of our hopes but also of our plans and efforts
that we sometimes feel that history is a fate moving toward its
own nonhuman ends regardless of all we can do. We are impelled to ask whether our plans and efforts matter.

27   Can human beings control the course of history?

This is to ask whether politics can be significant, for politics is
the activity in which we deliberate and act upon our collective
existence. It is the way in which we take part in history. If we
can control the course of history, then politics can be meaningful. If we cannot, we must ask whether the political sphere can
be anything more than a stage for puppets, for spectacles that
can be watched with interest and amusement but have no practical effect.

Deeply rooted modern attitudes make our relationship to
this question curiously contradictory. Our activism and our
confidence that every problem has a solution dispose us to answer in the affirmative. Americans are conscious of having mas-

tered and settled a nearly empty continent and of having made that continent a base of world power. Most of them believe, moreover, that America plays a decisive role in defending civilization and freedom. Thus Americans have felt so sure of their own impact on events that they have scarcely questioned the power of human beings over history.

Nevertheless, it is axiomatic in much of modern scholarship and thought that people are products of society and can be wholly understood in terms of past environing conditions. If so, people are made by history and do not make it. Thus, for example, the major ideas of any past philosopher are assumed to be called forth by the conditions of the philosopher's historical era and personal life; those ideas are not regarded as authentically original and hence inexplicable in terms of the circumstances from which they emerged. In similar fashion, political decisions are commonly seen as mirrors of a situation. If some particular leader had not acted as he did, we are often told, another leader would have done so instead. Politics registers, but does not direct, the forces of history.

These two attitudes express the voluntarism and the naturalism discussed in Question 25. In action we are usually voluntaristic; in observation and study, naturalistic. From one point of view a person is a first cause, from another an effect, or rather a complex set of effects.

An extremely cogent and influential statement of naturalism is found in the writings of Marx. In connection with Question 6, we discussed Marx's idea that individuals and society are shaped primarily by economic relationships. We must look again at this idea to comprehend Marx's concept of history. Marx was acutely conscious of the force of physical needs, for food and shelter, for example. Not that physical needs have greater absolute importance than other needs, like those for companionship and beauty, but they do have the force of biological necessity. Unless they are met, we cannot live. Hence the relationships we enter into in order to meet our physical needs—our economic relationships—are uniquely imperious. They are inescapable and, until they have been met, all-absorbing. They are bound to shape our life and very being. This is the gist of what is often referred to as Marx's "economic determinism." It does not mean that human beings are completely fulfilled by the satisfaction of physical needs, that anyone who is warm, sheltered, and well fed is bound to be happy. It means rather that human beings cannot be fulfilled without the satisfaction of physical needs and are therefore subordinate to the economic system as long as those needs are unsatisfied. To realize our potentialities we must live, and to live we must lead the lives that the economic system requires.

In studying human behavior, consequently, Marxists typically seek explanations in economic circumstances. Activities that many regard as the loftiest expressions of the human spirit—art, philosophy, and religion—are typically analyzed by Marxists in terms of the economic situation from which they have arisen. Politics for Marxists cannot be understood as an autonomous activity. It is a manifestation of economic purposes and tensions. As a historical activity, it is only a way in which we act out the roles economic conditions have allotted us.

The Marxist answer to our question, then, is negative. We cannot control the course of history—not, at least, in most circumstances or in significant measure. To make this a fair generalization, however, two qualifications must be noted. First, "history" will end. The determination of events by economic forces will cease, and indeed that is already coming to pass through the evolution of capitalism. A human entity capable of freely controlling history—the industrial working class, humanity in its full productive and creative potency—will gain ascendancy and human beings will no longer be puppets. Naturalism applies to the present and the past; voluntarism, to the future. This helps to explain why Marxism, in spite of its determinism, has so aroused and inspired many people. It gives them hope.

Further, sophisticated Marxists avoid invoking economic determinism as an invariable law by which everything can be explained without investigation (indeed they often object to the very term "economic determinism"). They use it rather as a methodological postulate, a guide in empirical analysis. Marx himself used the principle with great subtlety and flexibility. Today some of those who consider themselves followers of Marx have granted so much autonomy to noneconomic conditions that the principle has, in their work, been tacitly abandoned.

In orthodox Marxism, nevertheless, the conditioning power of economic forces and relationships remains a methodological axiom. History is seen as much more a product of economic necessities than of human ideals and intentions. Human beings thus have little control over the course of events.

Hardly anyone today would entirely reject the Marxist way of looking at history. Few historians now study any event, cultural, intellectual, or political, without carefully taking into account the economic conditions surrounding it. In this sense, as someone has said, "We are all Marxists now."

But the truth in economic determinism is hard and unpalatable, and perhaps it is dangerous. Much depends on the degree of emphasis given it. So far as it becomes an exclusive or even dominant principle of historical understanding, it does make puppets of us. Our aims and actions are shaped by history and when we deliberate and decide upon something politically, we play a role that economic fate has decided in advance. This, at any rate, is implied. Economic determinism has been widely acceptable only because, as we have seen, it was combined in Marx's thought with the faith that our economic captivity is bound to end. As technology is perfected and nature brought under human control, economic relationships will lose their determining power. Human beings will gain command of their lives and their history.

But hope of this kind has faded, not among Marxists alone, but everywhere. History now seems menacing rather than beneficent. Events since the outbreak of World War I in 1914 have wantonly violated human wishes and expectations. As a consequence, historical determinism has become a doctrine of doom. To retain hope and to live as human beings and not puppets, it has been necessary to resist doctrines that deny our autonomy and to say, perhaps with qualifications, that history is what we make it.

Followers of Marx have turned toward voluntarism as consciously and unreservedly as anyone. Lenin, the best-known example, was unwilling to wait for the natural course of events (natural according to Marxist thought) in Russia and in October of 1917 dramatically demonstrated the power of human beings to alter the course of history. A contemporary school of Marxist thought, often referred to as "critical theory," also emphasizes the efficacy of deliberate thought and action. Critical theorists devote much attention to culture as an autonomous sphere of human activity. Although culture does not at present promote freedom, they believe that it can. Humankind can rise above the historical forces that have deprived it of joy and dignity.

The voluntarism manifest in Lenin and the critical theorists has been present, often naively, in liberalism all along. Franklin D. Roosevelt and the early New Dealers seldom doubted the power of human beings to shape history. Historical self-confidence was manifest also in Roosevelt's liberal successors, Harry Truman, John F. Kennedy, and Lyndon Johnson.

However, under the last and most commanding of those successors, Lyndon Johnson, history got thoroughly and disastrously out of control. This happened in Vietnam, where America became involved in a war it was unable to withdraw from, win, or justify. That war has provided Americans with a more somber perspective. Now we wonder whether liberal voluntarism has ever been valid. Looking back over the years since World War II, during which strenuous efforts have been made to overcome unemployment, to provide housing for the poor, and in other ways to ensure everyone a decent level of material welfare, we are not sure that very much has been accomplished. Failures are conspicuous. The notion that we are products rather than makers of our economic circumstances has a new plausibility. Looking further back from our present position of self-doubt, we can see how dubious was the mood of mastery exhibited by Roosevelt and Lenin. Roosevelt's New Deal did not restore prosperity, and Lenin prepared the way, not for the uncoerced harmony he foresaw prior to the Bolshevik Revolution, but for a monstrous tyranny.

As the example of Lenin suggests, the boldest claims of historical mastery are made by modern revolutionaries. There have, of course, always been revolutions. But only in the last few hundred years have revolutions been undertaken by men and women who believed that they were able not merely to replace a government, but to destroy an entire social and political order and build another. Such was the self-confidence that animated both French and Soviet revolutionaries. And it reflected an attitude that is widespread in modern times and present in many (such as American business people) who are completely uninterested in, or opposed to, political revolution. The self-confidence of revolutionaries is only a dramatic manifestation of the self-confidence of the modern age—a confidence in human power and virtue that arose in the Renaissance, was expressed in the intense activity that peopled and industrialized the North American continent, and was apparently vindicated by the triumphs of science and technology.

The modern idea of revolution, that of swift and complete reconstruction, provides a convenient focus for reflecting on our power over history. Has the self-assurance of the revolutionaries any justification? There are good reasons for arguing that it does not, although these reasons do not, as I shall try to show, lay the whole matter to rest.

First of all, it is hard to see how revolutionary self-assurance can be justified in view of the limitations on our ability to know society. We have to beware of letting the triumphs of the physical sciences mislead us. It is highly doubtful that society can be comprehended with the precision and fullness that characterize our knowledge of physical objects. This is not just because society is highly complex, although that is part of it. It is also because we ourselves are elements of society and cannot stand wholly outside it, studying it without prejudice or passion, as we might a mineral. Even if we could, moreover, society is made up of beings who apparently are capable of choosing freely, of choosing in ways that cannot be foreseen and thus cannot be incorporated in any body of knowledge; behaviorists assert that such freedom is an illusion, but a number of distinguished thinkers disagree.

If society is somehow outside the scope of exact and certain knowledge, then we are hardly in a position to transform it at will. We cannot foresee all consequences of our actions and thus must often produce unintended results. It has often been pointed out that both the French revolutionaries of 1789 and the Russian revolutionaries of 1917, rather than transforming society, largely reestablished the old societies they had set out to destroy. In its centralization, its pathologically suspicious authoritarianism, its use of secret police, and its insistence on spiritual as well as political conformity, Stalinist Russia was not unlike Czarist Russia. Such unconscious repetition of the past seemingly testifies to our historical ignorance; if we could understand the past, we would not blindly repeat it.

Another reason for questioning the modern revolutionary élan concerns human character. Belief in the possibility of total and successful revolution presupposes a considerable confidence in ourselves. A revolution can hardly succeed unless its authors are very good—good enough not only to envision accurately and to pursue the welfare of humankind but also good enough not to be corrupted by the use of violence, which as revolutionaries they can hardly avoid. Nor can a revolution succeed unless the populace as a whole is capable of becoming, or of being made, good; otherwise the new society is a house of cards.

It is hardly necessary to say that there is room for doubt that human nature corresponds to these flattering presuppositions. If it does not, if there are serious moral weaknesses both in revolutionary leaders and in the people at large, then a revolutionary situation invites excesses of terror and violence, and the new order, even if better than the old, is bound to provide new opportunities for evil.

Should we be satisfied with a middle position—one that denies that we are either masters of history or mere puppets? Should we assert our power to *influence* history while acknowledging that we cannot entirely *control* it? Such a position would of course be sensible; it would accord with the commonsense impression one is apt to draw from reading history or observing current events. And it would have a certain poignancy. It would envision human beings as denied the unambiguous role either of standing entirely above and governing history or of being so completely immersed in history as never to think of struggling against it.

Probably some position short of either extreme is the true one. However, anyone who wishes to think and understand would do well to approach middle positions with caution. They encourage you to cease thinking, under the assumption that the question is settled. This is one reason they appeal to us; they promise to lighten the labor of reflection. Often, however, not much has been settled at all; you have decided merely to shun the extremes. The "middle position" may consist, in fact, of numerous different positions that the inquirer has not even distinguished, much less chosen among. And deciding, as nonthinkers habitually do, that "the truth lies somewhere in between" two extremes provides little light. You go on looking at things as you always have; reflection has not deepened or altered your understanding.

Also, it is not obvious that the middle position is defensible. On the one hand, the case against revolution is so strong that we may wonder whether even limited historical goals can be reached. Is it possible, for example, to maintain stability against the forces of technological change? A great American essayist has remarked that "what actually happens when the steam engine or the dynamo or, for that matter, the automobile, the airplane, and the radio, is invented is simply this: Our hearts lift up and we let out a glad cry, 'Hold on to your hats boys, here we go again.' "[2] Is even moderation historically possible?

On the other hand, the revolutionary ideal has a power and dignity that are not destroyed by rational arguments like the preceding ones. Even if you find good sense in the antirevolutionary argument, you may feel a lingering and inexplicable sympathy for the revolutionary side. As with arguments for direct democracy and for the politics of redemption, they may flout common sense but still say something that needs to be expressed.

One thing often expressed in revolutionary writing, without which civilization might be far poorer, is a sense of the possible splendor of humanity. Political moderates usually assume that human beings are mediocre and life prosaic. The ideal of human glory expressed, for example, in the Greek conception of the gods as immortal and powerful human beings, is lost. The potentialities of life come to be identified with the most uninspiring actualities. Revolutionaries refuse to acquiesce in any such identification; they reassert the possibility of splendor.

In doing this, they do more than express a truth about humankind; they also, to use a traditional Christian phrase, bring society "under judgment." They refuse to allow the existing order to define human potentialities. Even those dubious of revolution may agree that it is crucial to our spiritual self-preservation to maintain the critical perspective on society that revolutionary writings often provide.

Many also will feel that there is at least an intimation of truth in the revolutionary exaltation of man as lord of history. This goes further than mere glorification of life; it asserts that people themselves can bring the potential glory of life into full reality. In the Bible, men and women have "dominion over the fish of the sea, and over the fowl of the air, and over every living thing

---

[2]Joseph Wood Krutch, *Human Nature and the Human Condition* (New York: Random House, 1959), p. 144.

that moveth upon the earth."[3] In the books of revolutionaries, they have dominion over themselves and their history as well. Some may say that this is an invitation to chaos and violence. That may very well be true. But assuming it is true introduces certain problems that may not be insoluble but are certainly serious. Is the glory of life then purely imaginary and never to be realized? And if we humans are not lords of history, what meaning can history have?

No small part of the demoralization of the present era arises from the fact that we do not know what to think about these matters. Since the beginning of World War I, a series of profound and unforseen disasters has shaken our confidence. Living in a century that has included two prolonged and ruinous global wars, a protracted economic depression, and the tyrannies of Hitler and Stalin with their calculated and extravagant violations of human dignity, we doubt that history is under the direction either of human beings or of any beneficent force. A religious civilization might bear such discouragement, for faith in things beyond history would remain. But people today count far less on rising above history than on dominating it, and less on entering another world than on perfecting the one we now inhabit. In these circumstances, to lose confidence in the future is to suffer a basic spiritual disorientation.

Our whole view of ourselves and reality thus is at stake in this question. The revolutionary outlook, although explicitly maintained by only a minority, expresses a humanistic self-confidence that has been shared by the vast majority. For people today to become convinced that they lack the capacity for revolution is no small matter; it poses a threat to what we might call their "cosmic morale," and it challenges them to revise fundamentally their entire world view.

Having considered the possible extent of human historical mastery, let us consider the means. Here perhaps the most important question has to do with the role of violence.

28 Can we shape history without using extensive violence?

The two main sides of this question are represented by liberals and radicals.

[3]Genesis 1:28.

Liberals believe in the possibility of correcting injustice through persuasion; this belief, indeed, is one of the essential principles of the liberal ideal. Everyone has the right to speak freely and to join with others of like mind in promulgating personal views; by virtue of this right everyone can bring grievances to the attention of the goverment and the citizens. The critical point is that one can anticipate a reasonable hearing, which means not only that grievances will be fairly considered but that all necessary actions will be taken. That is one reason why liberty is practical and desirable: it offers a way of peacefully correcting injustice. Liberals thus are optimistic as to both ends and means; the most serious injustices can finally be eliminated, and this can be done without violence.

Radicals, on the other hand, typically doubt the effectiveness of persuasion where paramount interests are at stake. Marx, for example, did not expect capitalists to give up their holdings voluntarily. While suggesting that the proletariat might in one or two countries come to power peacefully, he thought that in most countries violence would be unavoidable.

Radicals thus are optimistic as to ends but pessimistic as to means. They believe, like liberals, that injustice will finally be conquered, but they do not expect this to come about through mutual agreement. It is a measure of the seriousness of injustice, at least of economic injustice (if we are speaking of Marx and his followers), that it divides human beings so deeply that they cannot perceive one another's interests or enter into common discussion.

The difference between liberals and radicals arises partly from their differing appraisals of violence. A liberal would probably regard violence as a uniquely evil form of power. Not that liberals rule it out in all circumstances, as do anarchists and pacifists. But they feel that it subverts decent relationships more fundamentally than do other forms of power; violence is worse, for example, than propaganda or economic pressure. It must therefore be used only as a last resort.

Radicals usually are more ready than liberals to accept violence as a temporary expedient. In the long run, they look forward to a great lessening or even to the total disappearance of violence; and they are likely to condemn vehemently the repressive violence used by the dominant classes. For the typical radical, however, the propaganda and the economic pressures employed by these classes are morally no better than violence. Effective resistance by those underneath is impossible if violence is barred.

Most radicals go at least this far; some go farther. Some see violence used for revolutionary purposes by oppressed people as a positive good. It is a proof of humanity. Only human beings can violently rebel; doing so, therefore, demonstrates that they are not mere things to be used as others desire.

Something more decisive causes the liberal-radical split over violence, however, than a difference concerning the morality of violence. There is a difference over the nature of human beings.

Liberals characteristically see human beings as reasonable. They see them as reasonable both in beliefs and in actions; that is, people not only use reason—and use it competently—in arriving at their beliefs, but they also shape their conduct in the light of these rational beliefs. This is why liberals see persuasion as the best way to attack injustice.

Radicals do not ordinarily dispute the proposition that humans are reasonable in essence; indeed their long-range hopes depend on that assumption. But they usually hold that the realization of this rational essence is thwarted under the conditions created by serious injustice. This is why persuasion cannot work. Marx illustrates this point of view. He believed that human beings were reasonable enough for social and economic life finally, after the consolidation of the communist revolution, to be brought wholly under the governance of reason, with violence disappearing. But he certainly did not believe that capitalists were reasonable, except in the narrow sense of rationally pursuing their selfish interests. They were assuredly not reasonable enough to understand the nature of the common good or the laws of economic development. Why not? Simply because their minds were confined by their circumstances. Capitalists were capable of being rational about their own interests, Marx held, but not about the needs of humanity.

Many radicals adhere to some such determinism as this. They think that serious injustices cannot ordinarily be corrected without violence because these injustices destroy rationality; they establish divisions reason cannot surmount.

In a manner of speaking, the question is whether everyone lives in a single universe. It is hardly too much to say that they do not, as seen by some radicals; at least not for the time being.

In Marxism, for example, workers and capitalists live fundamentally different lives. As capitalism enters its death throes, they come to have different philosophies, different emotions, and different ends. As a result, they cannot peacefully communicate with one another; their relations are inescapably violent. Some radicals have placed equally drastic emphasis on the division between blacks and whites. The experiences and interests of blacks and whites are so completely disparate, they claim, that reason cannot deal with the issues that divide them.

Liberals (although not liberals alone) persistently reject such dichotomies. Human beings are never so far apart that they do not still share a single universe of reason, in the liberal view. Hence it can never be taken for granted that discussion is useless and violence inevitable.

The issue is not only the nature of human beings in general but also the nature of reason. I have stated the issue as though reasonableness included concern for the interests of others; I have assumed that a reasonable person can talk with others because of a rational capacity for understanding and respecting their concerns. In short, reason is a moral faculty. To look on reason in this way is in the tradition of liberalism. But there is another concept of reason, and even those who reject it should be prepared to take it into account.

Reason may be nothing more than a faculty for engaging in means-end calculations, a faculty having nothing to do with morality. A reasonable person may merely be skilled in devising ways of advancing selfish interests, whether or not they coincide with the interests of others. From this point of view reason does not disclose the ideal order within which we should live but is merely, as Hume remarked, the "slave of the passions."

Deciding this particular issue does not decide the question we are discussing; but it does have an important bearing on it. If reason is merely expediential, it may exacerbate rather than moderate historical violence, for it will only make individuals and groups more conscious of their own separate interests.

Help in thinking about the role of violence in history may be gained by considering the doctrine of nonviolence. Some of the most distinguished figures of recent times have defended and practiced nonviolence: for example, Leo Tolstoy (1828–1910), considered by many to be the greatest novelist who ever lived, and Mohandas Gandhi (1869–1948), the architect of Indian independence and at once a great spiritual and political leader. In America, nonviolence is represented by Martin Luther King Jr. (1929–1968), who, like Gandhi, finally lost his life to the violence he stubbornly refused to use in his long struggle against racial domination and injustice.

Fundamental to the view represented by Tolstoy, Gandhi, and King is the distinction between nonviolence and nonresistance. Nonresistance means absolute submission to all injustice and violence; *nonviolence is a form of resistance*. Nonresistance means abandoning all means-end calculations; nonviolence involves sophisticated strategies (it is often associated with civil disobedience, which was briefly discussed in conjunction with Question 17). Nonresistance is a refusal to use power of any kind; nonviolence is a refusal to use *violent* power, but is aimed at swaying people in other ways. It may seem that nonresistance is absurd, but in fact it can provide a position of great spiritual purity. It represents a repudiation of politics and of all human devices, with the future entrusted entirely to God. The great, and perhaps only, exemplar of nonresistance is Jesus. But the spirit of nonresistance—unconditional love for human beings and a limitless trust in God—is present in nonviolence, and Tolstoy, Gandhi, and King were all inspired by Jesus. The unique character of nonviolence is captured in the term "nonviolent resistance." Nonviolence is a way of using power and is thoroughly political. Tolstoy sought, in effect, to overthrow the entire social and political order of Czarist Russia (although he was unable, in his isolation, to seriously threaten it); Gandhi compelled the British imperial government to withdraw from India; and King, although heroically restrained in his ways of resistance, was a revolutionary figure in American society.

In short, the doctrine of nonviolence offers a powerful affirmative answer to the question before us. We can shape history not only without using *extensive* violence, but perhaps without using violence at all. Proponents of nonviolence are practically always people in quest of deep and rapid change. They are in that sense radical. Unlike typical radicals, however, they anticipate change without violence.

It would be misleading, however, to say that proponents of nonviolence believe in the *possibility* of change without violence; the proper word is *necessity*. Violence is a corrupting and abortive instrumentality. Most radicals exhibit an antipathy to violence—but mainly in their ends; they envision a world without war and societies without classes or domination. In proponents of nonviolence, this antipathy covers means as well as ends. Violence is believed to arise practically always in the company of arrogance and hatred, and these sinister companions flourish wherever violence rules. Violence is always at enmity with reason and always destroys the possibility of that patient and loving speech, often called dialogue, that we carry on best with allies and friends but can occasionally enter into with opponents. Violence dissipates our common humanity. This is to say, since our humanity is *essentially* common, simply that it dissipates our humanity.

Nonviolence, on the other hand, opens the way to truly human relationships even in the midst of conflict. It is a way of resisting evil without humiliating and forever alienating the perpetrators of evil. This, at any rate, is the claim of its proponents. The link between nonviolence and dialogue, although implicit in the practice of both Gandhi and King, was strongly emphasized in the writings of Thomas Merton (1915–1968), one of the great spiritual figures of twentieth-century America. Merton was a Trappist monk and hence was unable to participate in nonviolent activities. From his monastery, however, he closely followed the struggle for racial justice led by Martin Luther King Jr., and in his writings he eloquently defended the principle of nonviolence. For Merton, nonviolence differs from violence by arising from humility rather than arrogance and by approaching opponents with respect; it is a victory over hatred in situations where hatred ordinarily is in command. Nonviolence does not aim to crush those on the other side but to awaken them in their conscience and prepare the way for speaking with them. Nonviolence is patient. Above all, it is intended to create a mood of dialogical openness in circumstances that tempt people to kill one another.

What are the techniques of nonviolence? This is a question without a good theoretical answer. The answer is practical. There are, to be sure, traditional techniques—marches, public meetings, boycotts, and so forth. But the essence of nonviolence is not its techniques, but the spirit animating it—humility and love. Techniques vary with circumstances, and the successful practice of nonviolence requires leaders with not only the skill to devise appropriate techniques, but the charisma to induce multitudes to practice them, without arrogance or hatred, and often in the face of repeated provocation.

Manifestly, there is much here to interest a student of politics. Politics is often unsavory and sometimes brutal; the doctrine of nonviolence is a vision of politics as spiritually noble. Deep historical changes ordinarily involve force and bitter confict; nonviolence is an ideal of revolution through moral illumination rather than death. Nevertheless, one must ask whether the case for nonviolence is entirely sound.

Unfortunately, it is not—at least, not beyond all doubt. Here we shall take note just of two of the questions to which it is vulnerable. The first is practical. Is the efficacy of nonviolence severely limited by circumstances? Is it limited, for example, by the kind of opponents being faced? It is hard to believe that campaigns of nonviolence might have replaced the invasion of Normandy and the battle of Stalingrad as steps toward the final defeat of Hitler. And is nonviolence dependent for success on leadership of a kind that is rare? A man such as Martin Luther King Jr., for example, is not apt to appear in every generation, and when he was killed, he proved to be irreplaceable. This question does not point toward the complete rejection of nonviolence but rather toward recognizing it as a technique of limited applicability.

The other question is less practical and more philosophical. Does the doctrine of nonviolence obscure, and encourage a refusal to face, the evil in human nature? Proponents of nonviolence seem to assume that the evil in human beings is relatively superficial. Victims can approach their oppressors with love and openness in spite of the wrongs they have suffered; inveterate oppressors can be drawn beyond prejudice and selfish interest into the sphere of dialogue. Is this just another version of the age-old illusion (as some see it) that we discussed near the beginning of this book in connection with Rousseau: the illusion that we are not evil but only unfortunate—unfortunate enough to fall under the influence of circumstances that cause us to behave in evil ways? As we have seen, this view (illusory or not) gives rise to utopian expectations; eventually, by changing circumstances, we shall recreate the human race and bring into existence a transformed world. Is the doctrine of nonviolence a kind of utopianism—a utopianism of historical change?

Now, having reflected on questions concerning both the possible extent and the requisite means of deliberate historical change, let us consider its significance. The question we face here is whether historical change determines the whole framework of human life. Are your relations with other human beings and with the universe totally subject to history? Or is there an immutable structure of right and truth to which a moral and rational being can appeal regardless of what happens in history? It would be reassuring to think that there is, that certain standards and truths, at least, are not engulfed in history. A number of thinkers, however, deny this reassurance. All realities, all principles, all moral rules are mutable, they say. Everything is submerged in the flow of events, and the futility and tragedy of history encompass our world. Is this true?

29 Do truth and right change in the course of history?

We may doubt that all those who answer this question affirmatively—"standards change," they assert—are ready to live in the kind of universe to which they commit themselves. We may doubt, in other words, that they are fully aware of what they are saying. If truth and right really do change in the course of history, then there are no fixed points in relation to which life can be organized and guided. Liberty, democracy, justice, respect for life, honesty—all of the rules you might rely on for conducting your life and appraising your surroundings—give way. And not only right and wrong, but reality itself dissolves and is swept away in the flux of events. You cannot hold to "human nature" or to any other rock. Indeed, if you fully pursue the idea that all basic principles change in the course of history, you will find that idea itself escaping like water through your fingers, for it too must change in the course of time.

Jean-Paul Sartre, the late French writer and thinker, wrote a novel called *Nausea,* in which he depicted with great dramatic force the vertigo and horror felt by a man who begins to perceive the realities around him as completely lacking firm structure or meaning. Nothing, not even his own hand, has manifest form or purpose. Such a fluid, molten, meaningless universe is literally sickening, hence Sartre's title.

Those for whom "standards change," and for whom that is an absolutely serious and final judgment, live in a universe that is like a ship in heavy seas: the objects around them are un-fixed or straining to break away, the deck presses upward be-neath their feet or drops away unexpectedly, and even the horizon seems to move. Such, perhaps, is truly the human situ-ation. If so, it is not something to celebrate; as Sartre saw, what one naturally feels is nausea.

Thus it is not surprising that human beings have always tried to find firm ground above the flood of change, and that politi-cal thinkers have sought principles of human relations that will not crumble and disappear in the stream of history. In-deed, it is hardly too much to say that political philosophy be-gan with an effort to find firm ground. Plato as a young man saw the dissolution not only of Athenian political institutions but also of Hellenic moral and religious convictions. Athenian governments were repeatedly overthrown, and the city was filled with people who said, and who acted as though they be-lieved, that there were no fixed standards of morality. Plato's response can be found in *The Republic,* which argued that the basis of political order, and of all valid and fulfilling life, is an understanding of the eternally true and good.

But what *is* eternally true and good? Plato's famous "doctrine of forms" tried to answer this question. Every reality—every person, tree, chair, or rock—is real only because it participates in a universal, changeless form—the form of a person, tree, chair, or rock. These forms, for Plato, were what we might call "ideas" or "essences." They could not be seen or touched, but were absolutely real and could be known intellectually. "The Good," which we have already discussed, may be thought of as the form of all forms and thus as the eternal source of being and of value. What is most important in the present context is that Plato envisioned the forms as neither coming into being nor passing away, as having no history and as unaffected by history.

Philosophers, in Plato's conception of life, dwelt in the world of forms. They had ascended from the things seen and touched to the forms and from the forms to the Good. They had ascended from the changing to the lasting, rising above history. Were philosophers to rule absolutely, then a whole city might be founded on a plane above the violence and confusion of historical change.

Plato's fear of change may have been extreme. His general outlook, however, is not unique and even in his own time was not novel. Plato took up a search that had been initiated by other philosophers and that has continued to our own day, a search for what often is referred to simply as nature. I have already touched on the ancient issue of nature versus convention as the determinant of human character. A notable feature of this controversy is that convention has had so few defenders, while nature has for millennia had a remarkable and rarely questioned authority. One of the principal reasons for this seems to be that nature, that is, the fundamental structure of being, does not change; such at least has been the prevailing belief.

The concept of nature underlies the most durable and powerful idea in the whole history of Western moral and political thought—natural law. This is the idea, noted earlier, that human relations are subject to a law that is discernible by reason and unaffected by historical change. Times and customs may change, but the principles governing human relations remain the same. Some of our most civilized institutions, such as personal liberties, democratic government, and international law and organization, can be traced back to this idea. If this one timber in the structure of our civilization were withdrawn, we might suddenly find ourselves standing in the midst of ruins.

The ancient Hebrews, too, with their profound historical consciousness, sought a standpoint above the flux of history. Granted, they were far less fearful of change and more likely to see it as part of reality than were the ancient Greeks. Even Jehovah (in some ways it would be more accurate to say *particularly* Jehovah) was outside of any fixed and knowable order; divine decisions were free and unforeseeable, and Jehovah is even represented occasionally as repenting of past acts. As for humankind and the rest of creation, here too the Hebrews differed from the Greeks; they did not share the typical Hellenic belief that reality is basically an inalterable rational order.

But even the Hebrews affirmed that some things were beyond historical change. "The mercy of the Lord is from everlasting to everlasting," and one expression of this mercy is the Law, the commandments given to Moses on Mount Sinai. These cannot be touched by any process of historical erosion. In this way the Hebrews, like the Greeks, grounded society on changeless order.

The quest for inalterable realities and rules has been pressed so persistently that one feels in it the expression of a basic imperative of human existence. It seems that we can hardly live if nothing endures. Nevertheless, the last two centuries have witnessed numerous attacks on "nature" and natural law. As for nature (what *is,* as distinguished from what *ought* to be), some of the most profound and persuasive philosophers have argued against the notion that there is a knowable, permanent structure of being. Hume did so in maintaining the thesis that no necessary connection links cause and effect. When we speak of cause and effect, according to Hume, we merely report recurrent sequences of sensations. We have no way of knowing whether the sequences that held in the past will continue to hold in the future. Hence we can make no assertions concerning the basic order of reality; we cannot even know that there is such an order. A similar view is implicit in the works of Kant, despite his avowed intention of refuting Hume. As already noted, a major theme of his *Critique of Pure Reason* is that the changeless structure people thought they had discovered in nature is imposed by the mind on the sensory data they receive from reality. It does not characterize reality in itself.

The idea that reality is essentially a fixed natural order was challenged from another angle by Henri Bergson (1859–1941), a French philosopher whose popularity has somewhat declined but who was a thinker of great originality and eloquence. According to Bergson, change is not only real, it is the very essence of reality. "There do not exist *things* made, but only things in the making, not *states* that remain fixed, but only states in process of change."[4] This is most obvious in respect to living things and to humankind. Bergson admitted that some realities are relatively fixed, but they are dead and inorganic, not alive and spiritual. He condemned the quest for changeless reality. He saw it as an effort to impose fixity—which the intellect happens to demand—on what is intrinsically "unceasing creation."

A final example of the modern attack on natural order is existentialism. One way of stating the theme uniting the various

[4]Henri Bergson, *The Creative Mind: An Introduction to Metaphysics* (New York: Philosophical Library, 1946), p. 188. The italics are Bergson's.

forms of existentialism is by saying that human nature is not a changeless, transhistorical form. A human being is free, or subjective, and thus beyond every fixed, objective principle.

The question we are considering concerns not only truth but also right. As the views we have just been discussing prevail, the belief in changeless moral principles declines. Kant showed that this is not an invariable rule; although he attacked the traditional concept of nature, he set forth a moral theory with a firm and uncompromising conception of duty. But the traditional ideal of natural law necessarily falls if there is no nature. Hume founded morality on the wants and propensities of the individual, as well as on custom and habit. Bergson thought a good act was a creative act, arising from an intuitive sense of the movement of life; and existentialists have typically argued that choice creates values rather than being subordinated to values. None of these thinkers argued that something was good merely because an individual or a society called it good; they were not total relativists. All, however, reflected the decay of the ancient conviction that moral standards remain despite all historical change.

A good example of the prevalent view that right is relative to time and place is provided by Marx. Much of the force of Marx's writing lay in his apparent demonstration that many realities and standards that had been regarded as part of the inalterable order of nature, such as the profit motive, private property, and government by parliaments, were in actuality merely the beliefs and customs of a particular historical era and were destined to disappear. As a human being, Marx was not without absolute moral standards, as is plain in the bitterness of his denunciations of callous employers. As a thinker, however, he had no such standards: his aim was not to show that capitalist civilization was evil, but that it was temporary. His revolutionary power comes from the skill and thoroughness with which he swept all aspects of the civilization he attacked into the torrent of history.

Is it merely a sign of weakness in humankind that for so many centuries we have tried to ground society on the changeless—on eternal forms, on "nature," or on God? Or is it because of an intuition that relationships without such a foundation have no substance or validity?

With questions like these we are groping our way amid the shadows of contemporary despair. We have little confidence in the course of history, and we are afraid that our being and our relationships are wholly at the disposal of a merciless and capricious tide of events.

But is history really so cruel and unreliable? Perhaps it is less malignant and irrational in its ultimate ends than appears on the surface. It may be that the natural and moral order that sometimes seems to be dissolved in history is, in actuality, being created by history and thus may be the innermost logic of the historical process.

These hypotheses define roughly the course of modern thought. Having come to doubt that truth and right are invulnerable to history, thus giving up the ancient and medieval faith that an eternal order of nature underlies historical change, modern thinkers tried to find truth and right in the structure of history itself. This effort produced some ingenious and fascinating conceptions of the historical process. Here we shall confine ourselves to the most general form of the idea, the doctrine of progress. To hold that history tends to produce a good society—not merely more comfortable but also more reasonable and humane—is to hold that history is rational, because it is a process leading toward a desirable end and also, and for the same reason, that it is moral. Truth and right thus regain the primacy that they seemed, for a moment, to have lost; it turns out that they determine the logic of the very historical process that threatened them.

But is the doctrine of progress valid?

30 Does history lead naturally toward "the good society"?

For some generations modern peoples have answered with an exuberant yes. Progress has been taken to be a natural, if not inevitable, characteristic of human history. A typical and influential representative of this view is the Marquis de Condorcet (1743–1794), an exemplar of the doctrines of the Enlightenment and a victim of the Terror during the French Revolution. The core idea in Condorcet's philosophy of history is the limitless perfectibility of humankind. Condorcet meant not only that humankind *may* become perfect, which Rousseau, an opponent of the doctrine of progress, also believed; he meant that humankind has a strong bent toward perfection and that history, as a result, tends naturally toward the realization of this perfection.

The key to progress, for Condorcet, was rational enlightenment. Science extends and deepens knowledge; printing and education spread it. He assumed, in Socratic fashion, that growth in knowledge must be accompanied by growth in moral excellence. Condorcet admitted that the path of progress might lead through distressing times. He looked back on the Middle Ages, for example, as a period of superstition, intolerance, and priestly oppression. But he seems to have had little fear that we might descend forever into an era of darkness. He saw the human race as moved by a nearly irresistible destiny toward enlightenment, and through enlightenment toward universal freedom and equality.

Well-known exponents of progress in recent times are Hegel and Marx. Both thinkers show the modern inclination to believe in progress regardless of what the determining force of history is thought to be. Neither attributed preponderant influence to conscious will or to knowledge. For Hegel ideas (not necessarily held consciously in mind by anyone), for Marx economic forces, governed the march of affairs. They assumed that these governing forces would eventually be recognized, thus entering into the conscious determination of events, but for long periods of time they might shape events despite the ignorance and resistance of historical participants. Hegel and Marx thought that progress, over the long run, was inevitable. The blindness and inadequacies of human beings might delay it but could not completely block it.

The authority of the idea of progress is particularly evident in the Hegelian and Marxist dialectic. Both thinkers believed that progress comes about, so to speak, in a zigzag fashion rather than in a straight line. Progress is not a steady and harmonious forward movement. It comes about through tension and conflict, and the most catastrophic moments may presage the most glorious ones. The fact that human beings are usually backward-looking and confused, therefore, is not an obstruction on the road of history. Far from inhibiting progress, error and conflict are among the devices by which progress is made.

Progress could hardly be more emphatically affirmed. Whether through ideas or through economic forces, whether by means of the resistance of participants or by means of their cooperation, the law of progress maintains its sway.

But, just as belief in the human power to direct history is counterbalanced by the older conviction that history is determined by some power beyond humanity, so the doctrine of progress, although popular during the last century or two, far from expresses the consensus among Western thinkers. On the contrary, the history of thought reflects a great deal of pessimism about the course of events. For example, the ancient Greeks and Romans generally assumed that history moves through more or less regular cycles; recurrence, rather than progress, was the law of history.

It is easy to understand how such an idea might arise. Recurrence is a pronounced and even awesome characteristic of our environment and life. It occurs in the changing of the seasons and the passing of generations. But while the idea of historical cycles is comprehensible, it expresses a mood very far from the hopefulness of Condorcet and other apostles of progress. If history is cyclical, then ultimately nothing is accomplished. There may be achievements within a single cycle, but the long ages of history, comprising many cycles, can be nothing more than the recurrent restoration and decay of what was achieved in the first cycle. A terrible futility reigns in human affairs.

Augustine and other Christian thinkers repudiated the cyclical concept of history. They had to, for otherwise the life of Christ, as well as all other acts of God, would have fallen under the law and so been cursed by the absurdity of endless repetition. However, the alternative view developed by Christian thinkers also was markedly pessimistic.

Orthodox Christians envisioned history as leading toward a finale of suffering and terror: "For nation shall rise against nation and kingdom against kingdom: and there shall be earthquakes in divers places, and there shall be famines and troubles."[5] With the end of history, of course, God would establish his kingdom, and this climax, to which all the ages since Adam's sin had been leading, would give history a meaning it could not have had were it governed by the law of cyclical recurrence.

[5]Mark 13:8.

History was in this way leading toward a better life. It was not, however, leading toward a better *earthly* life; the kingdom of God was conceived to be, in its perfection, unlike any earthly kingdom. Nor was history leading *naturally* toward a better life; it was leading naturally, that is, under the impetus of iniquitous people, toward catastrophe. Only the intervention of God turned it into a process of redemption.

Thus it is plain that while history has a purpose and meaning for Christians that it cannot have in the classical mind, where it is conceived as cyclical, there is nonetheless an immense chasm between the Christian view of history and the modern doctrine of progress. In the Christian view, the beginning is the moral suicide of humanity; in the doctrine of progress, humanity never loses its fundamental innocence. In the Christian view, the dominant motif is tragedy, and we must anticipate "affliction, such as was not from the beginning of the creation which God created unto this time";[6] in the doctrine of progress, the major theme is steady improvement. In the Christian vision, the end is a transfiguration of reality in which the earth, as we know it, vanishes; according to the doctrine of progress, we may look toward increasing harmony and happiness on this earth.

Christianity suggests a deep and little-discussed reason for questioning the doctrine of progress. This is the idea that ultimately nothing is significant except the loss and the redemption of individual souls. "For what is a man profited, if he shall gain the whole world, and lose his own soul?"[7] From this point of view all progress must be spiritual and personal; thus it becomes questionable whether any historical, as distinguished from personal, development can be progressive or not.

This perspective is not uniquely Christian, although it is suggested by Christianity. In its most general form it is simply the notion that everything must be judged by its effect on individuals—only individuals, never peoples or historical conditions, are ends in themselves. This casts doubt on the idea of progress, even from a materialistic point of view, for the increasing convenience and comfort some nations now enjoy cannot justify the squalor and misery in which countless individuals have passed their lives. But the idea of progress is challenged

[6]Mark 13:19.
[7]Matthew 16:26.

with particular sharpness if the individual is treated as a moral and spiritual entity, as one who is not necessarily better off merely by being more comfortable. On this premise, how can there be historical, as distinguished from personal, progress?

If morality is a matter of personal choice and spirituality depends on the soul of the individual, it is not clear how an age, as distinguished from a person, can be morally and spiritually ahead of or behind another age. Can historical conditions place individuals on moral and spiritual levels that they would fall below under other conditions? If so, moral and spiritual greatness are apparently the products of external circumstances, not of personal striving. Reflection along these lines can lead us to wonder whether the nineteenth and twentieth centuries, with all of their self-satisfaction, have achieved any genuine progress at all.

In other words, when we think of historical progress, we seem to be thinking more of vast multitudes of human beings than of the individual. When we think of the individual, the significance of the multitudes that constitute historical eras becomes problematic.

Today, we do not know what to think about the natural course of history any more than we know what to think about the question of how far history is under human control. Our doubts in both cases are the result of the unexpected disasters that have befallen the human race since 1914. The idea of progress has suddenly come to seem old-fashioned and unrealistic. But what can we put in its place? We do not appear to have the kind of faith that would be required to return to the Christian vision of history, although many sense the apocalypse in the nuclear cloud. The cyclical concept of history strikes us as no less implausible, and intolerable as well. It is implausible because for two millennia we have been taught that history had a direction and a purpose and because in the past two centuries we have seen events, like industrialization, that we know have never happened before, which seems to disprove any theory of cyclical recurrence. The cyclical view is intolerable because, after believing for so long that history is purposeful, we are crushed by the thought that it is merely endless, useless repetition.

In James Joyce's novel *Ulysses* a character says that history is a nightmare from which he is trying to awake.[8] This remark

---

[8]James Joyce, *Ulysses* (New York: Modern Library, 1914), p. 35.

expresses the mood of historical insecurity and fear that half a century of disorder and violence has engendered in many people today. It expresses the mood of those who have confidence neither in their own control of history nor in the beneficence of its natural tendencies. If we cannot direct or trust the course of events, it is difficult not to feel that the universe is like a capricious despot who may at any time disrupt our existence and lay waste our future. Personal life is burdened by the impression that the surrounding universe is senseless; political life is demoralized by the feeling that the consequences of any action are incalculable and menacing.

Thus we are pretty much forced to face the question of whether history has any meaning—a question that may paralyze modest and cautious inquirers while inducing reckless inquirers to indulge in grandiose and undemonstrable generalizations. Moreover, so sweeping is the question that it drives us beyond all observable realities. It forces us to ask whether there is any such being as God, or transcendence, or any such reality as eternity, which might give meaning to history and which even, perhaps, is essential if history is to have any meaning. At the outset of this book, I warned that thinking is not always fun. Questions about the meaning of history succinctly illustrate the point. They "take one's breath away." I do not deny that we scarcely know what we mean when we ask such questions. On the other hand, I do not see how we can responsibly avoid them.

Suggested Readings

Saint Augustine. *The City of God*
Burke, Edmund. *Reflections on the French Revolution*
Hegel, G. W. F. *The Philosophy of History*
Tocqueville, Alexis de. *The Old Regime and the French Revolution*
Marx, Karl, and Engels, Friedrich. *The Communist Manifesto*
Dostoevsky, Fyodor. *The Possessed*
Sorel, Georges. *Reflections on Violence*
Bury, J. B. *The Idea of Progress*
Berdyaev, Nicolas. *The Meaning of History*
Malraux, André. *Man's Fate*
Buber, Martin. *The Prophetic Faith*
Popper, Karl. *The Open Society and Its Enemies,* 2 vols.
Löwith, Karl. *Meaning in History*

Niehbur, Reinhold. *The Nature and Destiny of Man,* Vol. II
------. *Faith and History*
------. *The Irony of American History*
Strauss, Leo. *Natural Right and History*
Camus, Albert. *The Rebel*
Bultmann, Rudolf. *History and Eschatology: The Presence of Eternity*
Fanon, Frantz. *The Wretched of the Earth*
Arendt, Hannah. *On Revolution*
Ellul, Jacques. *Autopsy of Revolution*
Didion, Joan. *The Book of Common Prayer*

■ The Idea of Humane Uncertainty

In the face of questions that for twenty-five centuries have defied the efforts of philosophers to find demonstrable answers, how can we avoid intellectual despair? To show that there are perennial questions about politics may rebut heedless votaries of religion or science, dogmatists who assume that no great questions remain unanswered. However, it may only fortify those who shun political speculation, not because they assume the great questions have already been answered, but because they assume they can never be answered.

The major premise of this book may be phrased as an answer to such threatened despair. Although our answers are never adequate, we encounter being in questioning itself. Truth is found in the act of thought but can never be embodied in universally compelling principles. The value of paradoxes is that they forcefully remind us of the inadequacy of our verbal formulas. They impel us to continue thinking. This is why, according to the epigraph, "the thinker without a paradox is like a lover without feeling."

Why this troublesome discontinuity between our understanding and our answers, between reality and words? To respond to this query even briefly and tentatively is not easy. In order to clarify the groundwork of this book and the value of thought, however, it is perhaps worth trying. Certain ideas of Kant's may help.

According to Kant, knowledge in the strictest sense of the word, knowledge that can be embodied in unequivocal and universally compelling scientific propositions, pertains to objects. This may at first seem obvious because it may seem that all genuine realities must be objects. But according to Kant an object is only a particular form of being, and objective being is not being in itself. What, then, is an object? Greatly simplifying Kant's analysis, an object is an entity existing in space and time, characterized by qualities like unity and plurality, and resulting from certain causes and causing certain effects. It is of the essence of an object that its location in space and time, its general nature, and its relation to other objects can be rationally defined.

Is this not true of being itself rather than merely of objective being? Not according to Kant. An object can be rationally located and defined not because it happens to have just those qualities that correspond with the categories, like unity and plurality and cause and effect, that structure our minds. It is rather because objects are created and given those qualities by our minds. All that being itself provides is a chaos of sensations. We must organize those sensations if we are to have a coherent experience. Space and time, and concepts like cause and effect, are the forms by means of which we do this. An object can be rationally located and defined because that is its essence, and that essence is bestowed upon it by mind in the very act of understanding it. An object is an intellectual artifact and not a thing in itself; it cannot exist without mind.

This is not to say that we create only such objects as we please, however. Gaining understanding is governed by processes inherent in the human mind as such. Personal volition and inspiration play no role, and the objects in my mind are necessarily the same as those in the minds of everyone. Although space and time, for example, are not "out there," existing independently of my mind, neither can I call them into existence nor abolish them at will. As a human being, possessed of the rational faculties that characterize the human essence, I necessarily arrange reality in a spatiotemporal framework.

Much in Kant's analysis is debatable. How, for example, can we say that being in itself causes our sense perceptions if causation is only an intellectual device for interrelating those perceptions? How can we even speak of being in itself if we can know nothing about it? Such questions have been discussed in countless volumes. We cannot debate them here, nor have we any need to do so. The important thing is to see how Kant opens the way to insight and vision.

The study of Kant can bring liberation—liberation from the materialistic assumption that every reality must be an object and the universe as a whole merely a vast collection of objects. Many people think this assumption is forced upon us by common sense. For those who accept it, the consequences are drastic. Being loses its mystery; persons turn into mechanisms; religious ideas become absurd. We live within, and are mere elements of, an inhuman and ultimately meaningless causal order. Kant unlocks the doors of this cosmic prison. Without denying the reality of objects or questioning the authority of science, he points to a more human and hospitable universe beyond the world of things.

The study of Kant can liberate us not only from the world of things but also from the dispassionate, precise, and systematic knowledge through which that world is understood. Science of the kind that attains its greatest perfection in physics and chemistry ceases to be our one sure means of access to reality. Room is made for intuition, wisdom, and faith. Not that science is discarded; within its own realm it retains unshakable authority. But its realm does not comprise the whole of being.

If we adopt the Kantian perspective, our minds are no longer confined by preconceptions mistaken for ultimate reality. Ideas like world, God, and humanity are recast and our range of vision is immeasurably enlarged. The world, which we automatically envision as a kind of all-inclusive object that we ought to be able to know in its entirety just as we know every other object, turns out to be simply the way in which we organize experience. The world is the context of objects but not itself an object; it is a way of looking at reality. We cannot know the world as a whole because no such reality exists, and we need not think of it as a totality that encloses and determines our lives.

As for God, we are no longer compelled either to imagine the divine as some stupendous but strangely insubstantial—because spiritual—physical entity, or to deny the very idea of God as a manifest absurdity. A major difficulty met in religious discourse is the assumption that every reality must be some kind of object. If this assumption were valid, atheism would be inevitable, for it is plain that no object—nothing within space and time, and thus finite, and nothing causally determined from without—can be God. In challenging the identification of being and objectivity, Kant reopens for the modern age the whole question of divine reality. In limiting reason, Kant asserted, he made room for faith.

Finally, the Kantian revolution enables us to look with new eyes at ourselves. It would be impossible in a few lines to do justice to Kant's obscure and complex theory concerning our knowledge of human beings. Suffice it to say that a human being is not only more than an object of knowledge but is the source of the whole world of objects. A person is not completely unknowable, for each one has a body and a psychic mechanism that can be studied through science. These are only appearances of the person, however, not full and authentic personal being. We are no longer burdened with the notion that a human being is merely a thing. We are not forced to dismiss as illusions the mysteries we sense in ourselves and in those we love.

"Everything that is an object for us," wrote the twentieth-century Kantian philosopher Karl Jaspers, "even though it be the greatest, is still always within another, is not yet all."[1] This is one way of expressing Kant's overall vision. An object is something that our minds carve out of being in itself, and even the world in its totality is carved out of being in itself. Thus every reality we can know is encompassed by being in its fundamental mystery. Encompassing being is not only the environment of every knowable reality, however, but also comprises the true "inner" being of every such reality. I discover myself and my friends not only in what a psychologist may tell me but also in the encompassing mystery. None of this is easy to express or understand, but that is primarily because we are trying to get in touch with things that "thought cannot think."

How does this relate to the question with which we began, that concerning the discontinuity between words and reality? How is this discontinuity to be explained? We have to recall that words are fitted primarily for dealing with objects and hence are inadequate, even misleading, when applied to being in itself. "Words" is shorthand for the knowledge in which words are combined in unambiguous, demonstrable propositions, and

[1]Karl Jaspers, *Reason and Existenz: Five Lectures,* trans. William Earle (Noonday Press, 1955), pp. 51–52.

propositions in turn are combined in systems explaining whole areas of reality. Kant enables us to see why we are able, through science, to gain unassailable knowledge of the things around us, whereas in trying to understand ourselves and others, as we have been doing in this book, we end in uncertainty.

What does Kant tell us about the possibility of somehow gaining insight into the encompassing mystery? Although we can gain no knowledge of being as it is in itself, we can, according to Kant, become aware of it. We become aware of it in defining the boundaries of knowledge; we become aware of it in moral life, in discerning and acting upon our duties; and we become aware of it in contemplating the beautiful and the sublime. We do not attain knowledge, in the proper sense of the term, in any of these ways. We do, however, become conscious of realities that transcend knowledge.

Let us note here that far from everyone is persuaded by such views, in spite of the consensus among philosophers that Kant belongs among the few greatest thinkers of the past. Of particular interest in the context of preceding discussions in this book is the fact that feminists are almost uniformly suspicious of Kantian philosophy. There are Marxist feminists and Freudian feminists but, to my knowledge, no Kantian feminists. This may be partly because Kant appears to be an exemplar of the rationalism and legalism of which many feminists are so dubious. In his *Critique of Pure Reason* Kant defended, as we have already noted, the possibility of formulating absolutely certain and universal laws pertaining to the physical universe; and in his *Critique of Practical Reason* he argued that personal conduct was under the command of sure and unconditional laws of reason, laws he called, forbiddingly, "categorical imperatives." Thus, both in epistemology and ethics, he seemed to represent the epitome of rationalism. And there is no doubt that rationalism was an important and conspicuous aspect of Kant's philosophy, even though, as my preceding remarks suggest, it was not all of Kant's philosophy.

Worse than mere rationalism, however, is that Kant clearly implied, in a paper he once wrote, that women were incapable of acting on principle and in this way were inferior to men even though, he said, they were superior to men in qualities like compassion, sensitivity, and benevolence. The trouble from a feminist point of view is that morality consisted, for Kant, in acting on principle; actions arising from feelings such as those women possessed in greater degree than men were not truly moral. Hence, women did not have, at least generally, the moral capacities men possessed.

One cannot blame women for being offended by such views. It would be difficult to show, however, that they shaped Kant's philosophy in any basic way. Gender was not a significant topic in any of Kant's major works. Moreover, almost all of the great philosophers viewed women much as did Kant; perhaps Plato and John Stuart Mill are the only two who did not. That for twenty-five centuries the greatest minds of the West have so uncritically taken male superiority for granted is understandably a source of anger among women. But feminist thinkers have found value in the works of other male philosophers, such as Augustine, Locke, and Rousseau, and it is doubtful that Kant was any more disdainful of women than were any of these.

As for Kant's philosophy, by no means does it represent an unqualified rationalism. As I have said, Kant defended reason but at the same time drew boundaries around it. In doing this he made room for superrational forms of insight, such as empathy. He made it possible to claim authority not only for science but also for intuitive understanding, for an immediate grasp of persons and situations that in their uniqueness surpass the grasp of science. As we have seen, feminism is linked with a modern revolt against one-sided rationalism. The signal point here is that Kant, for all of his rationalism, laid the foundations for this revolt. His philosophy offers suitable grounds for the richer, more intuitive conceptions of human understanding foreshadowed in many feminist writings. It is arguable that feminists should regard Kant not as an enemy but as a potential friend.

It may seem that his ethics, demanding the cold and unyielding reign of the categorical imperative, stands in the way. Granted, the ethics is not, at least for many, the most attractive area in the Kantian domain. Nevertheless, Kant's moral philosophy embodies a claim that feminists cannot find uninteresting. Every person, for Kant, possesses ultimate and inviolable moral authority; to be human is to have the capacity for judging right and wrong. This implies, first of all, the autonomy many women have felt driven to claim for themselves. Every person is a kind of legislator, able to formulate categorical imperatives, and thus to live by laws that are both universal in scope and riveted to the innermost center of one's reason and conscience. And Kant's moral theory implies not only autonomy but equality as well. *All* persons are competent when it comes to moral judgments. Setting aside casual utterances outside his major treatises, Kant introduces no qualifications concerning gender or sex. Personally, Kant may have had reservations about the moral competence of women, but philosophically he provided himself with no grounds for such reservations. In sum, Kant's ethics displays a spirit that is liberating and egalitarian.

From the standpoint of this book, one of the most interesting parts of *The Critique of Pure Reason*, Kant's major work, is his development of the "antinomies of pure reason." An antinomy is a pair of propositions that are mutually contradictory even though both statements are rationally defensible. For example, to say that some things happen because they are freely chosen and to say that everything happens according to the laws of nature is to voice an antinomy, one formulated by Kant himself. Whenever we speak of being in itself as though it were a set of objects laid out before us we necessarily fall into antinomies. But we can only speak, and only reason, as though we were speaking and reasoning about objects. Thus the desire for ultimate truth involves us inevitably in the formulation of antinomies. Kant does not conclude that we should inhibit our desire for truth in order to avoid antinomies, but only that we should anticipate the contradictions into which the quest for truth will lead us. If we do this, the antinomies can become indirect disclosures of being in itself.

Antinomies, of course, are what we have been calling paradoxes. That is why Kant's theory of antinomies is interesting in the context of this book. It clarifies and supports the main premise of the book, that thinking provides no certain and unequivocal answers but nevertheless opens the way to understanding. Although Kant always expressed himself with a sobriety and care that is often not evident in Kierkegaard's highly flavored prose, his basic view does not conflict with the epigraph of this book. Kant believed that reason drives us toward being in itself and toward ultimate truth. In doing this it drives us toward antinomies through which being in itself is indirectly disclosed. Thus we strive toward the antinomies. In this sense, Kant would agree, "the paradox is the source of the thinker's passion."

Kant and Kierkegaard alike thus suggest that wisdom is not gained by answering questions once and for all but in establishing a thoughtful and continuing relationship to questions. They suggest that wisdom is a thinking state. But to think is to be uncertain; likewise, to entertain antinomies or paradoxes is to be uncertain. We are led in this way to the idea that wisdom lies in uncertainty. To acknowledge this and to maintain a stance not of absolute assurance but of inquiring openness is what I mean by "humane uncertainty."

We have been speaking of the inner life of the individual, and humane uncertainty seems like a very personal, rather than institutional or public, matter. But the concept is not without political meaning. For one thing, from awareness of my power of asking questions arises an intuition that any organization or authority that attempts to suppress my questions and to make me an automatic part in some monolithic group, as a totalitarian state does, violates my essential being. An act of thought is a declaration of freedom; to be serious about reflection is to be incapable of subservience.

Moreover, humane uncertainty contains an intuition not only of freedom but also of equality. One person may know more about mathematics or automobile engines than another, but in the face of the perennial questions, we are all, in our lack of definite, demonstrable answers, equal. The wise stand above others, it would seem, only in their consciousness of this primal equality.

Finally, in humane uncertainty are seeds of community. To accept uncertainty as the sphere of truth is to repudiate the ideologies that objectify and degrade us. An ideology is a political creed designed as a guide to action for masses of human beings. Seeking mobilization rather than thought, and a new order rather than communication, an ideology claims to be the whole and final truth. There is no such thing as a paradoxical ideology. Moreover, an ostensibly total truth, intended to activate multitudes of people and transform society, must have interpreters and enforcers. Every ideology in this way is implicitly dictatorial. Anyone who shares Jaspers's sense that human beings are always more than we can know or say about them stands apart from all ideologies and is ready, not for action and the exercise of power, but for communication.

Have we now reached the ultimate premise of political thinking? The question is important because, while wisdom may be a thinking state, the converse is not true: a thinking state is not always wisdom. Uncertainty is not necessarily humane. It may be a state of enervating doubt and a source of nihilistic rage, provoked by the feeling that nothing on earth is worthy of devotion or respect. Does humane uncertainty depend on principles that we have failed to notice? Two such principles suggest themselves.

The first is that truth is good. "Truth" is one of those words we often capitalize, taking it to represent something so obviously sublime that no question of its value could conceivably arise. But it is possible, after all, that the ultimate truth might prove to be uninteresting, useless, or even harmful. If the structure of reality were fundamentally antithetical to human interests, illusion might be not only pleasanter than truth but also essential to keep human beings from suffocating under a blanket of hopelessness.

The second premise is that the truth must be sought through public dialogue, with no one excluded. This premise is not required for thinking as such, but for thinking in the only way most of us would find acceptable—in a way open to participation by all and not merely by a privileged few. That inquiry should be open to all, however, is no more self-evident than that truth is good. Granted, we are all equal in our inability to answer definitively the perennial questions. It may be argued, nevertheless, that the ability to reflect fruitfully on these questions is confined to a few. Or in the absence of any countervailing moral imperative, one may simply prefer to work within some exclusive circle of inquirers—one confined, for example, to members of a certain nationality or social class.

In setting forth to think, I must respect both truth and all persons. On what assumptions, on what conception of the universe and humanity, does such respect depend?

Many today would say that it depends on no assumptions at all and that respect for truth and for persons is the ultimate ground of serious and open inquiry. This must be the view of atheists—that there is nothing beyond the truth and the individual human being.

Perhaps this view is sound. It does, however, leave room for doubt. Why should we look on truth as an ultimate value regardless of the nature of reality? Why should we care about truth if it neither interests us nor has any practical value? In the history of thought truth has usually, albeit not invariably, been a religious value; reverence for truth has expressed reverence for being, which has been regarded as either divine in itself or expressive of the divine. Such a view is logical and understandable, even though someone may dispute its religious presuppositions. But is it logical or understandable to retain reverence for truth after denying the divine?

And why should we respect every individual, regardless of character and intellect? The idea of a dignity inherent in every person can be regarded as no less religious in its presuppositions than the idea that truth is good. In Western thought that idea is derived historically from the faith that every person is of concern to God. If this faith is rejected and reliance is placed solely on dispassionate empirical analysis, someone could argue that every human being no more deserves respect than every horse or every automobile.

This question can be summarily restated. To enter seriously into inquiry that is open to all expresses substantial faith in the universe. One must believe that truth is good and that all persons have the potentiality and right to share in the search for it. Does this faith make sense if its final object is only what we can see and objectively know, rather than God?

This question also arises from an assumption underlying every page of this book and made every day by all of us: in one way or another truth is accessible. I have been arguing that some kinds of truth can be gained through reflection; scientists believe that other kinds are reached through empirical analysis. But how can we be sure that such processes do not occur within the boundaries of some all-encompassing illusion to which we are inescapably confined by the very nature of reality and our minds? And even if truth is accessible, how can we have the courage to seek it in the face of the total and everlasting oblivion that death seems to promise?

In sum, it can be argued that serious inquiry is an act of religious faith. What kind of religious faith? There seem to be many possibilities.

The Jewish faith, as based on the Old Testament, can readily be the faith of an inquirer. The God of the Old Testament is often thought to be overbearing and doctrinaire, necessarily an enemy of free thought and open inquiry. We might do well, however, to remember the charge often made by atheists—that we create God in our own image. No doubt we often do. This reflection may lead us, however, to question not the reality of God but the validity of our images. It is not clear that the divine despot of human imagination is anywhere to be found in the Old Testament. If one had to offer a concise characterization, it would be hard to improve on the statement that the God of the Old Testament is one who speaks and listens. Granted, sometimes God commands or condemns and no human answer is possible. But in Genesis we encounter a Creator who has placed humankind in a universe that is good and knowable and has given men and women natural powers, such as reason, to enable them together to inhabit that universe and to understand and exercise dominion over the realities within it. And very often, and in some of the greatest Biblical passages, God pleads for attention and free assent. In sum, God is frequently, and perhaps fundamentally always, dialogical.

Some suppose that in turning from the Old Testament to the New you confront a more dogmatic faith. No doubt Christianity has often been dogmatic. But again we must ask what is inherent in faith and what human beings, in their weakness and perversity, have read into faith. The Gospels present not a doctrine but a story, an account of the life of Jesus. The central event of that story, the Crucifixion, can be seen as a symbol of the necessary defeat of every human truth, a symbol of a truth that lies beyond every truth we can state and possess. Søren Kierkegaard, the source of the epigraph to this book, was a Christian and at the same time an indefatigable and uninhibited thinker. The ultimate paradox he had in mind was Christ, the presence of eternity in time. Both by his inquiring life and undogmatic theology, he suggests the possibility of interpreting Christianity not as a final disclosure of the truth but as an act of divine liberation, enabling us to search for the truth. The author of this book adheres to an inquiring and communal Christianity of the kind exemplified in the figure of Kierkegaard.

No human example of the life of inquiry or of the faith on which inquiry rests, however, is more instructive than that of a man who lived several centuries prior to Christ. Let us end these reflections by briefly considering Socrates, the homely, amiable, and disturbingly intelligent Athenian who was put to death on account of his uncompromising pursuit of rational inquiry. Apparently Socrates did not expound a complete and definite doctrine but devoted himself to asking questions; these were on matters of ultimate import, such as friendship, justice, and truth. Socrates devoted his whole mature life to such questions. Although he sought out people reputed for their wisdom, he seems always gladly to have entered into conversation with anyone he happened to meet who was willing seriously to talk. He concluded at the end of his life that no one could answer his questions and that those reputed to be wise were in reality ignorant. It was this conclusion, expressed in conversations that resulted in publicly humiliating some of the most eminent men in Athens, that led ultimately to his trial and execution.

Two aspects of Socrates' life are particularly noteworthy in relation to the ideal of humane uncertainty. First, Socrates concluded not only that all others were ignorant but that he himself was ignorant. He was superior to others, he held, only in his awareness of his ignorance. Thus on the face of things Socrates was a failure. A lifetime of questioning had led him to no answers, had indeed led him to a death sentence, imposed by his fellow Athenians, for sowing spiritual and intellectual confusion in the city.

Yet Socrates lived the last days of a life that had brought him to intellectual uncertainty and a shameful death with triumphant composure, as though in his long intellectual struggle, he had magnificently succeeded. At his trial his defense was characterized, as his conversation always had been, by a calm but disconcerting irony. In prison he refused to save his life by escaping, although this could have been readily arranged, because a voice, murmuring in his ears "like the sound of the flute in the ears of the mystic," warned him that in escaping he would betray the laws under which he had always lived. He devoted his final hours to discussing the immortality of the soul, apparently approaching the question with complete openness of mind. At the end he calmed his weeping friends and "readily and cheerfully" drank the poison brought by the executioner.[2] Socrates did not act as though thinking had brought him only to a state of total perplex-

---

[2]These events are recounted, on the basis no doubt of firsthand reports, in three works by Plato: the *Apology, Crito,* and *Phaedo.*

ity. His "ignorance" seemed to be the paradoxical sign of an awareness that was inexpressible but so sustaining that even the imminence of death did not affect his tranquillity.

We have no certain knowledge of Socrates' political outlook. He was probably as unwilling to identify himself with definite political principles of any other kind. But it is not difficult to discern certain broad political ideals in the outlines of his life. To begin with, his whole career was a moving enactment of freedom. He was ridiculed by his fellow citizens and threatened with exile and death by the government but imperturbably continued to live and speak according to the unutterable but irresistable imperatives that governed his life.

Further, although Socrates may have had elitist leanings (having been, perhaps, the original source of Plato's concept of the philosopher-ruler), his manner of life was in some ways egalitarian. He did not claim special authority, except for that implicit in his mission of demonstrating the universal ignorance in which he shared, and was apparently willing to talk with anyone willing to talk with him. In one of Plato's dialogues, he is depicted as showing that significant knowledge can be elicited from an uneducated young slave.

Finally, Socrates was a thoroughly communal man. Loyalty to the very city-state that had sentenced him to death kept him from escaping prison, and his stubborn questioning represented an indefeasible openness to communication. Whatever the truth that Socrates had discovered, it was not a truth that could be embodied in a definite set of propositions and securely possessed. Nor could it be imposed on others. It was a truth that could be found only in dialogue.

Socrates displayed that difficult balance between personal independence and social responsibility, between uncertainty and the capacity for action, that we may call civility. He was apparently interested in all ideas and wholly free of fanaticism. In his openness, however, he was committed to the most serious of all tasks, the search for truth. Through a similar paradox, he was "ignorant"—unable to pronounce finally on the truth or falsity of the ideas he discussed—yet he was capable of rare decisiveness and courage in the performance of civil functions, on one occasion risking death by defying, on grounds of illegality, an order from a governing clique.

Today we scarcely even aspire to such a stance. We assume that the test of political seriousness is dedication to practical results. We respect above all else impassioned and uncompromising action. Yet history has been heedless of our demands. After striving for two centuries to command events (dating modern activism from the time of the French Revolution), the human race is nearly overwhelmed with misfortune. Could it be that what is required, rather than the sometimes complacent and sometimes desperate assertiveness of the modern age, is Socratic civility?

For most of us, doubt is unsettling, and we avoid serious discussion because we are afraid of doubt. But Socrates seems to tell us that doubt can be a source of health and hope and that the confidence of a free and communal person may be born, strangely, of uncertainty.

We are living today in a period of uncertainty, but it is an anxious and debilitating uncertainty, not the serene and luminous uncertainty of Socrates. Not only traditional religious faith, but even confidence in science, is weak. Vast multitudes of people crowding the earth have no clear and stable concept of what is real or how we ought to live. Our spiritual situation could hardly be more ominous.

If the idea of humane uncertainty is valid, however, our situation is not hopeless, and we should not try totally to eradicate our doubts. They may provide a pathway to understanding. When we try to replace our doubts with objective principles that cannot be shaken or destroyed, we turn aside from this pathway. In doing this we turn aside not only from possibilities of deeper understanding but also from one another. So fundamental a diversion can be disastrous. The totalitarianism and violence of our time result in some measure from the efforts of men and women to escape from uncertainty. Those who cannot live with doubt cannot live with human beings who are thoughtful and independent enough to be sources of doubt.

Thus, for the sake both of understanding and of community, we may hope that our age of anxious uncertainty does not give way to one of perfect certainty. The greatest achievement of political thinking today would not be to overcome our doubts but to help us live with them in a state of freedom and civility.

Index